SEVENTY-FIVE YEARS OF SERVICE

75 YEARS *of* SERVICE

Cooperative Extension in Iowa

BY **DOROTHY SCHWIEDER**

Iowa State University Press / Ames

DOROTHY SCHWIEDER is professor of history at Iowa State University and a trustee of the State Historical Society of Iowa. A native of South Dakota, she received her Ph.D. from the University of Iowa. She is currently working on a one-volume history of Iowa, *Iowa: The Prairie State.*

First edition, 1993

Library of Congress Cataloging-in-Publication Data

Schwieder, Dorothy.
    75 years of service: cooperative extension in Iowa / by Dorothy Schwieder.—1st ed.
      p.   cm.
    Includes bibliographical references (p.) and index.
    ISBN 0-8138-0388-8 (alk. paper)
    1. Iowa State University. Cooperative Extension Service—History.
I. Title.   II. Title: Seventy-five years of service.
S544.3.I64S39   1993
630′.7150777—dc20   93-14941

Contents

Foreword

As the twenty-first century nears, the United States is a world leader in agriculture—in production, in international marketing, in food available to its population, in food safety, in agricultural innovation, and in contributions of food to disaster-stricken areas around the world. This is true even though we still have wasted natural resources, some hungry people, a declining farm population, and a farm economy that is in part subsidized by the entire population. Yet the nation has continued to produce the staples needed by a constantly growing population and, in addition, enough to make agricultural commodities the source of one of the most important parts of our export income. We have, as well, been able to provide relief provisions to nations struck by disaster. This did not come about by chance nor did it come about by the exploitation of resources or of people. It came about by the application of research and education to farm production by enterprising and educated farmers. The Cooperative Extension Service has been a key factor in these accomplishments, just as Iowa has been one of the leading states in agricultural production.

Many of the nation's early leaders, including George Washington, Thomas Jefferson, Edmund Ruffin, Eli Whitney, Justin Morrill, and others, were concerned with improving both farming and farm life. A number of proposals made over the years came together in 1862 when the Congress passed and President Lincoln signed bills establishing the United States Department of Agriculture, the state land-grant colleges of agriculture and engineering, and making homesteads available to settlers on the western public lands.

Thus the machinery was put in place to bring about a revolution in agricultural production, and that is what happened. The land-grant colleges and the Department of Agriculture undertook experimental work to discover how to increase agricultural production. This became increasingly important after 1887 when the Hatch Agricultural Experiment Station Act was approved. Under the act, each state was allocated funds for the basic support of an agricultural experiment station.

The better-educated and more innovative farmers began to take advantage of the results of the new research. They would read the bulletins issued by the Department, the colleges, and the experiment stations, would attend lectures given by research personnel, would visit special railroad trains given over to exhibits of improved farming methods, and would even take a week or two to attend short courses given by college and experiment station personnel.

Agricultural productivity increased in the later part of the nineteenth century, particularly in states like Iowa, but the increase was erratic and varied greatly from farm to farm. Many farmers were, for one reason or another, not taking advantage of the opportunities to learn how to be more productive.

It was left to Seaman A. Knapp to provide the impetus for taking knowledge directly to the farmer. Many farmers would change, he said, only through demonstrations carried on by the farmers themselves on their own farms and under ordinary conditions. They looked with indifference or even disdain at what they called "book farming."

Knapp, at one time president of Iowa Agricultural College, now Iowa State University, was called upon by the Department of Agriculture to devise a way of combating the boll weevil, which was threatening cotton growing throughout the South. Knapp established a demonstration farm in 1903, which led to the appointment of the nation's first county agent in Smith County, Texas, in 1906. Meanwhile, other states and counties were undertaking activities that were somewhat similar in result. As Dorothy Schwieder points out in this book, the first Extension activity in Iowa began in Sioux County in 1903. In 1906 the Iowa General Assembly appropriated funds to create a Department of Extension at Iowa State College, and in 1912 Iowa had its first county agent. In 1911 a "farm bureau" was established in Binghamton, New York, with a county agent in charge.

Thus it was obvious that Knapp's idea of having a trained agriculturist to work directly with farmers was being accepted across the nation. At the same time, the agricultural colleges and the state and local organizations established to promote the idea were calling for federal aid. The Agricultural College Association drafted the first bill, which was introduced in 1908. Others followed. As a result of these efforts, the Smith-Lever Act for Cooperative Extension work was approved May 8, 1914.

Cooperative Extension was truly cooperative. The federal government provided a base fund, the agricultural college or other institution handling Extension was responsible for about one-third of the costs of the service, and the county or other local government was responsible for a third. Generally, every state has participated. Iowa, a leader in agricultural production in the nation, has also been an active participant in Extension, facts probably closely related. This book is the history of that participation and what it has meant to farming and farm life in Iowa.

WAYNE D. RASMUSSEN

Preface

This book is a history of the Iowa State University Cooperative Extension Service during its first seventy-five years of existence. Cooperative Extension was a result of the Smith-Lever Act passed in 1914, which brought together the federal government, the states, and participating county governments as partners in a three-tiered organization to serve the nation's farm population.

Extension in Iowa actually was under way before the passage of the Smith-Lever Act. Farmers in Sioux County are credited with the first Extension activity in the state in 1903. Three years later the General Assembly appropriated funds to create a Department of Extension at Iowa State College. By 1912 Iowa had its first county agent, and four years later its first home demonstration agent. With the passage of Smith-Lever, Iowa quickly met the necessary requirements and the new partnership was launched. During the next seventy-five years, Iowa's Cooperative Extension would grow from a handful of county and state staff members to an organization of about four hundred.

In 1960, in a review of Iowa's Extension Service, consultants Philip Van Slyck and Warren Rovetch wrote,

> The uniqueness of cooperative extension lies in the flexibility and pluralism of the system. It is a network of essentially local and largely independent county bases, served by a collection of state resources. . . .The county extension office, in this system, is the key service point for all extension services and programs. Effective performance by the county office is the principal measure of the effectiveness of the whole system.[1]

While every Extension office and staff member had (and continues to have) a vital role in carrying out the objectives of the organization, this study will focus on the "key service point[s]" where county staff interact directly with the public. At the same time, of necessity, it pays attention to changes in administrative policies, personnel, and programs. While this study might have focused on administrators, administrative policies, or the interaction between federal agencies and Iowa's Extension Service, the most fruitful way to deal with the interaction between Extension and the public and to study Extension programs is to emphasize activity at the county level. To a large degree this study rests on Van Slyck's and Rovetch's view of the county Extension office as the key service point.[2] As part of this approach, this study will present the view of the generalist more frequently than that of the specialist.

Extension has been (and continues to be) an organization that must respond to economic and social change. Throughout the past seventy-five years emergencies, such as world wars and depressions, have dominated with fewer intervals of calm. Given that agriculture is the major industry in Iowa, Extension has been continually initiating new programs and modifying old ones to respond effectively to those changing conditions. It seems appropriate, therefore, for this study to take a chronological approach, often by decade, where major areas of Extension are examined in the context of wider economic and social conditions. Different areas of Extension are treated in a common time period rather than in separate topical chapters, and each chapter presents an integrated view of the total organization. While eight chapters deal directly with Cooperative Extension, the first one presents a general view of Iowa farm life around 1900, intended to provide the setting out of which Extension developed. Even though Cooperative Extension became a part of University Extension in 1966, this study focuses exclusively on Cooperative Extension, both before and after 1966.

This history also includes considerable material on Iowa agriculture and farm life. The economic, and to a lesser degree social, conditions of Iowa's farming population have been of vital concern to Extension, not only because of the Smith-Lever mandate to provide assistance for farm people but also because Extension's own well-being rests on prosperity in the countryside. Moreover, Extension's main concern through the years has been production agriculture.

The acknowledgments for this study would be long indeed if every individual who provided information was listed. Over thirty Iowans, mostly former or current Extension staff members, gave freely of their time to be interviewed; four generous individuals—C. J. Gauger, W. John Johnson, Marvin Anderson, and the late Louise Rosenfeld—agreed to two interviews. I gratefully dedicate this volume to all of the above. The interviews were indispensable in helping me to grasp the broad view of Extension as well as to understand the specifics of certain developments and time periods. Although I have quoted from some interviews more than others, each one was valuable in helping to understand the many facets of Extension. I apologize to those dozens of current and former Extension staff members whom I did not interview. Every individual associated with the organization has an important and interesting account to give. Time restraints, however, made it impossible to interview additional people, regardless of their positions or perspectives.

I owe particular thanks to former Dean of University Extension and Director of Cooperative Extension Robert Crom, who initiated this study. Six years ago Crom expressed the desire for an urgent oral history project with former Extension persons so that their stories would not be lost. The present study is the result of that initiative. I wish to thank him as well as Ronald Powers and Elizabeth Elliott, both interim deans of University Extension and directors of Cooperative Extension, for assisting the project by providing me with release time from teaching duties in the ISU history department. Elizabeth Elliott deserves special thanks for reading and commenting on the manuscript and providing encouragement at each stage of the project.

Other people also contributed to the study. Thomas Morain assisted in its initial stages by locating library materials and doing numerous interviews. George Ebert, former director of Continuing Education, collected materials related to areas of University Extension other than Cooperative Extension. As always, the staff at the ISU Parks Library offered prompt, cheerful assistance. The Special Collections staff was particularly helpful in locating Extension materials. Audrey Burton, manuscript typist in the history department, did her usual excellent work in typing and retyping the manuscript. Lillian Johnson spent many hours transcribing hundreds of pages of interviews. Finally, to my husband, Elmer, a thank-you for always at the end of the day inquiring cheerfully, "Well, how's it going?"

While dozens of viewpoints are included in this study, these are carefully identified if they originated from interviews or published materials. The remaining viewpoints and assessments are my own and not the views of the ISU Cooperative Extension Service or any of its staff. For these views and the remainder of material, I assume full responsibility.

SEVENTY-FIVE YEARS OF SERVICE

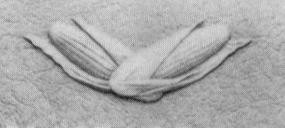

BIRTHPLACE OF AN IDEA

IN THIS LOCALITY, COUNTY COOPERATIVE AGRICULTURAL
EXTENSION WORK AS NOW CONDUCTED THROUGHOUT THE
UNITED STATES WAS FIRST ESTABLISHED. THIS PLAN WAS
CONCEIVED BY PERRY G. HOLDEN OF IOWA STATE COLLEGE,
THE SIOUX COUNTY FARMERS' INSTITUTE AND THE BOARD
OF SUPERVISORS OF SIOUX COUNTY, FEBRUARY 18, 1903.
THE FIRST WORK UNDERTAKEN WAS THE IMPROVEMENT
OF FARMERS' SEED CORN. THIS - - THE FIRST MASS
EFFORT TO IMPROVE CORN - - STARTED A MOVEMENT
THAT SPREAD OVER IOWA AND THE CORN BELT.

SPONSORED BY IOWA STATE COLLEGE IN COOPERATION WITH THE PEOPLE OF
SIOUX COUNTY AND THE MICHIGAN STATE UNIVERSITY CORN FOUNDATION.

PLAQUE IN SIOUX COUNTY commemorating the site where county Cooperative Extension work first began in Iowa. Courtesy ISU Photo Service.

1

Open Country Iowa

Circa 1900

In 1900 Americans perceived Iowa as a premier agricultural state. The designation was appropriate. By the turn of the century Iowa was a leading producer of two staples—corn and hogs—as well as a major producer of other agricultural commodities. Living in a part of the Midwest often described as the nation's breadbasket, Iowa farmers were known for an intensive, dependable type of farming made possible in large part by the presence of approximately 25 percent of the nation's premium farmland. It seemed fitting, therefore, that early in the new century Iowans should respond favorably to the economic and social needs of farm families by establishing an Extension Service. Following the first state appropriation for Extension in 1906, the organization would grow rapidly. By the 1920s Iowa Extension was known throughout the nation for its dynamic leadership and its innovative programs.

The farm population that Iowa Extension would be created to serve was still a distinct society in 1900. As historian David Danbom has pointed out in his study of agriculture and industrialism, despite many changes such as commercialization, technological innovation, and industrialism, "American rural life in 1900 was in broad outline similar to what it had always been."[1] Iowa farmers still relied on horsepower to plow fields, plant crops, and bring in the harvest. Work continued to be dictated by the seasons, not by the concerns or activities of those running the farm. Farm residents, moreover, still experienced social isolation, maybe the most distinctive part of life in the open country. And the great agents of change that would do so much to alter farm life—electricity, the gasoline internal combustion engine, and even hybrid seed corn—still lay in the future.

Given the social and physical isolation, Iowa's farm families in 1900 continued to live quite differently from the state's growing number of urban dwellers. While town and city families enjoyed the benefits of modern technology, such as electricity, and were beginning to participate in various social and business organizations, farm people found their social lives mostly unchanged from the previous century. Before 1900 the lives of both town and country residents had revolved primarily around the institutions of family, church, and school. For town and city residents, however, that would soon change. As Lewis Atherton has pointed out, in the late nineteenth century residents of small towns began "to participate in a national trend toward organizational activities." Atherton believes that by the first decade of the twentieth century this behavior was so obvious that he identifies it as the "twentieth-century cult of joining."[2] Because farm families could not share in many of these developments, the social lives of town and country residents would become more and more disparate.

For Iowans who lived in the open country, however, the new century brought renewed hope for a more prosperous life. According to historian Earle Ross, a major characteristic of the midwestern farm population in 1900 was optimism: midwestern farmers were manifesting "a spirit of buoyancy" about their calling. As a speaker at a midwestern agricultural meeting enthusiastically proclaimed, "Gentlemen, from the beginning of Indiana to the end of Nebraska there is nothing but corn, cattle, and contentment." This optimism was born out. By 1900 American farmers were on the brink of the Golden Age of American Agriculture, the most prosperous period ever. Midwesterners apparently believed that the new century was ushering in a permanent prosperity. As evidence they could point to the rising value of Iowa farmland, which increased from an average of $36.35 per acre in 1900 to $82.58 in 1910.[3]

Even in light of such optimism, Iowa farm families shared many not-so-favorable conditions with farm residents elsewhere. A major disadvantage at the turn of the century was social isolation, an immutable condition if one lived on a farm. It is worth noting that isolation was relative. For some families in the western Dakotas and Nebraska, isolation meant living perhaps forty or fifty miles from the nearest neighbor. In Iowa, given the pattern of nineteenth-century settlement and the size of farms at this time, families often lived within a mile or two of the nearest neighbor. Nevertheless, farm residents did not have the same opportunities to participate in social events as town residents.

By 1900, however, several developments had mitigated rural isolation. In the previous decade the federal government established Rural Free Delivery, which meant that farm residents received daily mail delivery six days a week. The federal government established the first route in Iowa at Morning Sun in Louisa County in 1896. By 1901 Iowa had 292 rural routes, placing the state fourth in the nation. Mail delivery established a vital link with the outside world; farm residents could then receive a daily newspaper that brought them market information as well as news from around the state, the nation, and the world. The importance of the mailman's visit is reflected in farm people's diaries and journals, where they dutifully recorded each day whether or not the mailman had been able to make his rounds. Even as late as 1921, a Guthrie County teenager recorded daily (following a weather description) whether or not the mail had been delivered.[4]

The telephone marked a second development that helped reduce farm isolation. Town residents came to enjoy telephones in the latter 1800s, and by the early 1900s farm families were also demanding the service. According to Thomas Morain's history of Jefferson, Greene County began a telephone exchange in the following way.

> [Farmers] had discovered that simple telephone lines could be built very cheaply. With wires, poles and telephones Farmers Mutual strung up service to the neighborhood on a cooperative plan. There were no full-time employees at first, but the service, though limited, seemed satisfactory.[5]

While farm residents may have initially justified the expense of a telephone by viewing it mainly for business, farm women quickly perceived it as a way of reducing isolation. One Greene County farm woman, Barbara Hamilton, recalled, "What a wonderful thing it was for the farm wife for it let her talk to her neighbors when her work did not permit her to leave the house."[6]

Residents of the open country were also beginning to benefit from community clubs in the early twentieth century. In Wright County the Evergreen Sporting Association started in 1905 when farmers there met to track down a wolf that was threatening their cattle. The group developed into a neighborhood community club that lasted for several decades. Members attended picnics, sponsored field days, and organized a literary society and the Prohibition Club. They also sponsored short courses taught by Iowa State College (ISC) faculty. Most of all, members enjoyed the social side of the organization prompting one member to write, "The only trouble that we encounter is to find a house large enough for the crowd, which often numbers one hundred and more. The people attending range in age from babies to grandparents, but all come expecting to enjoy themselves." By 1915 Greene County contained ten such clubs with an average membership of about sixty-five.[7]

Of all open country institutions, perhaps the most visible was the one-room schoolhouse. Along with education for the young, the school also provided country people with social opportunities. Like many rural institutions, however, the school can be viewed in both a positive and negative manner. For farm residents, the school represented a community center where they could come together for school functions, elections, and neighborhood social events. Each school typically held a yearly box social to raise funds for special school projects, a Christmas program, and a picnic to celebrate the end of the school year. All residents of the rural neighborhood usually attended these events. Yet educational studies conclude that farm children suffered from a lower quality of education than that received by town children. Farm youths attended high school in far fewer numbers than their counterparts in town.[8] A statewide study conducted as late as 1916 showed that in urban areas 30 percent of young people went to high school while in the open country only 5 percent did so.[9]

While country teachers typically had less education than town or city teachers (making them appear less qualified than their urban counterparts), some made a great difference in the lives of their students. At age nineteen Jessie Field started teaching the Goldenrod School near Shenandoah. Along with the traditional responsibilities of teaching the three *R*s, Field also believed that rural education should be relevant for her students. She believed that education "should foster a feeling of pride and self-worth in farm children." Later, as county superintendent of schools in Page County, Field created the Boys' Corn Club and the Girls' Home Club to continue providing "relevant" education for Page County farm children. These clubs would later be viewed as the forerunners of 4-H.[10]

School consolidation, which brought some improvement to rural education, started early in Iowa but progressed slowly. In 1896 Buffalo Center in Winnebago County organized into one township district. A short time later all but three of the districts in the county arranged to have pupils transported to the city school. The next consolidation did not take place until five years later and by 1913 only eighteen schools had followed Buffalo Center's example. As historian Earle Ross has pointed out, not only were individuals hesitant to give up local control, but many had some prejudice against innovations in subjects and methods, and many opposed the anticipated cost increase.[11]

The presence of dozens of ethnic settlements provided another visible characteristic of open country, Iowa 1900; these ethnic clusters appeared everywhere in the state. In northeastern Iowa Norwegian-Americans predominated; in the southwestern part of the state Danish-Americans were most numerous. Given their statewide numerical superiority, German-Americans could be found in every one of Iowa's ninety-nine counties, especially in eastern counties such as Dubuque, Clinton, and Scott. Each ethnic settlement formed something of an insular community, identified not only by its residents' common national background and shared language, but also by participation in one religious denomination. Norwegians in Winneshiek and Story counties were typically Lutheran; Germans in Carroll County were mostly Catholic. North of Algona, however, Germans were mostly Missouri Synod Lutherans while in Kossuth County many German-Americans belonged to Dutch Reformed churches. The shared characteristics of ethnicity, language, religion, and sometimes even architectural styles produced considerable social and economic solidarity. Of all these, religion would be the most enduring. Historian Frederick Luebke has observed, "Of all important institutions, the church was the easiest to establish, the most effective in its mission, and hence the most long-lived. Unlike most ethnic institutions, the church survived the transition to an English-speaking society."[12]

Kinship ties represented yet another important characteristic of farm society. Each rural neighborhood included numerous families related by blood and marriage. Neighborhoods typically included several sets of adult siblings, along with their spouses and children, living in close proximity to one another. Sometimes kinship patterns were more complex with two sisters marrying two brothers and both families, as well as several of the offspring and their families, residing in the same rural neighborhood. These families frequently attended the same church and their children attended the same rural school. In turn, young people grew up with cousins, sometimes by the dozen. Economic ties also existed; some family members farmed together, jointly purchasing farm machinery. When farm families faced economic difficulties they usually looked first to relatives for assistance.[13]

Strong bonds often existed between female members of families, which greatly affected work and socializing patterns. Mothers and daughters as well as sisters helped one another with child care, canning, and cooking for threshers. Family members, especially women, provided emotional support for one another in times of sickness and bereavement. For many families, socializing took place within the extended family circle as members came together to celebrate birthdays, graduations, and holidays. Throughout rural neighborhoods kinship ties not only strongly influenced social relationships but made frequent socializing possible.[14]

While the presence of kin and ethnically related neighbors might affect work patterns, one aspect of farm life was unalterable. At the turn of the century farm people continued to work very hard. David Danbom has observed that the "first fact that strikes the observer of agriculture in the early years of the [twentieth century] is the universality of hard work." In 1896 another observer put it more dramatically: farm life "was drudge, drudge, from daylight to dark, day after day, month after month, year after year."[15]

The farmer's daily work routine remained much the same as in the nineteenth century. As historian Gilbert Fite has noted, before 1920 agricultural change had been slow. Machines available were "simply an extension of manual labor and horse-power. As late as the second and third decades of the twentieth century, the three-mile-an-hour gait of the horse established the speed and power of most field work on American farms."[16]

Still, some change did occur in the implements used by Iowa farmers. One result of the prosperity of the new century was that more farmers could select from the increasing supply of larger and more efficient farm machines coming on the market. As historian Allan Bogue has observed, in the latter nineteenth century farmers had started farming sitting down. By 1900 grain drills, two-row cultivators, and corn planters were available. Farmers carried out their grain harvesting by banding together in threshing rings to use steam-powered threshing machines. According to Earle Ross, the greatest change in farm technology (between 1900 and World War II) came in the form of corn-harvesting machinery. In the 1890s the binder had been perfected. By about 1902 farmers could purchase corn pickers with husker attachments, although the machines were considered by many to be wasteful and inefficient. Also by 1900

IOWA FARMER PLOWING circa 1900. Courtesy ISU
Photo Service.

farmers could purchase twine corn binders. Husker-shredders were available as well as steam-powered corn shellers. Even though larger and more efficient farm implements were continually coming on the market, it should not be assumed that all farmers utilized the new machines. As Bogue has pointed out, "Farmers seldom outfitted themselves completely [with machinery] at any one time." Underscoring that observation is the fact that the average American farm in 1900 had less than $131 worth of machinery.[17]

Farmers continued to find their work dictated by the seasons. In January, usually the coldest part of the winter, farmers butchered hogs for home use and cut and stored ice. Winter was also a time to repair buildings and fences and cut firewood. With the coming of spring, farmers prepared fields for planting. During the summer they sheared sheep, cut hay, and with the help of neighbors harvested small grain. In September farmers brought hogs from the fields to be fattened for sale in late fall or early winter. And, in late fall, they began the hardest work of all—picking corn. Typically all able family members pitched in to help until the last ear of corn had been safely stored in the cribs.

Improvements in farm technology affected the lives of women far less than the lives of men. Documents abound relating that the purchase of new farm machinery was viewed as a wise expenditure that could bring economic rewards. Improving the farm home, however, or even taking on a hired girl was not viewed in the same light. The first represented good business; the second an unnecessary, perhaps even foolish expenditure. Hamlin Garland commented on that fact in *Son of the Middle Border*.

> Although a continually improving collection of farm machinery lightened the burdens of the husbandman, the drudgery of the housewife's dish-washing and cooking did not correspondingly lessen. . . . I fear it increased, for with the widening of the fields came the doubling of the harvest hands, [yet] my mother continued to do most of the housework herself.

The result was that most Iowa farm women at the turn of the century carried out their farm and domestic chores in the same fashion as their mothers and grandmothers before them.[18]

Like their menfolk, farm women found their work dictated by the seasons. During the winter farm women sewed and mended clothing; in 1900 women still made much of their families' wearing apparel. Farm women helped with butchering, being mainly responsible for preserving the different cuts of meat. In the spring women cleaned chicken coops and set hens, made soap, and prepared the ground for planting gardens. Like town women, country women strictly observed the ritual of spring housecleaning. Summer brought yet additional chores as gardens had to be weeded and produce either canned or dried. Every family viewed threshing as an important event and farm women played a vital role in preparing at least one noon meal for the threshing crew; often neighboring farm wives helped each other with this task. In the fall women had to preserve the last of the garden produce. Throughout the year women also cared for children, prepared three meals a day, and did the family's washing, ironing, and mending.[19]

While not much has been written about Iowa farm children, it seems fitting that some mention should be made of their work on the farm. The oldest son and daughter in each family usually had the greatest responsibilities for "helping out" but eventually all children were expected to contribute to the farm's operation. The family farm, an institution highly visible in the Midwest, called for a flexible labor system. While large operators might have permanent hired help, many smaller operators employed seasonal workers or relied on family members. Farm young people often made the latter possible, assuming work responsibilities at an early age. Weeding gardens and caring for younger siblings were common tasks. As farm youth grew older, they assumed more major responsibilities and eventually became an important component of the midwestern farm labor system.

Clifford Drury, who grew up on a Sac County farm in the late nineteenth and early twentieth centuries, recalled the work expectations in his family.

> My father believed in keeping his children busy as soon as they were able to perform simple tasks. Depending upon the season of the year, we were usually up at 5:00 or 5:30 A.M. Our first duty was to light the fires in the kitchen and the dining-room stoves. Then we went outside to do the milking, feed and water the horses, and clean out the barns before breakfast.

Drury added that when he and his brother, Grover, were twelve and thirteen years old respectively, "We together took a man's place in the fields, and on the threshing crew." For many farm families, the labor provided by young people like Clifford and Grover Drury "took up the slack" so that little or no money had to be spent on wages. It also meant that no one had to be fired at the end of the season.[20]

Even while midwestern farmers expressed optimism about their future, worry persisted over the continual movement of farm people to the cities. As Gilbert Fite has written, "a strange contradiction" was evident on American farms in the later nineteenth and early twentieth centuries. The term describes the fact that while Americans seemed to believe that farmers exemplified the nation's best virtues, such as independence, self-sufficiency, and honesty, thousands of farm people were leaving for the cities.[21] Sometimes called the "flight to the cities," the movement of people off the farm concerned many Americans in the early twentieth century, both rural and urban, including the nation's president. Because of his concern, in 1907 Theodore Roosevelt appointed a Country Life Commission to study rural life and to determine ways that it could be improved.

While undoubtedly many males became discontented and left farming, unhappiness with farm living seemed more prevalent among women. Iowa author Herbert Quick observed this phenomenon in 1913 when he wrote that the movement to the cities "has been largely a women movement. I have found the men on the farms much more contented and happy than the women." Quick noted that most progress on the farm benefited men more than women.[22] Tom Morain has also perceptively observed that situation in his study of a small Iowa community.

> The features of rural life that were most frequently cited as deficient were "feminine" issues—education and cultural opportunities. What made farm life seem inadequate was the tremendous improvement in precisely these areas that town women were experiencing. To understand rural discontent through the first third of the twentieth century, one needs to see it first through the eyes of the farm wife aware of new opportunities for town women and frustrated by her inability to participate in them. In no small part of this was the root of the "flight from the farm."[23]

As Morain suggests, women were more concerned about education than men, a concern that manifested itself in wanting better education for the children. Living on the farm in 1900 meant attending a country school and accepting the fact that only a small percentage of farm children went on to high school.[24]

While life in the open country would gradually include more social outlets, that improvement came more slowly than social change

WOMEN STUDENTS BAKING bread in the Domestic Economy Department at Iowa State College in the latter 1800s. This was a forerunner to the Home Economics Department in the early 1900s. Courtesy ISU Photo Service.

in nearby towns. The Country Life Commission, which issued its report in 1909, observed with considerable concern that town living held great attraction for farm people, pointing out these people often equated town living with better living. When farm couples retired, for example, they thought of moving to town. When parents desired better schooling for their children, they thought of town schools. And, perhaps most disturbing, when young people wanted to better themselves, they often thought of moving to town. To counter that attraction, the Country Life Commission recommended that life in the country be improved by creating better schools, better roads, and helping farmers to help themselves through rural cooperative organizations.[25]

Among the Commission's many recommendations was a call to establish an Extension Service. Such an organization would carry new scientific and technical information from the states' Experiment Stations and land-grant colleges to the nation's farm families. Since the mid-nineteenth century farmers had belonged to county and state agricultural societies, attended agricultural fairs, received agricultural bulletins, and participated in agricultural short courses, all in an effort to increase their knowledge. But each state extension service would do much more. A representative of the college would reside in each county, becoming familiar with local agricultural conditions. This representative, known as a county agent, would be available to local farmers for consultation and problem solving, acting as a conduit between the agencies doing the research and the state's farmers, who were viewed as the major beneficiaries of that research. If the agent could not answer a client's question, the agent could call on specialists at Iowa State College for assistance. In addition, Extension home demonstration agents would work with farm women to improve farm homes and help make women's work less arduous. Extension, in general, was to help bring greater prosperity to farm people, reduce the drudgery of farm work, and increase the rewards of country living.[26]

Iowa was in the vanguard of change. In 1906, three years before the Country Life Commission issued its report and eight years before the passage of the Smith-Lever Act, the state created its own Extension Service. The appointment of the first county agent, the most visible sign of an active Extension Service, was still six years away. Although Iowa's Extension Service would include only a handful of staff before the creation of Cooperative Extension, nevertheless, a commitment had been made. The first step had been taken to improve the quality of farm living.

2

The Formative Years

1903–1918

In April 1912 a small group of Clinton County citizens—members of the Clinton Commercial Club and several local farmers—met to discuss the hiring of an Extension agent. The meeting resulted in the hiring of M. L. Mosher, the first county Extension agent employed in the state. Within a short time businesspeople and farmers in Scott County followed Clinton's example. The hiring of Iowa's first agents preceded by two years the passage of the landmark legislation, the Smith-Lever Act. This federal act created Cooperative Extension, a three-tiered organization, involving local, state, and federal governments. Between 1912, when the first Iowa agent was appointed, and 1917, when America entered World War I, the number of agents gradually increased to twenty-four. A much greater expansion of personnel would come with World War I. The federal government, faced with the need to feed its own army as well as providing food for millions of hungry Europeans, funded the hiring of dozens of county agents. Soon every county had an agent and one county, Pottawattamie, had two; federal money also provided for the hiring of some forty home economists. By 1918, through the presence of county staff and a small central staff located at Iowa State College (ISC), Iowa's Extension Service had taken shape. Within the next few years Extension gained increasing visibility as the major organization serving the needs of Iowa's farm families.

The hiring of Iowa's first two county agents did not take place without significant groundwork being laid by earlier Extension personnel. Foremost among these was Perry G. Holden, who came to Iowa State College in 1902. Holden might well be called the father of Iowa Extension. Before his employment by ISC, Holden had been involved in many areas of agriculture. He had served as professor of agronomy at the University of Illinois; he had performed fieldwork for the Illinois Sugar Refining Company; and he had helped start the Funk Brothers Seed Corn Company. Traveling to Iowa to give several lectures on corn growing as part of a short course at ISC, Holden had come to the attention of ISC President William Beardshear. Before Holden's involvement in the short course, college officials had been cautious about allotting much time to corn production, feeling that the subject was simply too boring. College officials feared that if farmers became uninterested, they might simply walk out of the presentation.[1]

Once exposed to Holden's enthusiastic presentations, rather than leave the meeting, farmers began to ask for more material on corn growing. The farmers, in fact, approached Holden personally to request that more time be spent on the subject. Holden responded that the short course program left no other time available. Then jokingly he added that he could make the additional presentations from 2 A.M. to 8 A.M. The group conferred with other farmers and came back with the suggestion that the class be held at 5 A.M. Holden responded, "That's fine, but bring your lanterns and your lunches. Electric lights are not on at 5 A.M. and you probably won't have time to go home for breakfast."[2]

When President Beardshear heard about a college professor who could "coax farmers out to a 5 A.M. class," he decided to meet with Holden. Convinced that the college needed a man of Holden's talents, Beardshear then faced the matter of raising Holden's salary. Because of money shortages at the school, it was necessary to seek private funds. Henry Wallace of *Wallaces' Farmer* and two Odebolt area farmers, W. P. Adams and A. E. Cook, contributed $600. The additional money enabled the college to hire Holden in the fall of 1902 as professor of agronomy and vice-dean of agriculture.[3]

The decision to hire Holden resulted in many positive developments at Iowa State College. For the next ten years Holden with "untiring enthusiasm and remarkable powers of popular appeal," traveled throughout the state, concentrating his energies on improving corn production. According to historian Earle Ross, Holden soon started three lines of Extension effort: county farm demonstration work, regional short courses, and the Seed Corn Gospel Trains. Holden's experience in both scientific research and its practical application served him well. He not only proved to be highly successful in his presentations to farmers, but his campus courses also quickly became favorites among ISC students. According to one account, "Holden took Ames and Iowa by storm."[4]

In April 1903 Holden traveled to northwest Iowa to speak to farmers about seed corn selection and cultivation. In effect, he was taking part in a farmers' institute, a popular event held throughout Iowa in the late 1800s and early 1900s. A Hull area farmer inquired whether agricultural experiments carried out at the Experiment Station in Ames, some one hundred miles away, would be applicable in northwestern Iowa. Holden responded with something of a challenge for Sioux County farmers. He stated that farmers did need to understand local conditions and that "every county should put on demonstrations and have someone in the county to direct the demonstration plots, advise the people as to their problems, and work with farm boys and girls."[5]

Farmers attending the institute accepted Holden's challenge and created an experimental plot where agricultural experiments could be conducted. According to longtime Iowa Extension Director R. K. Bliss, the Sioux County demonstration farm "appears to have been the first well-organized county cooperative extension work conducted in the United States." The Sioux County experimental plot was only the first of many such developments organized by Holden.[6]

The next year Holden proposed another idea: create a traveling exhibit that would bring the "modern science of corn culture" to the attention of Iowa's farmers. With the support of Henry Wallace, the Rock Island Railroad, the Iowa Grain Dealers Association, and the Central Iowa Grain Company, Holden's idea became a reality. The exhibit, the Seed Corn Gospel Train, consisted of three coaches and a baggage car. Holden began his work armed with lecture charts, displays, a speaker's platform, and from all accounts a great deal of showmanship. The first tour began on April 18, 1904; it ran from Gowrie to Ruthven and on to Estherville, making fifty stops in all. Crowds were described as good, and at some stops train windows had to be opened so farmers unable to get in, could still hear Holden's talk. Holden himself estimated that three thousand people had heard his presentations on the first tour.[7]

The messages that Holden would present again and again on the corn trains were simple and to the point: he told farmers where to look for the best seed corn; he explained the need for and the process of testing seed corn; and he described ways to achieve a stand of three stalks to the hill. Holden also included demonstrations with a germination box, in effect, showing farmers how they could test their own seed corn. According to one authority, "No message could have been more appropriate and timely than that of improved seed corn selection." Agricultural supporters in the state, like Henry Wallace, had pushed a long time for this improvement. In later presentations Holden included topics on crop rotation and manure handling. Throughout all his work, however, the topic of seed corn remained the central issue. The seed corn trains continued to operate in the state until 1906.[8]

Holden was also involved in another development at ISC—the initiation of the off-campus agricultural short course. Short courses had been offered at the college, the first being organized by Dean Charles F. Curtis in 1901, but the first short course held away from campus was at Red Oak in January 1905. The request had come from two farmers in Montgomery County who had previously attended a campus short course. The affair in Red Oak drew about two hundred and fifty local farmers who each paid $2.50 a ticket. Holden and his staff quickly deemed the event a success and repeated it the following January. As farmers throughout the state became familiar with the short course opportunity, they sent hundreds of requests to the college. During the winter of 1906–1907 Holden's staff received thirty-seven thousand inquiries about such courses.[9]

Holden had long advocated a formal extension service, and with the success of the off-campus short courses, he felt it was time to act. Moreover, he certainly was aware of Extension activities in Texas, which offered a precedent for other states. Along with the support of the Iowa Grain Dealers Association, the *Des Moines Register,* and the *Wallaces' Farmer,* Holden drafted a bill calling for the creation of a state extension service. A revised bill passed the Iowa General Assembly, known as the Extension Act of 1906. In turn, Holden became the first superintendent of Extension. He remained in that position until 1912 when he resigned to begin work setting up an extension service at International Harvester.[10]

During the first six years of the Iowa Extension Service, a great many Iowans benefited from its programs and service. During the first year Holden alone gave 172 lectures, conducted 77 corn judging contests, and devoted 28 days to short course work. By 1909 Extension's annual budget had increased to $32,000 (over the original $15,000) and 167,000 men, women, and children were involved in

FARMERS GATHERED around the Lake Park depot with the Corn Gospel Train in the background. Courtesy ISU Photo Service.

Extension-sponsored activities of various kinds. Extension activities during Holden's tenure involved work by both the agricultural staff and staff members in home economics. Mary F. Rausch was one of the first Iowa home economists lecturing on "Domestic Science" at many of the short courses around the state. During the first year she took part in short courses at Red Oak, Mount Pleasant, and Lenox as well as conducting short courses exclusively in home economics.[11]

Personnel at ISC provided instruction for Extension activities beginning in 1906, but in 1912 a major change took place. In that year, M. L. Mosher, a farm crops specialist at ISC, attended a meeting of the American Association of Agricultural Colleges and Experiment Stations at Columbus, Ohio, to investigate the county agent system initiated in several other states. Mosher returned convinced that Iowa needed such a system and related his views to several college officials. Mosher believed that the county agent should be supported by an existing county agency, but that the agent work directly for the state Extension Service rather than for the county agency. This would provide, in Mosher's view, "coordination and prevent duplication." Mosher felt strongly that everyone should understand that the agent represented not the county group but the state Extension Service. Mosher was directly involved in implementing his views when in July 1912 he accepted the position as agent in Clinton County. Unknown to Mosher at the time, his view that the county agent work for the state rather than for the "existing county agency" would later be of great significance. Between 1912 and 1955 the supporting county agencies would become a part of the strongest farm group in the state, the Iowa Farm Bureau. Had the agent been more closely identified with Farm Bureau than with Extension or with ISC, the course of Extension may have developed differently through the years.[12]

The early Iowa county agents' work was partly financed by local private organizations concerned with the prosperity and well-being of their counties. The experience in Clay County reflects that pattern. In 1913 a group of farmers there, feeling "they needed some help along educational lines," joined forces with the Spencer Commercial Club to form the Clay County Improvement Association. Since the salary of a county agent needed to be guaranteed for two years, the Spencer Commercial Club promised to raise $874 the first year and $580 the second. For both years the First National Bank and the Citizens National Bank donated $75, with other businesses or businessmen donating anywhere from $2 to $20. In other parts of the

DR. PERRY HOLDEN PRESENTING a lecture on
producing better corn to Iowa farmers in 1909 aboard
the Corn Gospel Train, which traveled throughout
Iowa. The Holden sawdust corn testing box is held by
the man on the left. Six kernels from one ear of corn
could be tested at once. Courtesy ISU Photo Service.

county, individuals and banks pledged $233.50. The preamble to their bylaws stated the following: "The purposes of the organization are to make Clay County greater, richer, and a better place in which to live, to develop the agricultural resources, improve the agricultural methods, and foster the best commercial, social and material interests of our county." Members paid dues of $2 each, with memberships available for any county resident over sixteen years of age. The organization established an advisory council that consisted of one farmer from each township and two delegates from each commercial club in the county. Along with directing the association, the advisory council determined the program and generally directed the work in the county.[13]

The hiring of the first county agents would be followed closely by the enactment of state legislation that provided important organizational structure for the new county agent system. In 1913 the General Assembly passed legislation creating the county farm aid associations and gave county supervisors power to levy a tax for the support of the new organization. In his history of Iowa agriculture, Earle Ross described this organization as one that "combined public and private support and local and centralized control." The law provided for the annual election of officers and directors who would receive no compensation. Originally the law called for a vote of county residents to authorize an amount, not to exceed $5,000, for Extension work. The legislature soon amended the law, requiring gifts and memberships amounting to $1,000 from farmers and other landowners before county funds would become available. In turn, the farm aid bill led to the formation of the first county farm bureaus (originally called county farm improvement associations), which eventually led to the state Farm Bureau organization.[14]

In 1914 events at both state and national levels would greatly affect the future of Extension in Iowa. At the state level Ralph K. Bliss was appointed Director of Extension. He would serve in that position until 1946, guiding the organization through two world wars and a major depression. Born on a farm in Union County in 1880, Bliss graduated from Iowa State College and returned home to help operate the family farm. A short time later, in 1906, he came back to Ames as the animal husbandry specialist in the newly created Extension Department. During the next several years he acquired experience in all phases of Extension work. Bliss served for a short time as acting Superintendent of Extension Work and in 1914 became Director of Extension.[15]

THE IOWA STATE COLLEGE Extension staff in
1907. Dr. Perry Holden is in the center of the front row
and longtime Extension Director R. K. Bliss is second
from the right, first row. Courtesy Iowa State University
Library/University Archives.

At the national level Congress passed the Smith-Lever Coopera-tive Extension Act, which produced a new cooperative relationship between the states' Extension Services and the U.S. Department of Agriculture (USDA). In effect, the law created a partnership between the state and federal agencies. Under this legislation each state college accepting USDA funds had to provide for a "more definite and distinct administrative division for the management and conduct of Extension work in agriculture and home economics with a responsible leader selected by the college and satisfactory to the U.S. Department of Agriculture." The legislation made funds available for the expansion of Extension work, but left the adminis-tration and development of programs to state Extension officials. Iowa then received its first federal Extension grant of $10,000 in 1914, which together with state appropriations raised the state's Extension budget to $85,200.[16]

While the wording of the Smith-Lever bill presented in broad terms the purposes of the legislation, the intent behind it was more specific. In the House Committee report made by Congressman Asbury Frank Lever, chairman of the Agriculture Committee, six features were emphasized: (1) cooperative work with the U.S. Department of Agriculture, (2) demonstrational teaching, (3) county agent work, (4) marketing, (5) boys' and girls' club work in agricul-ture and home economics, and (6) home economics with farm women.[17]

With additional funding and a new director, Iowa's Extension Service experienced considerable expansion during the next three years. During the winter Extension officials conducted local short courses throughout the state, averaging about thirty, one-week courses a year. These included both agriculture and home economics. During the same three-year period, Extension officials offered "smaller" separate short courses in agriculture and home economics. Officials also continued with farmers' institutes and county farm demonstration work. New programs initiated between 1914 and 1917 included a farm building blueprint service and demonstrations for control of ditch erosion. Extension personnel also promoted hog cholera prevention and control and set up farm tours demonstrating better farming methods. A correspondence course for rural school-teachers was also established.[18]

Even before the passage of the Smith-Lever Act, Iowa had six county agents in the field. These individuals immediately faced a wide variety of tasks, including organizing many different groups in the county, dealing with farmers' individual problems, and strengthening ties between the Extension Service and the local commercial clubs. Clay County's first agent, W. A. Posey, began reorganizing boys' and girls' clubs with considerable success. Within the first four years these groups averaged an enrollment of about three hundred members. Among the young people, corn clubs and poultry clubs proved the most popular. Posey was also involved in setting up farmers' institutes in the county. The Extension Service, under Posey's guidance, sponsored an annual county picnic including barbecues and events such as plowing contests, tractor demonstrations, and stock shows. In 1916 the annual picnic led to the organization of the Clay County Fair Association. The Board of Supervisors then spent $12,000 to purchase land, resulting in the beginning of the Clay County Fair, later advertised as the "World's Greatest County Fair." Posey also worked to strengthen and further develop Extension's sponsoring organization, the Clay County Improvement Association.[19]

The county agent was required to become, as one early agent described it, "the crop doctor." It seemed that local farmers looked upon the county agent "almost entirely as the principal source of information." As Ralph K. Bliss explained in his history of the Iowa Extension Service, the county agent's office became a "clearing house for farm questions and difficult farm problems. If the agent could not answer the question himself, he got in touch with those that could. . . . And if there were no answers there, he contacted the Experiment Station." In Clay County in 1913 an epidemic of hog cholera broke out which required considerable time of the agent. The agent also supervised soil surveys taken throughout the entire county. From the beginning of their tenure, county agents were concerned with corn improvement; in Clay County in 1914 staff in the county agent's office tested eight hundred bushels of seed corn. The agent also set up alfalfa demonstration plots, one in each township during the first year. Other projects carried out by county agents in this period included applying limestone to the soil, spraying orchards, conducting soil demonstration tests, and culling chickens.[20]

In Black Hawk County in 1915 an early frost prevented the corn from ripening and drying properly so that every farm had soft corn. The county agent faced a difficult situation as during the winter rumors began circulating that none of the corn saved for seed would grow. He immediately set up testing stations in Cedar Falls and Waterloo and searched the county for corn that would grow. Officials at these stations tested "thousands of ears of corn"; they also sent out smaller testing machines to rural schools where they urged farmers to carry out tests themselves. As a result, farmers who had none of their own could purchase good seed. The county agent estimated that 1,104 bushels of corn were sold the following spring.[21]

In effect, in the first years of Extension work, the county agent provided personal service to farmers in his county. According to one description, the county agent essentially worked alone.

> In those early days the County Agent had to rely entirely on his own brains and stamina. All work done by him was original work. There were no yearly programs sent out from Ames. There were no trained organization workers, no familiar wheelhorses to depend on. There was plenty of skepticism and even open hostility. For instance, the now familiar process of vaccinating hogs against cholera was new in those days. Even some of the veterinarians were opposed to it. When Mr. Burger [the county agent] went to Ames and learned the method and later came back to the County to give demonstrations, farmers muttered darkly that he was poisoning the hogs.[22]

In Calhoun County the first agent had a hard time convincing local farmers that planting sweet clover would not bring a "permanent weed pest on the farm."[23]

While county agents carried out a full range of responsibilities, they typically did not seek out farmers to help with demonstrations (or make use of the local leader method) as national officials urged them to do. In 1915 at a meeting of land-grant college officials, Bradford Knapp, son of Extension pioneer Seaman Knapp and himself an Extension official, presented his views on various aspects of Extension work, including reference to the local leader system. Knapp believed there were really two types of demonstration. The first "conducted by the teacher himself" and the second by "the one who is being taught." Knapp made it clear that according to his definition of demonstration, a farmer or some member of his family would actually do the work (or conduct the demonstration) while the county agent gave instructions.

> The value of such demonstrations has sometimes been overlooked. It has a direct effect upon the farmer and also has an important effect upon the county agent himself and on his work. Such a demonstration serves two purposes: (1) It conveys a lesson and imparts information to the farmer who is conducting the demonstration and to his neighbors; and (2) it demonstrates to the farmer

and to the community the practical worth and value of the information the county agent has given him.[24]

In the first Black Hawk County agent's report in 1912, the agent wrote that Extension work "should be handled entirely on a county-wide demonstration basis and . . . local township organizations [do] not serve to improve the effectiveness of the work." Later reports indicate that setting up township organizations and relying heavily on local leaders to help organize and even help with teaching materials was an approach not used by county agents until about the mid-1920s. Even then they utilized the system much less than did home demonstration agents.[25]

A part of the county agents' responsibilities was determining the lines of work or the projects to be followed during the year. In the 1910s and 1920s two situations developed in regard to programming. During World War I wartime emergencies actually determined the program of work. Many agents wrote in their annual narrative reports that emergency measures, such as finding adequate seed corn, working with local labor boards, and promoting Liberty Loan drives, occupied most of their time. In other words, there was little time for what they viewed as their traditional duties. At other times in the 1910s and 1920s, the agent typically sat down with the local farm bureau board of directors to determine the line of work. In Calhoun County, once that meeting had taken place, the "agent then proceeded to set meetings at different places in the county and then followed up with personal visits to help carry out the practices." In Clinton County in the 1910s the program of work was "mainly determined by a few farm leaders and the agent. The farm leaders did not contact their farm neighbors as they [would do at a later date]." It was not until the mid-1920s that farm people became actively involved in determining future programs.[26]

Despite formal planning, local conditions often determined the agents' work. Even with the help of subject matter specialists—in the 1920s there were six specialists in the fields of soils, farm crops, animal husbandry, home work, horticulture, and dairying—county agents had to make do with very little and to a large extent utilize their own ingenuity. In Crawford County an agent wanting to demonstrate the effect of applying limestone to alfalfa simply took some plaster from an old house and spread it on the field.[27]

It should also be noted that especially during the late 1910s, the Extension Service and the county agents were new and not all farming people in the state were convinced of the necessity for such an organization. Many agents wrote in their early reports that it took some time to convince their clients of this need. In the view of one agent, this period extended from about 1917 (when his county was organized) until 1923. "In the beginning of the work, people were not familiar with just what the Extension Service was attempting to do. It was necessary for the Agent to do a lot of personal work to help them create a desire to do something about solving . . . problems."[28]

While the county agents' time was mostly taken up delivering "personal service to the farmers of the state," home economists were concerned with the farm family and farm home. For over a decade home economists from Iowa State College had been part of short course presentations, both on and off campus. Neale S. Knowles came to Iowa State in 1908 as head of Home Economics Extension and was personally involved in many short course presentations. In December 1914, for example, Knowles and her assistant, Esther Munge, presented a program in Crawford County during the week-long short course on Household Arts. Between 1906 and 1914 state Extension personnel used educational trains to travel the state. One train, designated as the Bacon Special because it carried many meat products donated by Morrell Meat Packing, also contained a women's car. Traveling with the train were home economics specialists, including Knowles and her assistants who, through the use of many charts and demonstrations, lectured on problems related to the farm home. After 1907 home demonstration agents became a regular part of the educational trains.[29]

Along with agriculture, Home Economics Extension had been specifically mandated in the Smith-Lever Act passed in 1914. In the committee report made at the time the bill was introduced in Congress, Representative Lever made specific mention of farm women's plight and that legislation should provide assistance to them.

> This is the first time in the history of this country that the federal government has shown any tangible purpose or desire to help the farm woman, in a direct way, to solve her manifold problems and lessen her heavy burdens. The drudgery and toil of the farm wives have not been appreciated by [legislators] nor has proper weight been given to her influence on rural life.[30]

Lever added that the neglect of farm wives and daughters—in light of attention paid to farmers and their problems—was "almost to the point of criminality." Smith-Lever would produce a Home Economics Extension that would teach "the elementary principles of homemaking and home management for farm women."[31]

In 1916 an important advance took place in Home Economics Extension when the first county Extension home economist was hired. In that year Director Bliss attended a meeting of the Board of Directors of the Black Hawk County Farm Bureau where he "presented the case for the HDA [home demonstration agent]." Following the meeting, the committee voted in favor of hiring a "female demonstration agent." Neale Knowles was also involved in negotiations. On September 1, 1916, the county hired Tura Hawk as the Black Hawk County home demonstration agent and the first such agent in Iowa. Apparently Agent Hawk had to be proficient in many areas as county records indicate she "actually demonstrated to the Board that she could shoe a horse." More in keeping with her Extension duties, Hawk quickly became involved in the food conservation program, giving demonstrations at local schools on the subject of meat and meat substitutes. She also presented material on candy making, poultry demonstrations, egg marketing campaigns, and planning convenient kitchens.[32]

Like their male counterparts in Extension, county home economists worked to bring about cooperation between rural and urban groups. In 1916 farm women in Black Hawk County began a "clean milk campaign," whereby they sought to convince the General Assembly that milk producers should keep only TB-tested herds. According to the county agent's report, Black Hawk County "was one of the worst infected areas of the state." Five nearby states had erected quarantine barriers against Iowa dairy cows because the state had no compulsory tuberculosis law. The next year the farm women joined forces with the Federated Women's Clubs of Cedar Falls to ensure that Cedar Falls residents could obtain "clean milk free from TB germs." The women apparently took to heart Extension's method of demonstration as they visited Rath Packing Company and obtained specimens of the "internal organs and body walls of TB-affected animals," which they put on exhibit in a downtown building. Following that action, two city dairies agreed to have their cows tested for tuberculosis. An Extension report noted that the two dairymen had such an increased demand for their milk, they quickly raised their prices.[33]

In 1917 America entered World War I, an event that had great significance for the Extension Service throughout the nation. Because of the immediate need for additional foodstuffs, the federal government appropriated approximately $11.3 million to the Department of Agriculture and the Food Administration, much of which went for the development of the nation's Extension Service. A slogan heard throughout the country, "Food will win the war," was especially appropriate for the Middle West. As Earle Ross has pointed out, given the need to mobilize American farmers for increased production, "The Middle West was the key region and in many respects Iowa . . . was the key state." With its "unique agricultural resources," Iowa would be central in helping the nation increase the production and conservation of food.[34]

In Iowa, as in other states, the Extension Service became the central agency responsible for mobilizing Iowa's citizens for the war effort. Once war was declared, Iowa officials hurriedly organized a county farm aid society for all counties previously unorganized. This created the framework for the Extension Service so county agents could be hired. Extension officials John W. Coverdale and Murl McDonald worked vigorously during the next nine months and by February of the following year they had reached their goal: all counties had organized farm bureaus and one county, Pottawattamie, had two. By June, due to federal funding and the organizational work of Coverdale and McDonald, Extension could boast of a county agent in every county (two in Pottawattamie County) and forty-one permanent home economists. Some counties also had youth workers. In total, Extension had a field staff of 199 persons along with 50 specialists housed at ISC.[35]

Even before President Woodrow Wilson issued a declaration of war, however, Iowa Governor William Harding called together a group of prominent Iowans to discuss "ways and means of increasing the food supply." As a result, a thirteen-man committee was appointed—including men from every part of the state—to the War Emergency Food Committee. ISC President Raymond Pearson served as committee president and Ralph K. Bliss as secretary. The committee listed the following wartime goals: (1) more farm labor, (2) more vegetable gardens, (3) more poultry, (4) more hogs, (5) better seeds, (6) less waste, (7) better adaptation of crops to soils, (8) more breeding animals, (9) fewer losses from animal disease, and (10) better distribution of food. In effect, the rapid action of Iowa's state officials meant Iowa was in a state of readiness when the declaration of war was actually made.[36]

A major difficulty facing Extension in its efforts to mobilize the state's farmers was communication. Director Bliss solved this problem by organizing a plan for the appointment of one farm person in each township to distribute materials to approximately sixteen other township families. These individuals were known as War Food Production Cooperators; each cooperator had responsibility for a school district or for four square miles of land. There were then 140 cooperators in each county and a total of 14,000 cooperators in the state. In effect, the volunteer cooperators plan provided a communication network throughout the entire state.[37]

As state planners had anticipated, with America's entry into the war, Iowans soon faced a shortage of farm labor. State officials established Volunteer Farm Labor Bureaus in each county to help deal with the situation. Because it was necessary to mobilize quickly, state officials asked local commercial clubs and other private organizations to "establish, finance and maintain" the Volunteer Farm Labor Bureaus in their communities.[38]

In organized counties the Extension agent took charge of the labor bureau. In Greene County the agent reported that in 1917, 44 farmers were supplied with labor; in 1918, 94; and in 1919, 124. Along with supplying laborers, county agents also helped establish wages for some workers. In 1918 the Greene County farm bureau directors recommended that laborers picking corn should receive "seven or eight cents a bushel." The Greene County agent reported that this action "had a very beneficial effect upon the labor situation in that men who were seeking work knew that the prices were the same all over the county and instead of looking for a place where they could get more per bushel, took the first job offered them and stayed by it." In the state as a whole during the war period, officials placed twenty thousand farm laborers on Iowa farms.[39]

Iowans, anxious to show support for the war effort, immediately began to comply with the government's guidelines of increasing production and conservation of food. In Buena Vista County, which hired its first county agent in January 1917, residents found that in April it was too late to change farmers' production plans for that year. Therefore Extension staff placed the emphasis on conservation of food. Extension staff urged people to reduce their consumption of all kinds of foodstuffs, particularly wheat and meat products, since these were more easily shipped to the Allies. Increased production of food remained the major goal, however, and Extension utilized several approaches to increase acreages of corn, potatoes, and garden stuffs. Even though the corn acreages had been established by April, farmers raised some additional corn by using land intended for small grain and also by plowing up meadowland. Local officials also encouraged an increase in potato production. The county agent in Buena Vista County reported, "Vacant lots were utilized and practically every spare yard of ground was put under cultivation." In Storm Lake citizens utilized a considerable part of parking areas between sidewalks and streets for gardens. People in every town in Buena Vista County carried out this "front door" type of gardening. The agent estimated the increase in potato production at over thirty thousand bushels, while the corn acreage increased at least 10 percent. Slogans abounded such as the one continually voiced by Extension agents: "Make two blades of grass grow where one grew before."[40]

In the fall and winter of 1917–1918, an unexpected and potentially catastrophic problem surfaced with the shortage of seed corn. A cold, wet summer slowed down the maturation of corn and an early frost further depleted the state's potential supply of seed corn. State agriculture officials described the situation as "a little short of desperate." Throughout that time Extension moved quickly to survey farmers regarding their seed corn supplies and to urge them to test their own reserves. County agents performed a variety of tasks ranging from testing seed to visiting farms to locate surplus supplies. When it was discovered that some southern Iowa farmers had a surplus, Extension personnel arranged for seed corn to be sent to farmers in northern Iowa who were facing a shortage. The campaign was apparently successful as Director Bliss announced the following summer that farmers had "procured one of the best stands of corn in the history of the state."[41]

By the spring of 1918 the Allied countries were so desperately in need of food that the U.S. Department of Agriculture agreed to provide money for the summer hiring of a home economist in each Iowa county. In Buena Vista County Bertha Knight was appointed as home demonstration agent. Knight presented demonstrations in saving wheat, meat, fat, and sugar. She also gave demonstrations in canning and drying of fruits and vegetables as well as the saving of fuel and clothing. Under Knight's direction four girls' canning clubs organized, which collectively canned 210 quarts of fruits and vegetables. At the same time nine garden clubs and twenty women's units organized for food and clothing conservation. One woman cited for her extraordinary effort was Mrs. Swallum of Storm Lake, who canned 388 quarts of vegetables, 547 quarts of fruit, 135 quarts of pickles, 20 quarts of jelly, 69 quarts of jam, and also "put down one barrel of kraut."[42]

In addition to work directly related to food production and conservation, Extension agents had many other responsibilities. When the state held its first Liberty Loan campaign, sales did not go well in rural areas with the result that Iowa did not meet its quota. This situation resulted from a number of conditions, including the fact that rural people were unfamiliar with bond investments and that it was difficult to carry out mass appeal campaigns in rural areas. County agents took part in future drives, which had considerably more success than the first. They also served as members of their local draft boards with the responsibility of recommending that "farmers with dependent families and without adequate help to care for the farm in their absence be exempted from military duty."[43]

By the end of the war the increase in food production and food conservation in Iowa had exceeded the most optimistic estimates. With Extension personnel serving as the major assistants, Iowa's farmers in 1917 and 1918 increased their production of corn, oats, wheat, barley, and rye by 26 percent over the average yearly production for the ten-year period preceding the war. At the same time hog production increased by 15 percent over the previous year. At its peak in 1919, Iowa farmers produced 10,822,000 hogs. In the area of food savings, the record was also impressive. Director Bliss wrote that while it was impossible to know exactly the food savings in the state, he estimated that in the campaign to use potatoes instead of flour, reports show that "26,048 families saved 2,288 twenty-four pound sacks of wheat flour by substituting potatoes; 968 families used no wheat flour at all; 440 families saved 253 twenty-four pound sacks in excess of the saving required by the regulations; and 16,544 families reported savings but not definite enough for tabulation." Bliss also noted that the federal government "placed Iowa at the top with regard to the percentage of women who signed cards pledging themselves to support the government in the food saving campaign." By all assessments the Extension Service had measured up to its first major challenge. As one historian observed, "Extension had proven its worth during World War I."[44]

The period from 1903 to 1918 represented the formative years for the ISC Extension Service. In effect, the period marked the initiating, the shaping, and the legitimizing of the organization. Clearly, Extension came into existence in response to local needs within the state, but with the passage of the Smith-Lever Act in 1914 and the creation of the federal-state relationship, the future of Extension seemed assured. During World War I Iowa's Extension

Service expanded rapidly and officials could feel great pride over its major contribution to the war effort.

In one sense the war years brought about an unexpected reciprocal arrangement between the federal government and Extension: while Extension contributed significantly to the war effort as requested by the federal government, in return the federal government greatly aided Extension by appropriating money for an expanded staff. By war's end, the Extension Service had a presence in every county in the state. Through varied activities Extension had gained considerable status in the eyes of Iowa's farm population. As Earle Ross has written, the creation of Extension "synchronized opportunely with the coming of the war."[45] Although Extension would have continued to expand even without U.S. involvement in World War I, that expansion—and subsequent visibility and increased stature—would have come more slowly. Without question, Extension's work throughout the war years gave legitimacy to its programs and a rationale for its existence. By 1918 the basic structure of the organization was in place. In effect, from that date on when important events took place in rural Iowa, Extension would be involved.

3

A Decade of Expansion

The 1920s

After responding well to the emergency needs of a nation at war, the Extension Service had only a few prosperous years before agriculture again experienced a crisis in the early 1920s. During 1920 and 1921 farm exports declined and farm prices fell, leaving many farmers with heavy mortgage payments as the result of expansion during the war. Extension personnel responded to the economic difficulties by urging farmers to reduce production costs and take part in cooperative production and marketing groups, both in an effort to increase profits. During the 1920s Extension greatly increased in type and number of services available to its rural clientele, all geared to improving Iowa's farm, home, and community life. Extension personnel also worked closely with other community organizations and trade associations to promote these goals. At the beginning of the 1920s Extension could still be described as an institution in the making; by the end of the decade it was an organization with its mission defined and experienced leadership—R. K. Bliss and Neale S. Knowles—in charge. As a result, through the decade the Iowa Extension Service had become increasingly visible both in Iowa and the nation.

Only one month after hostilities ended in Europe, Iowa farmers organized a new association that would have highly significant and longtime implications for the Extension Service. In December 1918 delegates from seventy-two counties met in Marshalltown to organize a state Farm Bureau. Extension officials had urged leading Iowa farmers to form such a group and had held earlier meetings with farmers to plan the federation campaign. Once assembled, the delegates agreed on the need for a state organization; accordingly, they drew up a constitution, bylaws, and named an executive committee. The group elected J. R. Howard from rural Clemons as president.[1]

From the standpoint of Extension, the new group could hardly have been organized at a better time. In July 1919 the federal government terminated funds given Extension to encourage war food production. The support had been sizeable; during 1918 alone Iowa had received $220,000. The federal money had helped support many county agents and home economists and given the pending cutbacks, Extension faced a sharp reduction in staff. Following its organization, the new Farm Bureau Federation began a statewide campaign that resulted in a total of 110,000 memberships. The funds generated by additional membership fees plus those traditionally raised by the county farm bureaus had the desired effect. According to R. K. Bliss, "Through the prompt action of the State Farm Bureau in increasing the membership of county farm bureaus, enough funds were provided to prevent any serious decline in Cooperative Extension educational activities." In reality, the Farm Bureau underwrote much of the cost of county Extension work including the agents' salaries. This was significant as throughout the nation about one-third of the counties lost their county agents and about one-half lost their home demonstration agents.[2]

The creation of the Iowa Farm Bureau Federation and its almost immediate involvement in fund-raising helped bring an even closer relationship between Farm Bureau and the Extension Service. In his annual report in 1921, typical of reports throughout his tenure as director, Bliss left no doubt that he felt the association between the two groups to be totally positive. "The county farm bureaus have made possible the extension of education work into every community in the state. They have been a constructive force for agricultural improvement and better living on the farms of Iowa." He added that furthermore his organization "considers it an honor and a privilege" to work with the Farm Bureau officers and personnel. Bliss frequently pointed out that Farm Bureau memberships added considerable money to Extension's budget; in 1924 he estimated that they contributed approximately a third of a million dollars for the development of agriculture in the state.[3] The annual narrative reports of county Extension staff also underscore the close relationship as some county agents referred to themselves as Farm Bureau agents. Since county Extension personnel and Farm Bureau staff often shared the same office, the public tended to think of the two groups as one.

Shortly after one financial emergency had been solved, a far more serious one appeared. At the end of the war economic conditions for Iowa farmers had looked promising, a condition that continued into 1920. But in May of that year the federal government ended its subsidies of agricultural products and farm prices soon dipped dramatically. Adding to the difficulty, fewer American agricultural products were needed in Europe as those nations began to recover and produce food for their own populations. Director Bliss noted that "the farm market almost collapsed in 1921."[4]

Farmers quickly realized that not all segments of society shared equally in the difficult times. The farm sector was particularly hard hit because consumer prices—what farmers paid for stock, machinery, and farm supplies—remained the same or even increased while farmers' incomes had greatly declined. In June 1921 a bushel of corn, measured in exchange value, "would purchase 44 per cent as much clothing, 42 per cent as much fuel, 40 per cent as much building material or 32 per cent as much [in] house furnishing as it did in 1913." Farm prices fell even more and by December of that year a bushel of corn would purchase only about one-third the items needed by the farmer, compared to 1913.[5]

Iowa farmers found themselves in severe difficulty not only because of declining prices, but also because of land payments, results of expansion during the war. The high price of farm products during World War I had brought about an "unprecedented land boom." At the peak of that boom, Iowa land averaged $227 per acre. As values rose, land was often "bought and sold 'on a shoestring' with very little cash changing hands." Iowa farmland values had increased 33 percent from March 1919 to March 1920; this increase compared to 21 percent in the country as a whole. With the sharp drop in farm prices, many farm families found themselves caught in a cost-price squeeze: payments remained the same because of obligations assumed during prosperous times, but they had far less income to pay off financial obligations. In his annual report for 1921, Director Bliss commented on the bleak situation, noting that the corn and oats crops were sold on a ruinously low market. Bliss then summed up the dilemma in simple terms.

The average farmer grew about 50 acres of corn in 1921. The

purchasing power of that 50 acres . . . when exchanged for the manufactured articles which the farmer has to buy is just about equal to the purchasing power of 18 acres of corn in 1913 if expended for [clothing, fuel, building materials, and home furnishing goods].[6]

A major response of Extension personnel to the agricultural distress in 1920 and 1921 was to work for more economical farming practices. If prices had fallen, then to make a profit the Iowa farmer must lower the costs of production. As a first step, Extension officials urged farmers to start good record-keeping systems to have more information on their operations. To assist with this task, Extension agriculturalist Sam H. Thompson developed a farm record book specifically for farmers. Thompson and others then held a total of 139 one-day short courses throughout the state to acquaint farmers with the process. The result was that 14,279 farmers purchased the book. Extension personnel explained that keeping complete records helped the farmer determine "what kinds of crops and stock and how much of each should be included in his farm business, the proportion of land, labor, and equipment that should be used, and by what means the marketing process [could] be made more efficient."[7]

In the early 1920s Extension personnel also urged Iowa farmers to make better use of cooperatives to increase the profitability of marketing agricultural products. In taking this action, the Iowa Extension Service was in step with the rest of the country as cooperatives were becoming more important nationally. Extension hired its first marketing specialist in 1917. During the next few years Extension hired marketing specialists in the area of livestock, dairy, and poultry. While the number of marketing cooperatives increased from 800 in 1920 to 1,200 in 1930, an even greater increase came in the amount of business transacted by these groups. Director Bliss estimated that their business more than doubled from $140 million in 1920 to $300 million in 1930. Six hundred cooperative livestock shipping associations were active at one time. Marketing specialists continually stressed that developing successful cooperatives depended on keeping good financial records.[8]

In the spring of 1921 Extension reorganized farm management and marketing under a new section known as Agricultural Economics and Rural Sociology. This reorganization followed changes already made both at the college and the federal Experiment Station in Ames. While the section was formed partly as a response to the two rapidly growing social sciences of agricultural economics and rural sociology, the agricultural depression was the major factor. The move coincided with the creation of the Bureau of Agricultural Economics in the USDA. Following the formation of this section, agricultural economics played an increasingly important part in Iowa Extension.[9]

In 1923 Agricultural Economics and Rural Sociology began a mimeographed monthly publication, "Agricultural Economics and Rural Organization Facts." Extension staff designed the newsletter to provide farmers with management information and program ideas for rural township meetings. Within a year Extension staff changed the title to "Agricultural Economic Facts." The editors stated that the publication would disseminate information about Iowa's agricultural economic conditions to people in both rural and urban areas and to businesspeople.[10] Knowledge of market conditions would help farmers make more informed decisions regarding their own planting, breeding, and marketing operations.

The publication of "Agricultural Economic Facts" in Iowa was related to changes in the federal Bureau of Agricultural Economics (BAE). Beginning in 1923 the BAE issued a yearly national outlook report covering the "anticipated trends and prospects for the coming growing and marketing year." This report served as the basis for regional and state reports that also incorporated state and local conditions. Extension officials disseminated the outlook reports through newspapers, over radio, and by Extension publications. In 1929 Extension initiated county outlook meetings. Extension specialists then "presented, interpreted, and discussed the implications of the [outlook] material directly with farmers." It appears that Iowa was one of the first states to begin publishing such information although not one of the first to hold county outlook meetings. By 1929 over forty states had some form of outlook publication.[11]

While agricultural economists issued monthly information on agricultural matters, their influence went well beyond the supplying of marketing and pricing information at any given time. Joel Kunze has pointed out that economic forecasts in the 1920s had far more lasting results than the immediate goal of providing monthly information: in effect, the agricultural economists were also teaching farmers about agricultural economics. During the 1920s, according to Kunze, the goal of the Bureau of Agricultural Economics was to reduce agricultural surpluses. Although that goal was not realized, in the process of developing and disseminating outlook information through countless publications and meetings, agricultural economists were educating farmers about economic issues and theory.

The outlook program attempted to establish a foundation of knowledge and economic understanding that had not existed before, to give farmers economic tools comparable to those used in other businesses. The USDA supplied not only the information necessary for decision making, it supplied the rudimentary instruction necessary to arrive at the decision.[12]

While agricultural economists and county agents usually worked together toward the same goals, there were exceptions. At certain times during the 1920s, agricultural economists urged farmers to cut crop production in an effort to reduce surpluses and halt fluctuating prices. This was the case in 1923 when economists urged farmers to reduce their 1924 corn crop because the economists feared that a large crop would produce more hogs and thus aggravate "an already overexpanded meat market." At the same time county agents and crop specialists were advising farmers to always test seed corn for germination. While perhaps not directly recommending farmers produce more corn, as one study points out, "Good seed could increase individual efficiency through higher yields. Both groups of specialists were simply doing their job, but gave contradictory advice."[13]

Although not as visible as agricultural economics, rural sociology also became an important part of Extension in the 1920s. The initiation of the program came partly as a consequence of the development of the discipline itself, but also in response to anticipated needs of Iowa farm people. In effect, rural Iowans were facing both a financial and a social crisis. Observers of rural life had long insisted that a drawback to rural living was its social isolation, particularly its impact on farm women. Because of that fact, the Country Life Commission in 1909 had urged that more social opportunities be created for them. By 1920 farm life was not only isolated but, in the view of many, clearly inferior to town and city life. A sharper contrast existed between the two: townspeople had access to modern conveniences such as electric lights, central heating, indoor plumbing, and electric appliances while most farm residents did not. Farm families also had fewer social and cultural opportunities than did townspeople.[14] Extension's development of social and educational programs that people could enjoy in their own rural neighborhoods—without going to town—spoke directly to the deeply felt needs of farm families. In 1922 Director Bliss appointed William Stacy as Extension's first rural sociologist, making Iowa one of the first states to have such a specialist. By 1927 only thirteen states had such a position.[15]

The development of the rural sociology program also reflected a national trend toward rural community organization. As a result of World War I, the Red Cross and other social service programs had given rural residents a sense of organized community life. Wartime prosperity had also raised the standard of living for many farm people and, in turn, the prosperity of their communities. In addition, increased mobility during the war exposed people to urban life. These changes produced a new set of interests and needs for rural community activities in Iowa. One survey of ten thousand farm homes indicated that farm women, as well as being concerned about economic matters, were also interested in cultural affairs and in matters related to their local churches and schools. And they were interested in organized recreation and social life. In response to these needs, the Extension Service in various states began to set up programs for rural residents. The work of community organization staffs was along two lines: (1) surveying local communities to determine social needs, and (2) offering "constructive service" to better conditions. Edmund deS. Brunner and E. Hsin Pao Yang observed that in the 1920s "farm homes and rural communities began to be treated as integral parts of the whole Extension program."[16]

A major responsibility of the Extension rural sociologist was to promote social interaction among rural people, providing them with more social outlets. While the programs in rural community development came in response to the social needs of local people, no doubt the economic difficulties faced by Iowa's farm population also made them more appealing. As R. K. Bliss noted, these programs were mostly "homemade" and therefore were far more affordable than going to town for entertainment. As Iowa's first Extension rural sociologist, William Stacy was involved in developing numerous programs and projects. Stacy and his staff provided a monthly program service for any organization in the state, with farm organizations viewed as potential recipients. Included were lists of speakers for events and plays which could be performed by local people. Gradually increasing during the 1920s, by 1931, 450 rural groups were receiving regular service. Music also played an important part in the recreational programming. In 1925 choral competition was held among farm people in Black Hawk County; within a short time county choruses had become an important part of farm women's social activities statewide. Rural orchestras were also developed in some areas.[17]

In 1927 Stacy set up a citizenship course for rural communities that contained five lessons: duties of American citizens, state and national government, county and township government in Iowa, the Farm Bureau as a public agency, and [ways to achieve] success in local meetings. Stacy designed projects to advance the motto adopted by the Extension rural sociology program: "Every Iowa community a good place in which to live." By 1927 Iowa, along with other states involved in rural sociology programs, selected a state project that would be followed by every county and local community taking part.[18]

In response to the decline of rural churches in the state, Extension personnel also began to develop a rural church program. In 1926 rural sociologists set up a statewide rural pastors' conference including a Class A Rural Church program. Requirements to become a Class A church included that the pastor be a member of a farm organization and that once a year the church present an annual rural-life Sunday program. William Stacy often presented the sermon on this day. St. Mary's Catholic Church at Panama became the first rural church to receive the Class A designation.[19]

Stacy also introduced a debate series, originating at the township level with the winners working their way up to a state championship. The topics, chosen by the state Extension staff, related to some aspect of rural life in America. In 1925 the third annual debate topic read, "Resolved: That the average Iowa farm boy of today will find greater opportunity in farming than in town or city occupations." Sometimes debate topics were of a more specific nature such as the one adopted the following year, "Resolved: That government assistance should be given in the creation of a mechanism for the purpose of making the tariff effective on farm products of which a surplus is normally produced in the United States." Stacy believed that the debates encouraged farm people to study important issues and receive experience in public speaking.[20]

The influence of Extension's rural sociology program on county Extension personnel was also evident. In 1921 the home demonstration agent in Benton County wrote that both she and her male counterpart encouraged township groups "to hold regular meetings in which a part of their program is recreation." Most of the townships in Benton County followed that advice. The agent explained that "people have put on programs of local talent in music, readings, etc. Usually there have been refreshments. Florence Township fixed up a permanent picnic place with bandstand, electric lights (a farm lighting plant being bought), seats and a dance pavilion. This was done from money cleared on the 4th of July picnic." Township meetings such as that in Florence Township served several purposes as typically they provided an opportunity for farm couples to discuss financial and legislative matters but also contained both recreational and educational components. Through the efforts of the rural sociology staff and the input of county Extension personnel, farm people organized more and more townships and, in turn, held regular meetings.[21]

The work of the rural sociology staff points out once again the close, reciprocal relationship that existed between Extension and the state Farm Bureau. It is instructive to note that of the five programs in citizenship, one was devoted entirely to "The Farm Bureau as a Public Agency," a move which no doubt brought criticism from the state's other farm organizations. Moreover, before a church could take part in Extension's rural church program, the pastor had to belong to a farm organization. Although Extension reports are not not very clear on this point, pastors no doubt typically were inclined to join the Farm Bureau rather than the Grange or the Farmers' Union.

Farm Bureau was also closely tied to Extension for program development. Iowa law provided that the county farm bureaus and ISC cooperate in planning the annual program of work for each county. Each August or September the county agent met with the county farm bureau program committee to prepare a tentative program for the coming year. Officials then presented it to the larger county farm bureau board with a representative of the Extension Service in attendance. The county board acted on the program, after which it went back to the different townships for consideration. The annual meeting approved the finalized program in January of the following year. In this way Extension personnel and county farm bureau members jointly determined the Plan of Work or yearly program.[22]

While the close relationship proved beneficial to both Extension and Farm Bureau, there were drawbacks. During the 1920s when Extension worked to involve more farm people in programs, the question invariably surfaced: Is it possible to take part in Extension activities without belonging to Farm Bureau? Home demonstration agents continually assured farm women that it was indeed possible; even so, this misconception probably kept some farm women from attending Extension programs. At the same time rival farm organizations, particularly the Farmers' Union, deeply resented the close tie between Extension and Farm Bureau. Founded in Texas in 1902, the

Farmers' Union became active in Iowa in 1917 when it received a charter from the State Legislature.[23] To Farmers' Union members, Farm Bureau held a favored position with Extension and therefore with Iowa State College, partly at taxpayers' expense.

The increased membership in Farm Bureau in 1919 and 1920, while providing more money for Extension, also meant more work for Extension agents. As Michael Lundeen points out in his study of the early years of Iowa Extension, this rapid expansion presented county agents with new responsibilities and problems. In Jones County, Farm Bureau memberships increased by 1,200 in four years. One county agent charged that the membership drive had "caught farmers unprepared" and therefore they were not willing to organize and take part in Extension programs. All of this meant the county agents had to carry an even heavier load, providing services to new members as well as doing additional organizing. As Lundeen points out, "Many county agents, therefore, became responsible for maintaining a viable farm bureau."[24]

Even though Extension faced serious problems in the early 1920s, the organization continued its traditional programs in agriculture, home economics, and youth work. Of the three areas, agriculture received the major share of support. Throughout the decade county agents continued to be present in every county while the number of agricultural specialists increased. In general, specialists were to work through county agents to help Iowa farmers move toward more efficient production, marketing, and spending. By 1921 Agricultural Extension contained the areas of animal husbandry, poultry husbandry, dairy production, dairy manufacturing, veterinary work, farm crops and soil, and horticulture. Also included in this division were agricultural economics, rural sociology, agricultural education, agricultural engineering, forestry, landscape architecture, and later, publicity and journalism. Each area contained at least one specialist and sometimes more.[25]

In 1921 Animal Husbandry Extension had four specialists who worked with county agents to upgrade livestock and improve its production. Included in their work were programs such as the Feeds and Feeding Service Project, emphasizing the need to better utilize feeds grown on each farm and to increase production of clover and soybeans to mix with farm rations. The object was to help increase efficiency, thereby bringing a larger return for time and money invested. In addition, these same specialists assisted in the organization of four new livestock breeders' associations along with serving the existing twenty-two associations. Animal husbandry specialists also worked with wool growers in the state, helping them with wool grading, feeding and management, castrating, and shearing.[26]

Animal husbandry specialists provided assistance to both farm men and women. Farm butchering demonstrations proved to be popular in 1920–1921 as specialists presented sixty-three of them in seventeen counties. Many counties requested demonstrations but had to be turned down. Specialists demonstrated by butchering some animals themselves, while supervising farmers as they butchered additional animals. Director Bliss noted in his annual report for 1920–1921 that "a large number of women attended each demonstration for the cutting of the carcass. They took an active part, asking questions and often telling the men how to cut the carcass." One farm wife commented on the benefit of the demonstration in her neighborhood: "I was delighted to find that our home killed hogs according to Professor McDonald's instructions furnished us with pork chops, where we had never before had anything but backbone." In effect, the demonstration on the "killing, curing and canning of meats" provided participating farm families with high-grade meat at a cheaper cost than if purchased from retailers.[27]

During the 1920s Extension revived a system used in the 1910s to disseminate information to farmers by making arrangements with various railroads in the state to pull extra cars devoted to agricultural use. In 1927 the Chicago, Burlington and Quincy Railroad carried special exhibits on lime and legumes throughout southern Iowa.[28] In 1929 Extension utilized the Pig Crop Special Train to help inform farmers as to better methods of hog production. The Benton County agent described the train when it stopped in his community in 1929.

> There were four cars . . . two of which were given over to charts illustrating various phases of proven methods of raising hogs at lower costs per pound, one to improved types of hog houses and another car containing pens of hogs that had been raised by farmers enrolled in the Iowa Pig Crop Contest. One group of hogs was shown that had been raised under the hit and miss plan.[29]

Many county agents noted in their annual reports that the train exhibits had been popular with farmers.

Specialists in dairy husbandry used yet another approach, the cow testing association, to work with the state's dairy farmers. This association was established to help farmers increase the milk production of each animal in a farm herd, rather than to increase production through a larger herd. Beginning in 1909 dairy farmers in the Waterloo and Cedar Falls vicinity organized the first two cow testing associations; by 1912 that number had increased to ten. According to Director Bliss, the associations "were successful from the beginning in increasing the amount of milk produced and in decreasing the cost of production." Associations were formed when a number of dairymen banded together and employed a tester "who tests each cow once a month and figures income and feed costs." As Bliss described it, "The farmer who joins a cow testing association takes his own herd of cows as his problem for study in cooperation with the college specialists. As a method of instruction there are few lines of work that offer such great possibilities as the cow testing association." Extension staff trained the testers on campus as well as supervising their work. By 1929, Iowa contained more than one hundred cow testing associations with about 2,500 members.[30]

Poultry work constituted another part of Extension agricultural work in the 1920s. At that time Extension trained farm people to cull their own flocks. The intent was to increase profits in poultry production, not by increasing the size of the flock but by eliminating unprofitable birds; an additional advantage was a reduction of disease. Specialists put on training schools at ISC and then initiated a statewide poultry culling and selection campaign. In 1920 county farm bureaus temporarily employed thirty-six people to do culling work; county agents and home demonstration agents also performed the work. In the early 1920s Extension staff assisted Iowans in starting poultry record projects as well as county poultry breeding associations.[31]

While agricultural specialists used different teaching methods such as demonstration, lecture, and exhibits, according to a 1931 review of Extension practices, the specialists still essentially did the teaching themselves. In a study of Extension initiated in 1931, the study committee was critical of these specialists because in the past they had not made much use of the local leader method of instruction. The study, authored by J. Brownlee Davidson, Herbert M. Hamlin, and Paul C. Taff, repeatedly urged Extension agriculturalists to make more use of the method whereby rural men and women were trained to help present Extension material to other farm people. The authors noted that the method had been used very effectively by personnel in Home Economics Extension throughout the 1920s. The committee believed that there were many advantages with the local leader approach, including the fact that far more farm people were reached. They observed that if one specialist spent "one day training a group of 15 to 20 leaders, a worker can expect these leaders to hold at least one meeting each. If each meeting is attended by 20 people, 300 to 400 people will have been reached with the message, all resulting from the one contact by an agent or specialist." The approach also resulted in helping rural people develop leadership skills and in conducting meetings. The committee conceded that during the 1920s farm men were disinclined to become local leaders, primarily for lack of time. They observed that "the scarcity of men who have the special and comprehensive knowledge of highly technical subjects required to present even segments of those subjects" was often a factor. Even in the face of these difficulties, however, the study committee noted that other state Extension Services were using the approach with good success in agricultural areas.[32]

During the 1920s in the Agricultural Division, Extension officials also added specialists in landscape architecture. Always striving to improve rural life in its entirety and at the same time respond to specific requests for information, the Extension Service in 1921 revived a landscape architectural service that had been in effect from 1916 to 1917. The service came in response to questions about the proper placement of new farm buildings, proper location of shelter belts, and the placement of buildings for keeping farm odors away from the farm home. While viewed as a utilitarian service, much of the information dealt with landscaping around farm homes and placement of trees and shrubs throughout the farmyard, adding elements of beauty and improving the quality of life for participating farm people.[33] A look at some "before and after" pictures in the county annual reports for the 1920s shows through the use of trees, shrubs, and flowers the remarkable transformation of rather stark, plain farmsteads into attractive, inviting homes.

Typical of many developments within Extension, the furnishing of landscaping information to specific people soon expanded to groups and institutions. In 1924 the Iowa General Assembly determined that Iowa State College would be responsible for landscaping the state's parks. In turn the college gave this responsibility to Extension. In 1929 Extension personnel visited thirteen state parks and began the work. In total Extension personnel provided assistance to thirty-eight parks in the state.[34]

The second major area of Extension, home economics, also underwent considerable change in the 1920s. During that decade the home economics division benefited greatly from the leadership provided by state leader, Neale S. Knowles. Widely recognized for her ability as an organizer, Knowles served the state from the early years of Extension in 1906 until 1934, a total of twenty-eight years. During Knowles's tenure, the home economics area quickly developed a highly proficient organization and acquired more specialty areas. Director Bliss continually praised Knowles for her outstanding organizational skills. By 1920 Home Economics Extension included specialists in the areas of clothing, food, home furnishings, home management, and health. Home economists used various means of presenting material including traditional lectures, demonstration lectures, exhibits, fairs, window displays, films and slides, style shows, plays, conferences, printed material, and work with boys' and girls' clubs.[35]

In 1920 Home Economics Extension began to utilize the local leader training method. Under this system, specialists from Iowa State College traveled into rural communities to present training sessions to local farm women who, in turn, presented the lessons to other farm women. Adopted because of the great demand for the programs, thousands of farm women were then able to benefit from the material. Through the training they received in sewing, nutrition, or home furnishings, farm women learned qualities of leadership that could be transferred into other areas of activity. In other words, Extension activities resulted in training female as well as male community leaders.[36]

Clothing projects proved to be the most popular in the 1920s and clothing specialists used three types of training schools: a five-month course; two- or three-day training schools; and a one-day training school. Clothing specialist Cora Leiby reported in 1921–1922, "The work in clothing has been very successfully carried on and proves to meet a need among farm women. They are eager for the help." Leiby explained that with clothing projects, the five-month course was set up in three counties. When the clothing specialist presented demonstrations to some township groups, Leiby noted that residents of other townships quickly realized what was going on and asked to be included. During the five months the clothing specialists visited each county on five different occasions. The home economists also put out bulletins on the topics of baby clothes, the use and alteration of commercial patterns, textiles for home use, and shortcuts in sewing.[37]

Farm women responded enthusiastically to Extension programs. In the 1920s Alice Ann Andrew remembered the early Extension specialists who came to Greene County with "all kinds of great

NEALE S. KNOWLES, early leader and organizer of Extension Home Economics, about 1915. Courtesy Iowa State University Library/University Archives.

inspirational things" for women to do. She particularly remembered making dress forms. "I'll never forget one session with dress forms. It was a hot old August day, and they were pasting all this stuff over a so-called T-shirt. About half of [the women] fainted with the heat, but that was how eager women were to learn to create their own clothes. *They were almost as spiffy as the town ladies.*"[38]

The use of the local leader or training school method, so efficiently utilized by home economics personnel during the 1920s, provided proof that, indeed, more farm women could be reached through this approach than by relying totally on presentations by specialists alone. Specialist Leiby related the following results achieved in Scott County after one year of presenting the five-month clothing course: 6 townships reached, 41 school districts reached, 8 project leaders elected, 81 local leaders trained, 143 clothing meetings held by local leaders, 274 dress forms made, 349 home demonstrations given, and 837 women reached. Leiby concluded that 1,989 women adopted suggestions. At times there were also additional benefits. When Scott County Extension personnel attempted to set up girls' clubs in the county, seven out of twelve leaders chosen for these clubs had participated in the five-month clothing course.[39]

While clothing projects proved to be the most popular with farm women, nutrition projects ranked a close second. County home demonstration agents and food and nutrition specialists promoted many projects including the initiation of hot lunches in rural schools, the consumption of more milk by all Iowans, and the improvement of infant feeding by encouraging breast feeding. Specialists promoted better nutrition by urging Iowans to follow six basic rules: Use at least one-half pint of milk daily for adults and one pint for each growing child; eat cooked cereal at least three mornings a week; eat at least one vegetable besides potatoes and dry beans daily; eat some fruit daily; eat raw fresh vegetables or fruit three times a week; and eat sweets only at the end of the meal.[40] These rules were reprinted frequently in newspapers around the state.

In their nutrition projects, Extension personnel were responding at least in part to the view that some Iowa children were undernourished. During the first part of the 1920s home economists sent out questionnaires to school personnel requesting data on children's health and their food consumption. According to one mailed out in 1920, Extension determined that out of the schools responding (83 counties out of 99), hot lunches were served in 10.9 percent of them. One method used to gain data on children's health was to have school officials measure and weigh children both at the beginning

LOCAL LEADERS PRESENTING a lecture on
clothing construction to Iowa farm women in 1921 at an
unidentified farm. One township reported that twelve
local leaders in three and a half months conducted forty
clothing meetings with an attendance of 508. Courtesy
Iowa State University Library/University Archives.

and end of the school year. As a result of this growth monitoring, nutrition specialists concluded that many Iowa children were underweight and therefore undernourished. Although home economists recommended changes in the total diet such as the consumption of more fresh fruits and cereal, the major emphasis was on increasing the consumption of milk and initiating hot lunch programs in the public schools. Following a hot meal at noon—rather than a cold sandwich—home economists believed that children did better work in the afternoon and had fewer illnesses. One specialist wrote, "The children work better and think more clearly." Typically, students' mothers and rural teachers alternated in preparing lunches. In 1922 one consolidated school superintendent wrote that in the previous year, 54 percent of his students were underweight but that percentage had fallen to about 25 percent in the current year. He added, "I hope to have it down 10 percent before the year is over."[41]

One of the most successful programs carried out as a part of the food and nutrition project was the milk utilization project. The purpose was to "interest children and adults in the food value of milk, to create greater interest in clean milk and to stress the different ways of using milk." Given the emphasis on nutrition by the Extension staff and the strong belief that milk was necessary for proper physical development and good health, this project fit well with the overall food and nutrition program. Perhaps no other food could be so easily promoted in the state.[42]

It soon became clear, however, that Extension personnel not only needed to encourage Iowans, especially children, to consume more milk but also to discourage children from drinking coffee and tea. The Scott County home demonstration agent wrote in 1920, "One girl of seven has been drinking six cups of coffee daily. She is working to earn a new dress which will be hers when she can report three weeks with no coffee."[43] As a part of the milk utilization project, many rural and urban school officials served milk to children at both midmorning and midafternoon breaks.

The report of Extension milk specialist Florence A. Imlay shows that in the milk utilization campaign, Extension specialists used almost every means at their disposal to promote their goals. Extension personnel worked with a myriad of groups across the state including public school officials, librarians, women's clubs, parent-teacher associations, community groups, and county fair boards. In 1920 October 19–25 was proclaimed "Milk Week" to call further attention to the project. Local officials established milk clinics at

Clinton and Davenport where Extension personnel reiterated the advantages of both consuming more milk and improving the state's milk supply. Specialist Imlay estimated that as a result of the campaign, milk consumption increased by 25 percent. Moreover, project personnel apparently did succeed in weaning some children away from tea and coffee. In her annual report, Imlay included the comments of a rural teacher on the subject: "All but one of my pupils bring milk to school. They have given up tea and coffee."[44]

The milk utilization campaign also placed emphasis on another project of importance to Iowans in the early 1920s—the campaign for clean milk. Believing that tuberculosis in cows could be transmitted through milk to humans, the state legislature in 1919 had initiated a voluntary campaign for testing and eradication of bovine tuberculosis. The testing law was changed several times and later in the 1920s it became mandatory for all farmers. The Extension Service strongly supported the testing and also the move by city officials to regulate the quality of milk sold in the cities. Home economists as well as Extension veterinarians took part in the clean milk campaign where cities such as Davenport and Cedar Falls and towns in Cedar and Jones counties passed ordinances requiring local dairies to have their herds tested.[45]

Like their counterparts, the county agents, home demonstration agents stressed economy measures in the early 1920s in response to hard times. Extension personnel handed out recipes for homemade products like soap that would produce a savings within the home. Sometimes projects paralleled those presented by county agents. In her annual report in 1921–1922, home management specialist Gertrude Lynn reported that she had stressed "thrift and home accounts" to help farm women manage their households more efficiently. Extension put out a home account book for 20 cents to help facilitate the record keeping. Other efforts were also undertaken to produce more direct savings. The home butchering demonstrations given around the state in the 1920s also allowed families to save money on food. In 1921 Mrs. Bert Keizer of Buena Vista County made a comparative study of the cost of purchasing a supply of meat and the cost of securing that meat through home butchering. She purchased a hog for $21 and paid $1 for butchering. Mrs. Keizer cut up the meat and rendered the lard, a process which took three and a half hours. Keeping detailed records of her work, the farm wife weighed all the different cuts and calculated their value, if purchased at the local meat market. According to retail prices, the meat would have cost $35.50; this amounted to $13.50 more than Mrs. Keizer had paid for the hog and the butchering. She explained to the local home demonstration agent that she considered herself well repaid for the three and a half hours spent doing the work. She also reported that "her self-respect is increasing by leaps and bounds as she is learning how much of an asset she is financially, rather than a liability as she had sometimes thought."[46]

Scattered throughout the specialists' and Director Knowles's reports were many apparently unsolicited letters from farm women testifying to the need for and effectiveness of the home economics programs. In 1921 a Mrs. Bedell wrote Specialist Gertrude Lynn:

> Please send me information that will enable me to keep our expenses within our income. I do not know how to make a budget as I might if we were on a salary. My husband says it can't be done, but he is willing to be "shown." We are a family of four. I do my own work, the sewing, [feed] extra outside men at harvest time, ensilage feeding, shredding, etc. I want help, something definite. I'd like to have money left of my own so Mr. Bedell and I could attend the 1925 Farm and Home Week. This year's program is most alluring. Send me advice and bulletins. I'd like to "run my house" instead of having it run me. I want leisure enough to be a *Mother* to my children.[47]

Farm women also commented that they enjoyed Extension activities because it gave them the opportunity to socialize with neighbors. Mrs. J. L. Reed wrote, "We don't count in our reports of time and money saved, the other results, such as contact with other people, and friendships formed and all those things that are more of a real benefit than time and money are." Sometimes farm women verbalized their feelings directly to Extension personnel. A local leader in Cherokee County "who had been looking on in amazement asked in all sincerity, 'Who in the world ever conceived the idea of sending you girls out here to teach us these things. I think she must be a wonderful woman.' "[48]

Throughout the 1920s as in later decades, county Extension personnel put in countless hours working with other organizations. After 1921 home economists assisted in setting up "well baby clinics." Federal funding was obtained through the passage of the Sheppard-Towner Act in 1921 which provided money for maternal and infant care and education. Sometimes the clinics were known as Sheppard-Towner clinics. In Allamakee County in 1921 local officials held clinics for a full week where residents could bring in their babies for physical checkups. Home demonstration agents helped in setting up and publicizing the clinics.[49]

While Iowa farm women in the 1920s expressed considerable satisfaction with the programs offered by Extension, apparently in the 1910s some farm women in other states had felt differently. In his book on the industrialization of American agriculture, David B. Danbom writes that some farm women were offended by Extension advisers and the farm women "gave home demonstration agents a particularly frosty reception." Danbom quotes a Wisconsin farm woman in 1915: "I am wondering what the Department of Agriculture proposes to do for us. . . . Perhaps they may send out some city woman to teach us how to cook. We will resent that."[50] While obviously not all Iowa farm women took part in Extension activities, thousands did and the evidence points overwhelmingly to a generally positive reception of home demonstration agents and their programs. The women not only attended Extension programs but a large number took a more active role by serving as project and local leaders. Each project, like nutrition and child care, had a woman in each township serving as chair of that project. A select number received training from state specialists so they, in turn, could present project material to other farm wives. In some counties farm women continued to give demonstrations on food and nutrition several years after the projects had officially ended.[51] Extension activities also meant more social interaction for women who previously had little opportunity to do so. It does not appear that they needed much encouragement to see the advantages offered by Extension.

Perhaps a different measure of success is needed for farm women than for farm men in regard to attitudes toward Extension programs. Although thousands of farmers took part in Extension programs in the 1920s, there were still some who resisted "book learning," feeling that the old ways of farming were best. Perhaps of greater importance, unlike their wives, most farmers did not need the social outlets provided by Extension. Midwestern farm men traditionally went to town far more often than farm women. Once there, men handled legal and business matters, purchased supplies, and had the opportunity to socialize with others. Farmers also frequently visited neighboring farms to share information, exchange labor, or barter supplies. For farm women who did not share all visits to town or to the neighbors, Extension brought organized activities into the countryside, providing them with educational opportunities and much-needed socializing.[52]

A second, more general criticism of Home Economics Extension relates to the influence of the domestic science movement and the subsequent concentration of women's Extension programs on domestic activities. At the time Smith-Lever was debated in Congress, the domestic science movement (or home economics) had developed into a strong program with some seventeen thousand young women studying the curriculum in land-grant schools. According to Jane Knowles, although many areas of home economics began with "fairly high scientific standards, especially related to nutrition . . . [over time] virtually all of them became 'how to' programs in cooking, clothing construction, home management, etc." Knowles observes that this is the aspect of the domestic science movement that is embedded in Smith-Lever. In turn, Deborah Fink has written that the structure of Extension work, given the influence of domestic science, "did not reflect the division of labor on most farms. From the time of the first federal extension program in 1914, the work was divided in a manner that reflected an urban middle class ideal rather than the farm reality." As a result then, the emphasis on domestic science prevented Home Economics Extension from dealing with farm work done outside the home, or put another way, Extension did not help farm women "integrate their home and field work."[53]

This general assessment of home economics during the 1920s (and even much later) as being narrowly focused on domestic issues is supported by the Iowa home economics projects discussed earlier. Had Extension decided to approach some areas, particularly poultry production, as a female rather than a male endeavor—or even as a gender-neutral task—the program would probably have been more beneficial to women and Extension seen as more in tune with the realities of farm life. The same view might be extended to dairy science, as some women did part or all of the milking and helped with the production of dairy products.

In evaluating the effectiveness of Home Economics Extension in the 1920s, it should be noted that programs, even though narrowly focused, still made available to women an abundance of valuable new information not obtainable elsewhere. Furthermore, farm women were engaged in numerous other Extension activities outside of home economics. While home economics dealt specifically with activities within the home, other Extension programs offered involvement in areas outside the farm home. Women raised the poultry on most farms, and even though the poultry experts directed their material toward men, farm women did receive that information. They also learned culling procedures from both male and female Extension agents. Many women attended butchering demonstrations, along with their husbands, and used that expertise extensively on their farms. Women also utilized Extension material on horticulture and landscaping to beautify farmsteads. At the same time women shared in educational and social programs disseminated by rural sociologists. Even home economics projects should not be viewed too narrowly. They provided women not only with technical and scientific information but also with cultural enrichment through art and music projects, opportunities for personal development through working as local leaders, numerous social opportunities with neighbors, and an enhanced sense of community.

Club work for farm boys and girls, the third major part of Extension in the 1920s, had been a part of Extension from its inception. In his 1921 annual report, Director Bliss wrote that increased attention had been given to these groups. In fact, in that year only 8 out of 100 farm bureaus "failed to do some work with boys' and girls' clubs"; in total, 14,773 young people were enrolled in such organizations. From the beginning Extension personnel believed strongly that if Iowa's farm population was to be better organized and better served, programs for improving farming and farm living had to be addressed to future residents as well as to the adult generation. It was also hoped that the 4-H work done by youths would encourage their parents to adopt better farming methods. Young people took part in programs at the county level as well as presenting their projects at the State Fair. In 1921 sponsors offered over $8,000 worth of premiums to boys' and girls' club members. In summer young people attended special camps around the state where they learned more about citizenship and took part in leisure-time activities. Young people also attended events such as the Waterloo Dairy Cattle Congress and the National Dairy Show where they participated in judging contests.[54]

Extension's main work with young farm people, however, took place within the local clubs. If a county had a professional club leader (always a male), he accepted most responsibility for youth clubs. In 1921, however, only three counties—Audubon, Appanoose, and Kossuth—had county club leaders employed for the whole year while eight counties had club leaders permanently employed for a part of the year.[55] For counties without club leaders, the county agent and home demonstration agent worked to organize boys' and girls' clubs (known as 4-H clubs later in the decade). Although the two groups might hold occasional mixed meetings, in Iowa the clubs had totally separate organizations, with parents typically serving as leaders. Yet even after clubs had been organized and leaders selected in counties without professional club leaders, the county agents and home economists spent considerable time working with youth groups.

Throughout the 1920s and beyond, almost every county included more girls' than boys' clubs. In some counties there were almost twice as many of the former. There were perhaps several reasons for this disparity, which had little to do with the interests of the young people. Edith Zobrist, active as a 4-Her in the 1920s, commented, "I figure that it was possibly a little easier to get a leader for a girls' club than for a boys' club, because the fathers maybe just didn't volunteer quite as readily as did the mothers." Zobrist explained that many of the female 4-H leaders had been teachers before their marriages. "They felt more confident at being a 4-H leader. There weren't as many men who had been schoolteachers and who felt as confident at conducting a meeting." Esther Whetstone, later a state girls' 4-H leader, recalled that at one time she and other 4-H staffers had gone to Marshalltown to help present leadership training for boys. She related, "It was much harder to get the men to come and sit through a day training school than it was the women. The women used to come and have [lunch] and then sit through the whole day and get a lot of their material." The matter of sociability undoubtedly played a part. As one woman observed, "Well, those were farm women and the whole day was probably her social event for the whole year."[56]

Both the boys' and girls' programs benefited from dynamic leadership in the 1920s. Josephine Arnquist, who served as the state 4-H girls' leader, was responsible for the development of many programs. Arnquist was described by another 4-H staff member as the type of person who "picked up ideas and went with them." At one point Arnquist visited Scott County where she observed the work that home demonstration agent Edith Barker was doing with girls' clubs in the area of music. Esther Whetstone related that Arnquist returned to Ames convinced that this type of musical training should be done all over the state. Edith Zobrist and Bernice Lund, also a 4-Her then, recalled that as club members, they benefited immensely from the 4-H music appreciation lessons that developed as a result of Arnquist and Barker's work; Zobrist and Lund explained that it gave them a lifetime appreciation of music. As Zobrist related, "You didn't have to have talent because you learned to listen properly."[57]

During this time both boys' and girls' clubs received premiums in the form of money for prizes received for members' winning projects. Barker and Arnquist suggested that girls' clubs use the money for a club project rather than dividing it up among members; girls' clubs then began to use the money to buy Victrolas, which they took along to each meeting. As they continued to receive premium money, they purchased records of classical music as well as folk music that could be used for dancing and other folk games. Clubs also raised money to send members to various meetings and to short courses at ISC. They had bake sales, served lunches at Farm Bureau meetings, and put on yearly ice cream socials.[58]

Herb Plambeck and E. Howard Hill, also members of 4-H in the 1920s, recalled boys' club activities including beef and pig projects as well as social activities. Frank Reed was the boys' state 4-H leader then and was regarded by Plambeck as having a major influence on 4-Hers. He remembered that Reed was "down to earth" with the 4-Hers, that he had a natural talent for the work, and that he was a good storyteller. Both Plambeck and Hill recalled the immense influence that 4-H had on their lives. Plambeck explained:

> For some of us, 4-H was our life. Those of us who were very much tied to the earth, in other words, who didn't even get a chance to go on to school, 4-H was our opportunity and *the* opportunity to develop and frankly, in the case of the little club that I belonged to, that was a big event every month. 4-H was everything in those days.

E. Howard Hill, later president of the Iowa Farm Bureau Federation, recalled that the first speech he ever made in public dealt with his 4-H hog project. He added that the speech "was about five minutes long and was I ever scared!"[59]

The annual narrative reports of county Extension staff also contain abundant comments on the activities of 4-H youth. While projects were stressed throughout the 1920s and after, home demonstration agents especially commented on the learning experience of club work that went beyond the sewing or beef projects. In 1921 the Benton County home demonstration agent gave considerable time to organizing and working with girls' clubs, noting that she had organized nine clubs during the year. She also related, however, another development. "The club which has 22 girls none of whom were over thirteen years of age were so timid at the beginning that they could scarcely be coaxed to carry on their business meeting . . . [but they were] conducting them with dignity and in good form before the summer was over."[60]

Youth clubs included a wide range of interests. In 1921 boys' clubs included, among others, Corn Club, Baby Beef Club, Purebred Calf Club, Dairy Calf Club, Market Pig Club, Purebred Gilt Club, and Sow and Litter Club. For girls, groups included Clothing Club, House Furnishing or Own Your Own Room Club, Food Club, Canning Club, and Meal Preparation Club. Every county did not necessarily have each specialty club organized within its borders. Interests of farm youths determined which clubs they organized. Overall, during the 1920s, the most popular clubs were Purebred Gilt, Poultry, Garden, Livestock and Grain Judging, and Clothing.[61]

While boys' and girls' clubs were then organized in much the same manner, one divergence did appear. When both groups first formed, members were free to select their own projects. But during the 1920s girls' clubs became more structured. State leaders decided that the state should be divided into three sections with each section taking the same project of either foods, clothing, or home furnishings. This was done partially to make certain that each girl received some training in all three areas. As Esther Whetstone explained, "The women decided that the girls needed more than just canning, canning, canning. And so they got this rotation thing going. Because housekeeping and taking care of a home isn't just canning or it isn't just clothing or it isn't just home furnishings." Also, if girls' clubs in one-third of the state had the same projects, state leaders could make better use of specialists traveling to that part of the state to meet with the girls and also to train the local leaders. This arrangement differed from boys' 4-H in that they could select their own projects from year to year. In this way a male 4-Her might decide to have a beef project for all the years he took part in 4-H.[62]

Ever mindful that an important part of educating Iowa farmers was the need to also influence future farmers, Extension took its campaign for record keeping to rural youth. In the mid-1920s, along with more traditional clubs or projects, club leaders established a farm record club. A son or daughter then kept the business records of the parents' farm for the year. Officials assigned an Extension specialist to work with the young people and to assist them in making an analysis of the records at the end of the year. In his 1925 annual report, Director Bliss noted that "several members have belonged to these clubs two or three years and have in cooperation with their parents rearranged the fields so that labor can be used more effectively." Also in 1925, in an effort to train younger Iowans, Extension personnel made plans for "introducing simple farm accounts into the seventh and eighth grades of rural schools as part of the arithmetic work." This work was introduced in eleven

GUTHRIE COUNTY YOUNGSTER named Burkhart
with his 4-H livestock project, circa 1920. Courtesy Iowa
State University Library/University Archives.

counties. During the previous year two counties, Emmet and Cerro Gordo, participated with 64 teachers instructing 326 pupils in the use of the farm account book.[63]

While much of the educational material generated by Extension was delivered directly to clients through meetings and training sessions, increasingly throughout the 1920s Extension developed different ways of disseminating information. As part of this general effort, Extension created the Publicity Extension Service, which in turn initiated several new programs. The main purpose of the service was to encourage media people around the state, particularly daily and weekly newspaper editors, to print more agricultural news. The Extension Service itself had begun issuing two mimeographed monthly publications, "Extension Bulletin," designed primarily for Extension personnel, and "Agricultural Economic Facts." The latter publication was widely distributed to both rural and urban people and businesses in Iowa.[64]

Perhaps the greatest change in the dissemination of information, however, came with the establishment of the Radio Service. Beginning in 1923 with the creation of WOI radio on the ISC campus, Extension personnel provided market news to farm families. By 1925 market reports were broadcast from principal markets twice a day along with weather reports. Once each weekday Radio Service staffers also answered questions of interest to Iowa farmers. Questions related to home problems were dealt with two days a week. Two nights per week Extension personnel presented special courses on agricultural instruction over WOI. With the initiation of radio broadcasts, Extension personnel were able to spread their message over a greater area and with far greater frequency than before. For Iowa farmers, daily market reports provided up-to-the-minute information on market conditions and prices.[65]

By the end of the 1920s the farm scene had changed considerably from a decade earlier. For the interested farm family, Extension information abounded on all aspects of agriculture and rural living. Beginning early in the decade, farmers could receive a monthly publication, "Agricultural Facts," informing them of market conditions. WOI radio continued to broadcast daily market prices and weather and crop conditions to farmers. Some newspapers, like the Waterloo *Evening Courier,* devoted one page each week to agricultural news, typically furnished by local Extension officials and state specialists. Printed material was also available dealing with the major home economics areas of clothing, food and nutrition, child care, and home management and furnishings. Presumably these publications and programs created a greater awareness of agricultural conditions and ways to increase agricultural production, as well as ways to improve the farm home and enrich family life.

Even though Extension experienced considerable success in reaching farm families, problems persisted. In effect, the agricultural depression continued to be a major concern throughout the decade. Extension personnel could work with farmers to increase production and reduce costs but that did not solve all farm problems; low prices continued throughout the 1920s because farm incomes really depended on uncontrollable factors. Moreover, solutions offered in the early part of the decade had not provided the anticipated relief. The marketing cooperatives that Extension had encouraged farmers to organize had brought some economic savings but not as much as had been hoped. As David Danbom has pointed out, cooperatives "could seldom address the farmer's basic problem of overproduction with any degree of effectiveness." Even the USDA had concluded by 1926 that marketing cooperatives had not been sufficient "to overcome the unfavorable conditions that had existed since 1920."[66] Agricultural conditions improved somewhat by 1925, but for the most part the entire decade is looked upon as one of depression for the American farmer.

The decade of the 1920s also revealed institutional priorities. While the number of county agents remained constant and specialists in agricultural and livestock areas steadily increased, the number of home demonstration agents and club agents often vacillated. It seemed that the latter two categories were expendable, depending on the money appropriated by state and federal governments and the amount raised by Farm Bureau memberships. In other words, when appropriations were reduced, reductions came primarily from the ranks of the home economists, not from the ranks of the county agents. Throughout the period from 1918 until 1933, the home economics staff was never more than 25 percent of the total Extension staff. In 1918 with the assistance of federal funding, Iowa had thirteen permanent full-time demonstration agents and fifty-six temporary ones. At the same time there were six home economics specialists. By 1921 there was a total of sixteen home demonstration agents in the state along with four county specialists and two two-county specialists. Four years later, in 1929, the number of home demonstration agents had decreased to thirteen, along with five two-county specialists and one city home demonstration agent working in Council Bluffs. By contrast, the number of home demonstration specialists had increased to twenty-five constituting 25 percent of all specialists.[67] Given farm women's high level of interest in Extension, it appears that a shortage of funds rather than a lack of interest accounted for the low number of home demonstration agents. Since Extension officials viewed the office of club agent as the training ground for county agents, turnover occurred frequently in that area.

The lack of home demonstration agents should not obscure the fact that thousands of Iowa farm women took part in Extension programs and gained great satisfaction from their involvement. In what was perhaps an early form of female empowerment and development of self-esteem, farm women expressed the opinion that Extension activities made them believe in themselves and feel that they made a real contribution to their families. According to annual Extension reports, the message seemed clear: "Farm women developed organizational skills from working within their townships; farm women gained confidence from speaking in public; and farm women developed personal talents, particularly in music."[68]

Throughout his tenure as Director of Extension, Bliss insisted that the basic purpose of the organization was education. In effect, the purpose of Extension, through education, was to help farm families help themselves. Extension personnel were not to assume a direct role in solving problems. Moreover, in the 1920s, Extension worked to promote "business-like procedures" and "business-like efficiency." The motto might have been "efficiency and uplift."[69] In February 1923 the *Extension Bulletin* included the following:

> The greater part of the work of the county agent is directed toward the efficiency of the average man. The man who produces most cheaply will be the one who suffers least hardship and the Agricultural College is directing its efforts to disseminate as widely as possible information which results in the plenty which is the basis of all prosperity.[70]

During the 1920s Iowa's Extension Service benefited greatly from the stability provided by capable leadership, particularly that of R. K. Bliss and Neale S. Knowles. Even in other positions, the same quality was evident. Growing up on Iowa farms and graduating from Iowa State College, men such as Paul Taff, Murl McDonald, and John W. Coverdale also provided stability through the 1920s and 1930s. Taff and McDonald served on the Extension staff in the 1920s and were later assistant directors; Coverdale also served Extension in the late 1910s and 1920s, working in a number of different capacities including state supervisor of county agents. Along with Bliss, these men brought a common background and sense of mission to the Extension Service.

By the end of the decade Extension had emerged as a strong, greatly enlarged institution, highly visible in both the state and the nation. Responsive to new directions in the sciences and social sciences, Extension had developed many new programs designed to help Iowa's rural residents improve their financial condition and their quality of life. Whether eating more nutritious foods, keeping better farm records, or beautifying farmsteads, most Iowans who participated in Extension programs benefited from that experience. Moreover, the institutional characteristics of stability, flexibility, and strong leadership begun in the 1920s would continue to serve the state especially well in the decade of the 1930s.[71]

4

A Time of Trial

The Great Depression

With the onset of the Great Depression, Iowa's Extension Service found itself once again confronted with the need for emergency measures. By the latter 1920s Iowa farm families had experienced some degree of recovery from the problems that plagued them throughout much of the decade although many farmers still had heavy debts incurred during the prosperous years of World War I. That upward trend would soon end, however, as the nation experienced the catastrophic Depression of the 1930s. In addition to the Depression and a drop in demand for farm products, Iowa farmers would experience extreme drought in both 1934 and 1936. By the 1930s, one clear pattern had emerged: when adversity struck the state's rural population, Cooperative Extension would provide the first line of defense. The Great Depression would be no exception as Iowa's Extension Service began immediately to issue information explaining conditions to the farm population. Throughout the decade Extension would be involved in major federal programs designed to help solve the crisis as well as developing additional programs for its rural clientele.

Although Iowa farmers had done better financially in the latter part of the 1920s, serious problems remained. Throughout the decade federal officials had attempted to deal with the farm depression but with little success. The major farm program proposed was the McNary-Haugen Act, designed to deal with the farm surplus and to raise farm prices. This legislation called for the creation of a government corporation that would buy up surplus agricultural products at a fair (1909–1914) price, reselling the products on the world market. Anticipating that the latter price would be lower than the former, the legislation called for an "equalization fee" to be assessed all farmers taking part in the program. This fee, in turn, would make up the difference between the price received on the world market and the price paid farmers. Although supported by numerous farm groups and many midwestern congressmen, President Calvin Coolidge twice vetoed the bill.[1]

While farmers had experienced difficulties in the 1920s, by the early 1930s conditions had become to many almost intolerable. Iowa farmers had never been known for radical behavior, but in 1931 some responded to the deepening agricultural distress with a growing militancy. The first major confrontation involving farmers and law officials, known as the Cow War, centered around the testing of cattle for bovine tuberculosis. Testing started in the state as early as 1917 and two years later the state legislature appropriated $100,000 annually for that purpose. In 1923 state officials determined that after a certain percentage of farmers in a given county approved testing, it would become mandatory for the entire county; later in the decade testing became mandatory for all farmers. Under the testing law, once veterinarians determined that an animal was diseased, they confiscated and destroyed it; the owner then assumed one-third the cost of replacing the animal while the state and the federal government each assumed a third.[2]

Apparently the testing plan did not meet much opposition in 1930 as the full force of depression had not yet hit the state. But by 1931, faced with an ever-growing farm crisis, Iowa farmers were in an angry mood over this issue, insisting that the testing law was "indiscriminate, unreliable, and often injurious." Instead, they argued, the state should adopt optional testing which they believed would achieve the same end. Unhappy farmers singled out state veterinarians and county agents for specific criticism, viewing both as a part of state government.[3]

Farmers in eastern Iowa soon gained notoriety for their opposition to the testing program. State officials had delayed testing in areas like Tipton hoping that "time would make [the farmers there] less scornful of urban laws and more amenable to general government."[4] This delay did not work, however. When state veterinarians traveled to the Tipton area in the fall of 1931, they were greeted by about four hundred farmers determined to prevent the vets from carrying out the testing of local herds. Immediately Governor Dan Turner declared that the testing law would be enforced, sending three regiments of the Iowa National Guard into the Tipton area and having several individuals arrested. The veterinarians then proceeded with the work "under the cover of military protection." Soon after, Turner sent troops into Henry, Muscatine, Jefferson, and Des Moines counties to ensure that testing was also completed there.[5]

While the Cow War was brief, it perhaps served as a catalyst for further militancy. Iowa historian Leland Sage has written that the event "contributed to consequences far beyond the incident itself; it might well be thought of as a spark dropped into a tinder box created by the depression." As Sage suggests, given corn at 13 cents per bushel and pork at 3 cents per pound, all that was needed "was a leader to act as the spokesman and organizer of the masses who were demanding action."[6] That individual would soon appear in the form of Milo Reno whose major plan of action was a "farm strike."

Throughout the 1920s Reno had been active in state agricultural circles. For ten years he served as president of the Iowa Farmers' Union and was also involved in the McNary-Haugen campaign. In his role as president of the Farmers' Union, Reno had become increasingly vocal about the farm situation.[7] Described as feisty and aggressive, he had often criticized Iowa State College and the Extension Service, particularly county agents, for their agricultural policies. Reno believed that the works of the academic theorists were not "going to be worth a damn in the [early 1930s] in solving the practical problems that confront us." At one point Reno accused agricultural colleges and professors of preparing the farmer to accept "the lowly position of the peasant." Reno had called for a farm strike as early as 1927 but without success. Given the intervening developments, he reissued his call, this time suggesting that the strike begin on January 1, 1932. In effect, farmers were asked to withhold farm products from market, creating scarcity and thus forcing up farm prices; Reno believed their actions would also call attention to the farmers' plight.[8]

While a later farm strike did take place in northwest Iowa, Reno and many of his supporters were also involved in another development with longtime consequences. On May 3, 1932, farm protest leaders held an organizational meeting in Des Moines for the Farmer Holiday Association. Those attending elected Reno as president and John Bosch of Minnesota as vice-president. From then on the Farmer Holiday Association was part of the farm strike.[9] Although a majority of Iowa farmers did not join the association or take part in the farm strike, the action of the minority clearly indicated that Iowa's farm population was in a desperate way.

Extension's first response to the deepening Depression and increasing militancy was to prepare materials to inform Iowa's population of the extent of the Depression, its consequences, and its possible remedies. Pamphlets issued included such titles as "The Cause of the Emergency" and "The Iowa Tax Situation—An Analysis for Farmers." Extension personnel held township meetings throughout the state whereby people could gather to hear Extension staffers explain conditions, followed by a general discussion. Extension continued its county outlook meetings initiated in 1929, resulting in an almost 50 percent increase in attendance by 1930. Most agricultural economists urged farmers to continue increasing their production efficiency and to reduce costs, the same advice they had given farmers in the 1920s. Yet some economists, like William G. Murray, concluded from a study of 1932 farm records that "the solution to overproduction in industry and agriculture required legislative action."[10]

The Depression soon affected the Extension staff in more personal ways. In the summer of 1931 the central staff discussed the feasibility of reducing the number of county staff around the state but decided against it. The views expressed were that while there was less money, the Depression was a time when farm families needed the services of Extension more than ever. Even though county Extension staff stayed on the job, the fact remained: some county farm bureaus were in serious financial trouble and there was less money to pay Extension personnel. In 1932, for example, Appanoose County had "its regular $900 indebtedness" plus an additional debt of $600. As a result, some county agents offered to take salary reductions.[11]

In the midst of great uncertainty in the fall of 1931, Iowa State College President Raymond M. Hughes called for a thorough review of the Extension Service. While that stressful time might have seemed an illogical one for such a request, there were compelling reasons for the action. By 1931 Extension had been in existence in Iowa for twenty-five years and had developed a pattern of action. Still Extension was not without its critics, particularly members of farm organizations other than Farm Bureau. And in times of great stress, it seemed proper to ask whether an organization's programs were the most effective.

In discussing his request, Hughes praised the work of the organization but added that he believed some changes could be made. In an address to the college faculty he explained his motives: "Now, I believe, is a good time for this division . . . to be fully reviewed and studied with the hope that we can make some improvements. I am not suggesting the present study because I question the value of the present work. I do know that in any college work there is a very strong tendency to continue to do what has been done. Times change and possibly our extension work can be altered with profit." Hughes appointed a general committee of three persons to carry out the study: J. Brownlee Davidson, professor of agricultural engineering; Herbert M. Hamlin, associate professor of vocational education; and Paul C. Taff, assistant director of the Extension Service. At the same time Hughes indicated that all future persons hired for Extension positions should have master's degrees.[12]

Two years later the committee issued its report after interviews with dozens of Extension workers and a thorough study of the organization. The report, several hundred pages long, included detailed discussions of the various Extension divisions followed by some ninety recommendations for change. While some suggestions were limited in scope, such as the recommendation that the relationship between the college and Extension be more clearly defined, the committee also raised major concerns and made many far-reaching suggestions. They called for greater cooperation between regular faculty and Extension staff, voiced concern over the close relationship between Farm Bureau and the county agents, and suggested that the college should pay agents' salaries rather than having some money come from Farm Bureau (thus giving Extension more control over its agents). The report advocated that Extension workers periodically have additional technical training in their fields as well as taking courses such as psychology, sociology, speech, and journalism; they also urged agricultural areas of Extension (following the lead of home economics) to use the local leader method of instruction rather than continuing to use only the lecture and demonstration methods. In general, the committee found much to praise about the Iowa Extension Service even though they believed some changes were in order.[13]

Following the release of the study, it does not appear that either Hughes or Bliss took much action regarding recommendations. Bliss continued to indicate both through his writings and speeches that he strongly favored the close relationship with Farm Bureau. Moreover, he believed that in spite of the Depression, Extension was correct in continuing to carry out "the five point program of efficient production, better marketing [in agriculture], home project work, boys' and girls' club work and community organization." After reading the report, Hughes did suggest that more of the county agents' salaries be paid by the college. Given the fact that the Depression had intensified and that Iowa farmers were growing increasingly militant, Hughes, Bliss, and other college personnel may have sensed that 1933 was not the time for major changes in Extension. According to one source, about the same time that the study was being done, rumors circulated that Hughes wanted Bliss's resignation. When approached by Bliss, however, Hughes denied the rumor.[14]

While action at the state level produced little change in the economic situation, relief would be forthcoming from the federal government in the spring of 1933. The nation's new president, Franklin D. Roosevelt, quickly identified the farm problem as one of the most pressing. He selected as his secretary of agriculture a man from Iowa who had long-term experience with agriculture. Henry A. Wallace was perhaps best known throughout Iowa and the Middle West for his editorship of *Wallaces' Farmer,* but he also had the distinction of being the second generation to serve in the nation's cabinet. His father, Henry Cantwell Wallace, had served as secretary of agriculture from 1920 to 1923.[15]

Wallace, along with other members of the USDA, immediately set to work on a new agricultural program that Congress passed in May 1933. Known as the Agricultural Adjustment Act (AAA), the legislation was designed to "raise the prices of farm products to a fair exchange value and . . . [define] fair exchange value (except tobacco) at the price which would give farm products the same purchasing power they possessed during the pre-war period of 1909–1914." The increase was to come about primarily because products of seven basic farm crops would be reduced. In Iowa, this basically meant a reduction in the production of corn and hogs. The program was to be voluntary on the part of farmers and was to be administered by local and county committees. Limited changes took place on Iowa farms during 1933 including the destruction of many baby pigs (for which Iowa farmers received $3,500,484) but the main effort was directed toward determining the corn and hog output for 1934.[16]

Soon after passage of the farm bill, the USDA announced that the Extension Service would conduct educational work for the AAA and supervise the signing up of farmers. In effect, the USDA believed that only an agency already in existence could quickly implement the law. Critics of Extension soon expressed their disfavor. Milo Reno charged, "In my opinion, Henry Wallace intends to perpetuate the county agent system that has been the curse of agriculture, taking away the power of the people to eliminate them, and making them a part of the federal political machine." Reno was probably referring to the fact that the county agent system, which seemed to be "on the verge of collapse" because of the shortage of local funds, would be revived with its involvement in the federal program.[17] Wallace himself had expressed some reservation about the use of Extension personnel, anticipating that some farmers would refuse to take part because of the association between Extension and Farm Bureau. Wallace had heard many complaints about the county agent system, one of which stated that the county agent was about as popular "as a skunk would be under your Ford."[18]

Criticism also came from other quarters. Some groups disagreed with the agents engaging in so many different activities such as the AAA. An editorial in the *Co-Operative Manager and Farmer* in 1933 contained the following assessment.

> The county agent, created for a good and laudable purpose, has been forgotten and today, in addition to being the local representative of the political machines, he is in many instances the active competitor of the local elevator, the retail feed dealer, the retail coal merchant and practically every other merchant and enterprise in the community. He is the advance guard of every type of farm relief measure and an educator turned into that of a rural ward-healer.[19]

Regardless of criticism, however, the Extension Service immediately became immersed in the farm program. Extension's work with the AAA generally fell into three categories: (1) educating farmers as to the purposes and provisions of the legislation, (2) explaining the corn-hog contracts and the administrative rulings to farmers, and (3) organizing and training a large number of farmers who would actually conduct the sign-up campaigns. In a short time an additional fifty-three assistant county agents had been hired to help carry out these responsibilities, financed mostly by AAA funds.[20] For the next two years county agents spent much of their time dealing with the emergency measures necessitated by the program.

The decision to make full use of Extension personnel to expedite implementing the AAA seemed a judicious one, even in spite of farmers' criticism. In World War I Extension personnel developed a network of local volunteer war food production cooperators, one for each four square miles of land. By the 1930s, therefore, not only was the basis for a cooperators' network still in place, but also an

Extension staff familiar with the system. Wallace himself had first-hand experience with Iowa's cooperator system which, according to Director Bliss, led Wallace to select Iowa as the first state to adopt the plan of local farmer administration.[21]

Once initiated, planning for the corn-hog sign-up proceeded rapidly. County agents first attended regional schools to learn about the program and receive charts and explanatory material; Smith-Hughes vocational teachers also took part. (The Smith-Hughes Act of 1917 had provided federal funds for training teachers in vocational subjects.) Around November 15, county agents began to present talks to their individual counties concerning the AAA. In Black Hawk County agent Paul Barger conducted eleven educational meetings during December, explaining why controls were necessary. Given the fact that traditionally the goal had been to increase production, Barger believed farmers needed help to understand why it should be cut. Donald E. Fish, who went to work as a county agent in Dallas County in January 1933, also presented many meetings on the AAA to farmers in his county.

> I have never seen such interest. The turnout was overwhelming. There were over two thousand people attending those meetings, about 99 percent of all the farmers in the county. I am sure that nearly every farmer in the county attended one meeting, and some attended more than one. Probably at least half of the farm women attended also.

Bliss estimated that during the latter part of November and December, almost every township in the state held educational meetings to discuss the corn-hog program. A short time later officials made presentations to commercial clubs, women's clubs, and parent-teacher associations. Bliss described this educational program as "one of the most comprehensive adult educational campaigns ever carried on in the state."[22] Soon after county agents organized sign-up committees.[23]

The training of personnel to supervise the AAA program moved rapidly. On January 1, 1934, Extension held a special meeting to discuss the training schools that were held during the next two days. These sessions included twenty-three corn-hog fieldmen who were actual farmers, twenty-eight Extension staff members and the state corn-hog committee. On January 4 and 5 all county agents and temporary county committeemen traveled to Ames to be briefed on the materials. On January 10 an Extension supervisor and a corn-hog fieldman began conducting two-day training schools in the various counties. These meetings lasted until January 20, after which training schools were held in each township to make certain that at least one volunteer worker from each school district knew how to complete sign-up forms. As a result of this rapid training schedule, when the sign-up campaign actually began, Iowa contained from 125 to 150 trained men in each county and approximately fourteen thousand in the entire state to carry out the work.[24] This network had been developed with great speed, a fact that reflected favorably on the efficiency and capabilities of the state's Extension staff.

Among Extension personnel, county agents were particularly involved with the preparation for the sign-up campaign. Once sign-up forms were available, county agents typically went into the various townships to explain them, expediting the actual completion of the work. No one in the county knew the farm population better than the county agent, and no one was more familiar with the township system of organization. County agents would continue to play a significant role in all aspects of the administration of the AAA program during the next two years. Director Bliss estimated that in 1934 county agents spent "a little more than one-fourth" of their time on the corn-hog program.[25]

Once farmers had sign-up forms and instructions in hand, they were urged not to fill them out by themselves but rather to attend the local sign-up meeting; there, farmers found workers to assist them. Usually these meetings took place in rural schoolhouses, usually several in each township. Extension agents designated specific days when farmers could attend and receive help. To complete the forms properly, each farmer needed considerable information on his farm operation for the previous two years, including acreages planted and actual production figures for corn crops and hog production. Each farmer also had to provide a five-year history on the acres that he intended to set aside under the plan.[26] Director Bliss later reflected on this difficult task.

> Getting farmers' signatures on the corn-hog contracts was a mammoth job. It was necessary to count each farmer's hogs and determine the number of hogs sold during the past two years in order to make a hog allotment. Measuring the corn acres and determining the number of acres grown and bushels produced for ten years back in order to make the corn allotment was also a tremendous job.[27]

Following the sign-up work, most counties and townships selected permanent organizations that provided the follow-up work. In most cases the chairman of the temporary committee was selected as permanent chairman. Township committeemen and volunteers visited every farmer who had not signed a contract, informing the farmer of the advantages of the program. For those farmers not taking part, township officials often provided some persuasion by relating unofficial estimates of the benefits from participation.[28]

After additional work had been completed including the appointment of county allotment committees and completion of the state's AAA committee budget, contracts were forwarded to the State Board of Review. That board finished its work of establishing county quotas on corn acreages and hog production on May 18, and immediately forwarded the contracts to Washington. Extension supervisors and state committee fieldmen then carried the county quotas to every county in the state. Following the completion of all sign-ups, contracts, and adjustments, Director Bliss reported that 176,000 Iowa farmers had signed corn-hog contracts with approximately $75 million being distributed to participating farmers.[29]

The following year Iowa's Extension officials were again deeply involved in carrying out the AAA. Extension staff prepared and disseminated educational materials informing Iowans of the provisions of the legislation and, in turn, again carried out an intensive leadership training program. The second year 155,369 farmers signed contracts controlling their corn and hog production. As Bliss has pointed out, the major effort of the Extension Service in 1934 and 1935 was the training of local leaders.[30]

While Extension received some criticism for its involvement in the AAA, it also benefited from that activity. Michael Lundeen has pointed out in his study of Extension that while some state Extension directors had originally planned to "treat the AAA as any other USDA program, selecting the agreeable features of the program and rejecting the rest," the Iowa Extension Service quickly realized that cooperating fully with the program "would demonstrate anew Extension's value to farmers and would stimulate an expansion of extension services." According to Lundeen, the corn-hog program especially marked the farmers' "returning confidence" in Extension and brought an end to "vigorous agricultural dissent."[31]

County agents also reported direct benefits to farmers from participation in the AAA, some of which helped further programs that Extension had been promoting for years. Linn County agent George Dillion wrote in 1934 that the experience changed farmers' "mental processes from that of thinking in terms of production to that of agricultural economics which heretofore had been wholly lacking in their consideration." An additional result was that more farmers began to realize the importance of good record keeping. Because farmers generally did not have good records in 1934 when they signed up for the corn-hog programs, Extension had conducted an intensive farm records campaign and many county agents had distributed farm record books to their clients. The Extension Service had promoted good record keeping almost from its inception with varying degrees of success; in the 1920s record clubs were started with farmers as well as with young people. It seems that the immediacy of the 1930s Depression along with the fact that farmers experienced "the lure of AAA payments" produced a greater commitment to record keeping than ever before.[32]

Some county agents also believed that their involvement in the AAA reduced hostility toward Farm Bureau. County agent E. C. Gardner of Cedar County noted that in his county farmers formerly opposed to the Farm Bureau had taken part in the corn-hog program. He also believed that involvement in the program had created "farmer cooperation." In Cedar County not only Farm Bureau members served on the temporary county committees but also eighteen Farmers' Union and Farm Holiday Association members as well as twenty-seven unaffiliated farmers.[33]

By 1934, given extremely low farm prices, Iowans probably assumed that conditions could not get much worse. But nature itself was to intervene and in 1934 the first of two major droughts struck the state. Dallas County agent Donald Fish described the impact of that event on his county. "Imagine . . . a period when no rain falls from March until late fall. This was what happened in Dallas County in 1934. On top of this the temperature passed a hundred, and it seemed like there was always wind—hot, burning wind." Fish explained, "The oats and grass seed planted in March and April never germinated but lay in dry soil. Pastures dried up almost before they had a chance to turn green. Some corn came up but it did poorly."[34]

The drought of 1934 illustrated that Extension personnel wore many caps. State officials asked Director Bliss to chair the state drought committee while county agents served as county drought directors. In effect, the drought program was handled through regular Extension channels with some special funds appropriated by the federal government. Much of Extension's assistance related to carrying out a corn fodder conservation program with farmers building special silos to store the feed. Also, feed was purchased in those areas less affected by drought and trucked into areas most severely affected. In thirty-four counties Extension personnel assisted with cattle purchasing programs, resulting in payments of $326,609 from the federal government. In turn, Director Bliss, one district Extension agent, and an Extension animal husbandry specialist directed the emergency drought program in cooperation with the Emergency Relief Administration and the Farm Credit Administration.[35]

An additional part of the emergency drought response was taking seed-and-feed conservation surveys throughout the state. Extension personnel held meetings in every county to acquaint farmers with the seed-and-feed situation, "to urge them to save all feed and to secure seed supplies early." Extension personnel also maintained exchange lists of seed-and-feed supplies to help farmers buy and sell such items. The work of Extension also concerned transportation; because of their designation as county drought directors, county agents had the authority to issue freight rate certificates that granted farmers reduced rates on shipments of feed into drought-affected areas.[36]

Following the second drought in 1936, particularly severe in southern and western Iowa and accompanied by searing temperatures and a heavy infestation of insects, Extension personnel carried out much the same program as in 1934. Director Bliss noted that the drought "overshadowed all other problems" as forty-six counties in western and southern Iowa were designated as drought stricken. As usual, Extension took part in all aspects of the emergency planning. Personnel in counties desiring drought status first had to submit applications to be signed by the chairman of the county board of supervisors and countersigned by the director of relief and the county agent. Officials then sent the proposal to the state Director of Extension who, in conjunction with the federal agricultural statistician for Iowa, either approved or disapproved the applications, which were then forwarded to the USDA. Once a county had been designated as drought stricken, farmers there were again, as in 1934, entitled to reduced freight rates on feed and livestock shipped in and out of the county and had the right to sell cattle and sheep to the government for relief purposes. The designation also let farmers apply for grants and loans to the Resettlement Administration. Moreover, in many drought counties farmers received employment through the Works Progress Administration.[37]

In 1936 the Extension Service and Iowa farmers would face yet another major change: in January the U.S. Supreme Court declared the AAA unconstitutional. Director Bliss recalled that he, along with some five hundred committeemen and county agents, was attending the annual farm program training session at Ames when he heard the news. A speaker at the meeting, USDA official Claude Wickard, read the telegram to the group, announcing the Court's action. Bliss described it as "a dramatic moment. The committeemen who were training to put the program into effect were, to say the least, stunned." According to Bliss, Congress soon came to the rescue by changing the law so that corn and other basic crops could be taken out of production for "further conservation of soil resources." He added, "This was something of a subterfuge with the real immediate object being to control production." Bliss believed, however, that the legislation did deal with an important problem, that of soil conservation. As a result of the change, the government dropped the hog-control portion of the program. As with the AAA in 1933, the soil conservation program called for the direct involvement of Extension personnel. Bliss estimated that all county agents spent an average of two months in 1936 working on the conservation program.[38]

Typical of the first AAA, the soil conservation measure passed in 1936 left little time to plan for the law's implementation. In each county, agents, Extension specialists, and county and township committeemen hurriedly explained the main program provisions and how they applied to farmers. These same individuals held a second meeting in each county to answer additional questions about the program and to help farmers fill out worksheets. Fortunately, the county and township networks used with the AAA were still intact, and these worked well for dispensing information on the new legislation to ensure its correct application.[39]

County agents were also involved in other ways with soil conservation. In 1936 Iowa contained twenty-one Civilian Conservation Corps (CCC) camps doing conservation work on Iowa farms. In counties where these camps were located, agents organized county soil associations, which then cooperated with the CCC officials. County agents and project managers conducted tours in these counties, held meetings, and made information available to interested farmers.[40]

The actions called for by the Soil Conservation and Domestic Allotment Act of 1936 and the work done by the CCC underscore the important soil conservation work carried out by the Iowa Extension Service in the 1930s. From the early years of Extension, personnel had been concerned about soil erosion and soil fertility. In the 1910s county agents had demonstrated that the application of limestone to soil reduced its acidity and had worked to educate farmers as to the desirability of growing clover and alfalfa as a way of restoring nutrients to the soil. Typically, some agents were more interested in soil conservation than others and therefore gave more attention to the project. In 1920 in Van Buren County, for example, the first terracing in the state was done by county agent Arthur Secor. In 1930 Extension personnel promoted the first four-county plan, involving Appanoose, Monroe, Wapello, and Mahaska counties, to work specifically in the field of soil conservation. The group employed a soil specialist who worked full time in cooperation with Extension personnel. This plan called for demonstrations in all four counties dealing with different fertility methods, terracing and contouring, and tree planting in sloughs and gullies. Ever alert to the need to train future farmers, Extension personnel worked to incorporate material on soil conservation in the agricultural teachings in rural schools. Also during the 1930s Extension helped to establish several more four-county soil groups in the state, including the East Central Soil Association created in 1936 in Tama, Benton, Iowa, and Poweshiek counties.[41]

In effect, the four-county soil associations served as forerunners of the county Soil Conservation Districts set up in 1939 by the Iowa General Assembly. Again the Extension Service played a role, providing advice and supervision for "the remedial practices of contour cultivation, terracing, and strip cropping and the introduction of special cover crops."[42]

The development of soil conservation programs provides an instructive example of how the Extension Service often initiated much-needed programs. These same patterns would be repeated over and over during the 1940s and 1950s. When a need was identified, such as soil conservation, Extension agents and specialists usually offered the first assistance and developed the initial programs. Within a few years, however, it often became clear that without additional funding and positions the Extension Service could not continue in the same manner. Typically an organization like the Soil Conservation Service was then formed, which in turn became the major agency for the service. In the meantime Extension had provided information, service, and expertise in response to the problem. Even after the formation of the federal Soil Conservation Service, Extension agents and specialists continued to supply information and to work with conservation employees.[43]

Extension's work with soil conservation also points to another aspect of the work of county agents. Given the changes in agriculture, with new programs like soil conservation needing implementation, with emergencies such as the need for additional food production in World War I, and the particular demands of the Depression, Extension personnel found themselves continually pressed for more involvement and more answers. By the 1930s a county agent was no longer regarded as the "crop doctor" who responded primarily to the needs of individual farmers, yet agents were still expected to be centrally involved in all major agricultural developments. When drought hit Iowa in 1934, for example, the Extension Director was appointed to the state drought committee and county agents served as chairmen of their county drought committees. When the AAA went into effect in 1933, federal officials immediately expected county agents to play a major role in carrying out the program. In this way when important events took place in the rural community, Extension (often through the county agent) was involved. Put another way, nothing of any significance took place in rural Iowa without the involvement of the Extension Service.

In the latter half of the 1930s, county agents and agricultural specialists continued to emphasize the keeping of farm records with an ever-increasing number of farmers taking part. As previously noted, the experience with the AAA in 1934 and 1935 convinced many farmers that record keeping made good sense any time. Extension personnel emphasized that farmers needed a solid understanding of their operation if they were to make a careful analysis of their past actions and to plan intelligently for the future. As Director Bliss pointed out in 1937, if farmers were to know which parts of their farming operation were making money and which were not, they would have to keep adequate records. In keeping with that view, Extension assisted in the organization of farm business associations in different parts of the state. The first group formed was the Cedar Valley Farm Business Association with a membership of 338 farmers. Each association had a fieldman who visited the groups regularly to explain the record-keeping process, inspect books for accuracy, and provide assistance with management problems. By the end of 1937 the number of associations had grown to five, which included a total of 683 farmers in forty-six counties.[44]

The keeping of farm records underscored the fact that agricultural economics was a rapidly growing area within Extension. In 1935 Extension started publishing the *Iowa Farm Economist,* a quarterly publication devoted "to popularization of economics for farmers." The journal contained "popular interpretations of research, discussions of public policies and analysis of individual farm problems."

The *Iowa Farm Economist* joined two other publications, *Agricultural Economic Facts,* a monthly circular on farm economic conditions, and *Farm Facts,* described as a "weekly economic service for the members of the farm business associations and county agents." Later in the decade Extension agricultural economists would begin publishing a yearly farm outlook statement designed to help farmers understand and prepare for economic conditions predicted for the following year. In 1939 Extension economists combined the *Iowa Farm Economist* and the *Agricultural Economic Facts* into one publication taking the name the *Iowa Farm Economist.*[45]

The advent of the Depression and the heavy involvement of Extension personnel in the AAA should not obscure the fact that Extension continued many general programs during the decade including those carried on by agricultural economists, veterinarians, marketing specialists, and livestock and crop specialists. As Director Bliss has pointed out, in the 1930s significant agricultural progress was made in many areas. Of major importance was that far more farmers began to use hybrid seed corn. Marketed commercially for the first time in the 1920s, in the 1930s "farmers bought [hybrid seed] as fast as it could be procured." In turn, corn production went up substantially. When new and better varieties of oats came on the market, Extension personnel helped disseminate the seed as quickly and as widely as possible. They also carried out more soil testing to see if Iowa soils contained sufficient lime. In the area of livestock production, researchers were finding ways to bring hog cholera and tuberculosis under control. And, college and Experiment Station scientists were developing better varieties of alfalfa, which again Extension helped to distribute.[46]

Throughout the decade Extension personnel also helped raise the income of farm families by introducing grading procedures into the production and marketing of major Iowa products. Earlier, Extension poultry specialists had worked with producers to introduce a grading system for eggs. In 1935 the state legislature passed the cream-grading law which required that "cream be bought on three grades, according to flavor and acidity standards." Following the passage of the bill, Extension personnel assisted the Iowa Department of Agriculture in explaining the law to creamery personnel. In 1936 approximately fifteen hundred farmers in fifteen Iowa counties worked together in the Quality Lamb Production Project. The group carried the project through to the last phase, the marketing of lambs in June 1937. Program personnel placed emphasis on breeding, feeding, and management, which would all lead to better quality lambs; these could then be marketed in early June when prices were typically the highest. Extension specialists also conducted lamb grading demonstrations.[47]

As in previous decades, the Iowa Extension Service worked hard to establish cooperation with other federal, state, and private agencies. In 1937 Iowa Extension personnel worked with employees of the Farm Security Administration (FSA), the successor to the Resettlement Administration. The federal government established the latter organization to provide rehabilitation for disadvantaged farm families in 1935. The Farm Security Administration continued this program, putting more emphasis on reducing farm tenancy and working to strengthen the family farm than on a general policy of fighting rural poverty. While cooperation existed between Extension and the FSA, there was also occasional dissension. As Edmund deS. Brunner and E. Hsin Pao Yang point out, some Extension agents did not approve of the "intensive attention paid by Farmers Home advisers to their clients" and others worried that by comparison, Extension personnel would seem too inattentive even though they lacked the means to operate on a household basis.[48]

In Iowa, it appears that a fairly good spirit of cooperation existed between Extension and the Farm Security Administration agents. Director Bliss wrote in 1936 that the "Extension Service maintained close contact with the rural rehabilitation workers [of the Resettlement Administration], especially in determining subject matter to be taught and practices to be recommended by the representatives of the federal agency." After working several years as an Iowa Extension home economist, Louise Rosenfeld worked for the Farm Security Administration from 1936 to 1943. She believed that cooperation was good between the two agencies, noting that the creation of the Farm Security Administration convinced Extension that there really were poor people in Iowa.[49] She recalled,

> That was in the period where rehabilitation loans were given for people who didn't have food to eat, whatever the drought didn't take, the grasshoppers did. I never thought I'd ever see that a farm family wouldn't have food. It never occurred to me that that could happen. Having grown up on a farm, etc. But there were people that if there hadn't been rehabilitation grants they would have had no food. It just wasn't there.[50]

Rosenfeld believed that because many FSA home economists later went into Extension work, they carried along the knowledge that

IOWA FARMER PLANTING corn with a four-row corn planter, circa 1930. Courtesy ISU Photo Service.

Iowa did indeed have farm families who were not prosperous and who were in need of assistance. Wayne Rasmussen has also pointed out that when Extension personnel worked with FSA officials, it brought Extension "into contact with a segment of the farm population with which they previously had few dealings." In Iowa home economic specialists also helped train home management supervisors for the rural resettlement program.[51]

While much of Extension's attention throughout the 1930s was focused on federal farm programs, the Division of Home Economics continued to play a major role working with farm families throughout the state. Home economists carried out general educational programs in the areas of food and nutrition, clothing, home management, and child care, as well as implementing and carrying out emergency activities designed to provide self-help and assistance for Iowans. Throughout, the overall goal was on economizing and retrenchment. The first line of defense in cutting costs always brought emphasis on lowering the cost of living, which directly involved farm women. The 1930s also witnessed an important change in leadership as Neale S. Knowles retired after twenty-six years of serving as the state leader of Home Economics Extension. Director Bliss appointed Sarah Porter Ellis to replace Knowles on July 1, 1934; Ellis remained in that position until the early 1940s.[52]

In light of reduced farm income, home economists suggested many ways that farm women could economize. County home demonstration agents urged women to raise more of their families' food supply and to can more vegetables and fruit. Throughout the decade farm women responded favorably to the home economists' suggestions. In the summer of 1932 Extension personnel launched a canning project, sending workers into each county to conduct classes for local leaders who, in turn, held schools in their townships. Director Bliss noted in his annual report that year that local leaders held a total of 1,286 meetings with an attendance of 11,524. At the end of the year home economists estimated an increase of 41 percent in canning over the previous year.[53]

Going hand in hand with more canning went an emphasize on home butchering and meat curing. In 1935 agent Jennie Nelson Knupp reported that Benton County women had increased their canning of meat by 70 percent, which led to an estimated savings of $6,000 on their meat budgets. The home demonstration agents' work in canning meat related to the Depression in yet another way. Because of the lack of feed, the state Extension staff recommended removal of surplus beef to both conserve feed and to ensure an adequate food supply for farm families for the following year. True to form, the Extension Service came up with a catchy title for the latter project: "Can A Cow Campaign."[54]

With less money to spend, farm women were also concerned about remodeling older clothing rather than buying new garments. In 1935 farm women took part in a clothing-remodeling project. Specialists demonstrated not only remodeling but also clothing construction and sewing shortcuts. In Adair County in 1935 women gave particular attention to remodeling coats since the project "gave them an opportunity to be well dressed at a minimum cost." Agents also gave demonstrations on producing personal grooming items such as hand lotion. That year the home demonstration agent reported the women chose fourth-year clothing as their major project. One of the first steps was to recondition their sewing machines. One agent reported that some machines had not been cleaned for twenty-five years. Louise Rosenfeld, then a home demonstration agent in Shelby County, remembered that she saw this activity as a good way to involve husbands as well. She explained that in bad weather the men brought their wives to the meetings and then adjourned to the kitchen where they visited for the duration of the meeting. Rosenfeld decided that the sewing machine project was a good way to get the husbands interested in their wives' projects so she suggested ways they could help.[55]

Farm women continued in the latter 1930s to be increasingly interested in clothing projects. This included more interest in "buying information" especially regarding synthetics and new fabric finishes. By 1937 Director Bliss noted that "Iowa farm women no longer can be 'spotted' on the street—extension clothing courses have helped her become an alert, erect, well-groomed and appropriately dressed individual, one in whom her family, as well as she, will have pride."[56]

Farm women selected both a major and a minor project annually; by the 1930s, topics were typically chosen on a countywide basis. Frequently the women continued the same projects for several years, each year studying them in considerably greater depth. With nutrition, for example, counties could advance from first-year nutrition to fifth-year nutrition. In 1935, when Benton County women voted to study fifth-year nutrition, agent Knupp reported conducting sixty-six nutrition training schools with an attendance of 1,070 women, including 127 township leaders; twenty-eight additional meetings associated with the home project were held at which 1,915 women attended. Knupp estimated that through her work she had reached 1,200 homes in the county, or 50 percent of the total farm homes.[57]

In the 1930s, farm women also chose annual minor projects such as art and music appreciation. This change may have been in response to criticism of home economics programs in 1933 that (1) projects were so highly structured that farm women felt they had little say about what they studied; and (2) home economics specialists should incorporate into their programs more material on "music, art, literature, recreation and dramatics." Women in Scott County in 1935, for example, selected music appreciation and recreation as minor projects. During 1935 home economics groups across the state worked on the production of a light opera, *Bohemian Girl,* with some groups presenting the opera at the county level. In Franklin County the home demonstration agent noted that *Bohemian Girl* was the "big event" of the year. She explained that the production attracted about seven hundred people who stood in the rain for fifteen minutes before getting into the building. The agent concluded, "Some of the people laughed at the idea at first, but they found out that it was really worthwhile." In addition to work done by home economics specialists, Extension sociologists also prepared programs for rural women.[58]

While home economists provided specific technical information on nutrition, clothing, and other topics, intangible results of Extension activities were also evident. Throughout the 1930s farm life continued to be described as isolated and farm women in need of social outlets. Not only did women feel that Extension provided them with new homemaking skills and information, but that the meetings gave them opportunities to socialize with neighbors. In 1935 the Audubon home demonstration agent remarked that Extension work "is a means for women to become better acquainted with one another. One woman at the county fair said, 'I'm glad the training schools are going to start soon. I'll get to see my neighbors again.' " Through their Extension activities, farm women also made contributions to community life. Agent Clara Blank wrote in 1935 that in their Extension work local women worked "to keep community life active. Their township meetings bring more people together and get them better acquainted." Farm women were experiencing the same personal benefits from Extension in the 1930s that they had experienced in the 1920s—taking part in Extension, particularly serving as local leaders, increased their self-confidence and their public speaking ability.[59]

In spite of financial difficulties, the number of home demonstration agents continued to increase throughout the 1930s. In 1934 thirty-two home demonstration agents served forty-six counties which meant that some agents divided their time between two counties. In 1936 the number of Iowa agents had increased to forty-seven working in sixty-eight counties, and by 1939 the number had risen to seventy-seven agents. The number of farm women taking part in Extension activities also continued to grow. Extension officials had high hopes that during this decade the number of participating farm women would reach a hundred thousand but that goal was not attained. Home demonstration agents continually urged more women to take part, however. In 1935 Extension invited all rural women in each community to attend a "homemakers' open meeting."[60]

During the 1930s Louise Rosenfeld worked as an Extension home economist in Shelby County. Although Rosenfeld had taught school for several years after graduating from Iowa State College, she still saw Extension work as a major challenge. Six months after going to Shelby County, she also became responsible for East Pottawattamie County. Her annual salary for handling both counties was $1,370. Five days a week Rosenfeld met with county women, and on Saturday she worked with 4-H groups. Sunday was the only day she had to prepare for the following week's work.[61]

Rosenfeld remembered that when she first arrived, the Shelby County women could not believe that they would have the services of a home economist at no cost. While it was a new experience for farm women, it was also a new experience for Rosenfeld. She had not baked much bread, so she practiced before she went out to give the first demonstration. Before long, however, the women wanted to know more than just how to put ingredients together. They were asking, "What made the bread have big holes in it? What happened if there was too much salt? Or too much sugar?" Rosenfeld quickly learned that farm women often lacked confidence in speaking before groups. She recalled, "I think of some of the women who said, 'I just couldn't get up in front of a group and I sometimes would say well, why don't we do it together? Why don't we do a little and you do something that's easy for you and I'll do something.' "[62]

From the beginning Rosenfeld, like other home economists, used the local leader training method. Rosenfeld observed, however, that because there were so few home economists local leader training was really taking part on two levels: first, the state specialists would train the home economists; and second, the home economists would train farm women. Thus despite the shortage of personnel, the meetings with farm women could take place.[63]

Rosenfeld also quickly discovered that in rural Iowa in the 1930s ethnic culture and local traditions remained strong. On one occasion when she was making an evening presentation with a mixed audience, the host family served beer even though prohibition was in effect. Although she accepted a glass and only took a sip, she was very concerned this might reflect negatively on her as an Extension employee. Arriving back in Harlan that evening, she immediately called the county agent to tell him about this potentially damaging situation. She related, "Before I got my story told he said, 'Louise, what did you do? What did you do?' And I said, 'Well, I slightly sipped it and put it up on the piano.' He replied, 'Thank goodness you didn't refuse it! They don't care whether or not you drank the beer but if you had refused it, they would have thought you were an old prude and you might not come back in the county.' " Rosenfeld agreed that it was extremely important that the county agent and the home demonstration agent did not appear to be too dignified to do certain things and to appear "as one of the group." Rosenfeld also explained that although she had not been a coffee drinker, after being offered coffee so often she finally felt she had to develop the habit.[64]

Reflecting on her career in western Iowa, Rosenfeld expressed great satisfaction about her work with farm women and their responsiveness and eagerness to learn. Even though resources were limited, she recalled that women managed to find much pleasure in their programs. One experience especially reflected that fact. When Shelby County women were having a lesson on serving a company meal, they didn't have much to work with.

> In one of the townships we had to put two tables together that didn't come flush up against each other. We had oilcloth on one table and a feedsack cloth on the other. But you know, when we were doing that it was just as if it were elegant. I'll never forget because there they were and they didn't see that the tables didn't match. They were having company with what they had. From my point of view, that was the important thing anyway.[65]

Although men's and women's Extension activities remained separate, in 1935 Director Bliss noted in his yearly report that farm women were becoming more knowledgeable about general economic conditions. Previously the Extension Service had provided outlook meetings for farmers in which future price and marketing conditions were discussed. That year Extension economists presented special outlook meetings for farm women where economic material was presented. Bliss also noted "a growing interest on the part of farm women in [purchasing] information." With the increasing importance of synthetics and new fabric finishes, farm women were being informed of changes. More and more women were taking part in Extension activities, with 99,849 rural women in some aspect of the program in 1938.[66]

Throughout the 1930s Extension's 4-H programs also continued to serve thousands of Iowa's rural youth through separate boys' and girls' clubs. Although the number enrolled in both programs fluctuated somewhat during the decade, overall the numbers gradually increased. In 1930 4-H membership totaled 24,343 while by 1939 that number had risen to 26,927. In 1931 the average age of club members was between fourteen and fifteen years. Projects remained similar to those in the 1920s; the three most popular projects with boys' clubs in 1930 were swine, dairy calf, and baby beef projects. By 1932 baby beef was the most popular project and remained so throughout the decade. By mid-decade corn clubs were becoming popular. With girls' clubs clothing, home furnishings, canning, and bread projects proved the most popular. Director Bliss noted that throughout the 1930s the rate of project completion was high, around 85 percent. The State Fair remained the climax to 4-Hers club work and in 1930 premiums totaled $15,373. The same year Extension officials held the third annual 4-H Girls' Convention at Ames where delegates heard the noted suffragist, Carrie Chapman Catt, deliver the main address. Also during the summer, 4-H boys attended the annual Boys' Short Course in Ames, and both boys and girls participated in other conferences and contests in and out of state. By 1940 boys were serving as delegates to the National Club Camp in Washington, D.C.; the National Dairy Show in Harrisburg, Pennsylvania; and the Club Congress and Junior Livestock Feeding Contest in Chicago.[67]

During the 1930s girls' 4-H clubs followed a two-year rotation program. Members spent two years studying clothing projects, two years with home furnishing, and two years with nutrition. 4-H officials followed the same procedure as Home Economics Extension in relying heavily on local leaders. In fact, local leaders were indispensable to the continuation of the program through the decade as the number of club agents was very low. By 1937 girls' 4-H officials had developed an eight-year cycle, dividing counties into groups of twenty-five so that members in each group studied each major topic for two consecutive years. Also by 1937 topics had been expanded to include home efficiency. Given the rotation program, state leaders believed that 4-H girls were receiving "well-rounded home economics training." By 1939 girls were also being trained in good citizenship with an emphasis on a "world-conscious" program that included learning about other countries and developing a deeper appreciation for "the democracy in which [they lived]."[68]

Throughout the 1930s, girls' 4-H leaders stressed health issues. Officials held health contests throughout the state, which led to 4,434 girls receiving complete physical examinations. Each project contained a health component so that a study of health was a part of every member's program. Clothing projects, for example, emphasized correct posture and correct footwear while home furnishing projects stressed sanitation, ventilation, and proper lighting. In 1930 Iowa received special recognition when the state health champion, Marion Syndergaard of Grundy County, was named the national health champion.[69]

Leaders also emphasized music with girls' programs. By 1930, music appreciation had been a part of 4-H for nine years. That year 4-H girls studied the opera *Martha,* and took part in music appreciation contests and club and county orchestras and choruses. At the annual state 4-H convention, girls participated in a state orchestra and a state chorus, with 2,470 individuals involved.[70]

Julia Faltenson Anderson, who later worked for Extension, grew up on a farm in Iowa County in the 1920s and 1930s and was an active member of a local 4-H club. Anderson related that at the time, as far as rural youth were concerned, 4-H was the only organization available. "There weren't alternatives in rural Iowa. And not even in our small communities, because I cannot remember any active Scouts or Campfire. It was a 4-H program." In the 1930s there were two rally day events at the county seat. The first had to do with nominations and elections of county officers with some competition between various 4-H clubs. The second event was known as Achievement Days where 4-Hers gave demonstrations and displayed their projects. County winners then went on to the State Fair in Des Moines. At age fifteen Anderson won a trip to the State Fair to demonstrate baking whole wheat bread, the first time she had been in Des Moines. The experience began a lifetime interest, as Anderson has baked bread ever since. Like so many 4-Hers in the 1930s, Anderson fondly remembered the many 4-H musical activities such as the county chorus.[71]

4-H activities also provided rural youngsters with role models.

Eleventh Annual 4-H Girls' Convention
Iowa State College, Ames, June 15-18, 1938
Design by Fisher; Engineer, Kerekes; Photo, Richardson

IOWA 4-H GIRLS CELEBRATING the 100th anniversary of the founding of the Territory of Iowa (June 1938) with the words "Iowa's 100 years 4-H." Courtesy Iowa State University Library/University Archives.

Julia Anderson recalled that Iowa County did not have a regular home demonstration agent but state specialists frequently visited the county, thus providing teenage girls with a sense of possible future careers. Because of their involvement in 4-H and often a close association (through their parents) with other Extension personnel, Anderson believed that many rural teenagers thought only of attending Iowa State College. No doubt many of those same youngsters also first thought of attending college because of their association with Extension staff. Anderson herself would follow this path as she attended ISC and later worked as an Extension home economist.[72]

As in previous decades more girls than boys took part in 4-H. In 1931, for example, approximately 2,600 more females were involved than males. Accordingly in that year, 1,821 women and 1,020 men served as local leaders. By 1936 approximately 2,900 more girls were involved than boys. Apparently Extension staff still found it more difficult to find men to serve as local leaders than women. In their report on Extension published in 1933, Davidson, Hamlin, and Taff pointed out that agricultural specialists used the local leader method of teaching much less than home economists. One result of that condition seemed to be that men, lacking the experience of being a local leader in adult agricultural and livestock projects, did not feel comfortable taking on that role with 4-H clubs.[73]

While both boys' and girls' clubs followed the same organizational form, their activities varied. In annual reports both by county agents and the state Extension director, boys' 4-H activities were characterized in terms of projects. Girl 4-Hers, on the other hand, were engaged in a wide variety of activities ranging from health, music, canning, bread making, home efficiency, and drama. In some communities girls' 4-H clubs made presentations before local farm bureau meetings. In 1935 Director Bliss placed the boys' livestock projects in the context of the market price for each type of livestock. Two years later in the same vein Bliss wrote, "The total value of livestock in crop club projects supervised by 4-H club members was approximately $1,460,000. This did not include premium money won at fairs and shows totaling $75,217." Bliss continued that "through these projects, the club members are obtaining invaluable experience in selecting, feeding, and managing animals and are building up good purebred cattle, hog and sheep breeding herds. In legume, garden and fruit, forestry, farm record and farm efficiency clubs the boys and girls are getting information which will be helpful in other phases of the farm enterprise."[74]

While Bliss included both boys and girls in this description, it pertained far more to the former than the latter. It appears from these records that competition between male 4-Hers was more intense than among female 4-Hers and that male members continued to work individually far more than did females. For girl 4-Hers, taking part in a chorus, orchestra, or dramatic presentation gave them considerable experience in cooperation and working as part of a team. It seems that in the major programs sponsored by 4-H through the 1930s, boys were being trained to be good farmers while girls were being trained not only to be good homemakers, but also to be good community leaders and all-around good citizens. Clearly the 4-H goals of learning leadership, cooperation, and citizenship were being more fully advanced by the diversified program of girls' 4-H than by boys' 4-H.

During the 1930s a change took place in club work at the national level that affected some activities of 4-H clubs in Iowa. By that decade, the National Committee on Boys' and Girls' Club Work had become a major influence in 4-H. Organized in 1921 so that individuals and private businesses could contribute to the support of 4-H, the group soon began raising money to provide premiums and prizes for clubs as well as organizing annual club tours to Chicago (later called the National 4-H Club Congress). The presence of this committee as well as the role played by Extension, according to Thomas and Marilyn Wessel, made "4-H unique in its public and private support." But during the 1920s and 1930s the National Committee and the Extension Service moved in opposite directions regarding their roles with 4-H. As early as 1925 federal Extension Director Clyde W. Warburton had complained to the National Committee that it was giving the impression that "4-H work was its special preserve and [it was ignoring] the Extension Service." Disagreements continued between the two groups and in 1937 a committee reviewing Extension work prepared a report on 4-H. The committee expressed considerable concern about the place of contests and awards in the organization, believing that contests had been overemphasized. They also felt that the national committee had taken "undue advantage" in using the 4-H organization as a "means for undesirable commercial advertising." The review committee further noted that too much attention was given to representatives of commercial firms at the yearly 4-H banquet in Chicago. They believed that because of this situation, those groups involved with the National Committee were exploiting 4-H members.[75]

By 1939 Extension and land-grant college officials such as ISC president Charles E. Friley, insisted that an agreement must be reached between the two groups in regard to their roles and responsibilities. In effect Extension made it clear to National Committee officials that unless changes were made in the way they conducted business Extension was ready to carry on 4-H work by itself. In the same year the Extension Committee on Organization and Policy established a subcommittee devoted entirely to 4-H. This then became the policy proposal body for 4-H and a means of communication between public and private groups. The National Committee continued to play an active part with 4-H programs but in a somewhat diminished way. At the same time direct contact between private businesses and 4-H club members ceased.[76]

While writing a history of the Iowa Cooperative Extension Service in the years following his long tenure as Director of Extension, Ralph K. Bliss reflected on the work of Extension during the hard times of the 1930s. He observed that "the greater progress is often made when conditions are the most difficult." Bliss's statement seems particularly appropriate for that time. Iowa's farm families suffered through a devastating economic period, yet paradoxically the decade also included many positive changes in farm living. That development was especially significant since farm families in the previous decade had experienced increasing dissatisfaction with farm living. A major change, for example, concerned road improvement. During the 1930s many country roads were hard-surfaced, which meant farm families could get to town more easily and more often. In 1925, 23,909 farm families lived along roads that were either hard-surfaced or finished with gravel, shell, or shale. By the end of the 1930s the number of farm families along improved roads had risen to 121,863.[77]

The diaries of Iowans in the 1930s underscore the changes in farm living since the 1920s, particularly regarding geographic mobility and subsequent social activity. Clara Ackerman, an eastern Iowa farm woman, recorded that she attended many social activities in her neighborhood "including church, a PTA meeting at the local rural school, and a bridal shower and wedding for a neighborhood couple." The Ackermans often shared Sunday dinner with neighbors. Elmer Powers, a farmer near Boone, kept a detailed account of his family's activities in the 1930s. It seemed that the family went to town several times a week, sometimes daily. Frequently the family traveled to nearby Boone to shop, to attend Sunday School, and sometimes to attend Farm Bureau meetings. The two Powers's children took piano lessons, which necessitated a weekly trip to town. The Powers also socialized frequently with their rural neighbors. In regard to the types of social activities pursued, the Powers family did not seem much different from their counterparts in town.[78]

The greatest change in farm living occurred, however, with the passage of the Rural Electrification Act of 1935, which brought electricity to the countryside. Iowa poet James Hearst, raised on a farm in Black Hawk County, wrote that with electricity "farm life took on a new dimension. Not even the telephone changed our way of living, thinking and acting as much as the coming of electricity. This break with the past seemed an entrance to the modern world."[79] In 1937 *Wallaces' Farmer* asked farm women to share the ways they used electricity in their homes. A farm woman from Tama County responded.

> The good fairy, electricity, has waved her magic wand across my path and now I lead a charmed life. . . . No water to be carried uphill; no waste water to be carried out; no kerosene lamps to be cleaned and filled; no hand scorching sad-irons to be used; no fuel to clutter up my kitchen in pails and boxes; no ashes to be swept up and carried out; no exposure from lack of bathroom facilities. It seems to be too good to be true.[80]

Changes also took place in the social and cultural spheres. Extension sociologist William Stacey had initiated a new area in the 1920s whereby the Extension Service prepared programs for rural community gatherings. These programs continued during the 1930s and often included dramatic and musical presentations and topics for debate. Any group in the state could use the materials but they were particularly designed for use in rural communities. Rural sociology also continued to work closely with rural churches.

A cultural area greatly expanded by Extension during the 1930s was music. Extension hired Fannie R. Buchanan as Extension Assistant for Home and Community Development and rural people throughout the state soon became acquainted with this energetic, enthusiastic woman. Each year hundreds of Iowa farm women voted music appreciation as a minor project, using material put together by Buchanan. One such program, Musical Moments with American Composers, was a third-year minor music project. For each musical program, Buchanan established three goals: singing a song; playing a game, usually a folk game requiring music; and doing an appreciation study of the topic under discussion. Buchanan listed the goals this way: "Each month memorize text and tune of one song; play one folk game; become familiar with one selection of composed music." The fifth and final lesson included for the song, "My Old Kentucky Home" by Stephen Foster; for the folk game, "Pop Goes the Weasel"; and an appreciation study on John Philip Sousa with "El Capitan March" as the illustration. The eleven-page program prepared by Buchanan contained instructions for the songs, games, and the material for the appreciation lesson. In effect, any group anywhere, regardless of musical knowledge or ability, could participate in the music program.[81]

Farm families also carried music appreciation a step further when they organized county choruses in 1937. In that year a total of 1,102 farm women sang in forty-five choruses in a state chorus tournament sponsored cooperatively by the Extension Service and the State Fair.[82]

During the 1930s Extension personnel also created a new program for rural young adults, including unmarried men and women between the ages of twenty and thirty. Extension officials believed that this age group would no longer be involved in 4-H and yet would not share the interests of the older, married farm couples. Extension assigned a full-time specialist to the Rural Young People's group and by the end of the first year thirty-nine groups were organized within the state with a membership of 1,800. The group concentrated on three major activities: education, recreation, and community service. Members held informal and panel discussions on subjects of farm organization, world peace, international relations, highway safety, home beautification, and state and federal legislation. At their meetings members also took part in recreational activities including dramatics, songfests, dances, picnics, and seasonal parties. Some members assisted with their local 4-H club activities. In 1937, the group began a program of rural-urban cooperation which they carried out in conjunction with the state Junior Chamber of Commerce. The same year members were sponsoring short courses on such subjects as home management, family relations, beekeeping, and wildlife conservation. By the late 1930s members were attending summer weekend camps.[83]

By the end of the decade both economic and social conditions in rural Iowa had improved significantly. Of primary importance, the state's farm economy had rebounded from the dark days of 1931 and 1932. The drought periods had also come to an end and by 1939 farming conditions had improved in every way. Throughout these difficult times the Extension Service had maintained a high visibility in rural areas. While Extension certainly played no direct role in bringing the Depression to an end, it had served well as an educational and support agency.

Perhaps a beneficial approach in determining Extension's importance in the 1930s would be to look again at the Iowa countryside and envision it without the presence of Extension. Most importantly, the implementation of the AAA programs would have been slowed considerably. Without the involvement of county agents, it would have been necessary to create a statewide network of workers to both interpret programs and help farmers sign up for benefits. Extension also served as the major education agency dedicated to carrying new technical and scientific information to its clientele, and without this service new developments in hundreds of agricultural and livestock areas would not have reached farmers quickly. Soil conservation programs would have developed more slowly without Extension's involvement. Residents of the open county would have had far fewer recreational and educational opportunities without programs supplied by Extension sociologists. Farm women would have lost an important social and educational organization and would have lacked assistance in finding ways to stretch their meager resources even further than before. And thousands of farm youngsters would have found that without 4-H there were simply no organizations to join. In assessing its role in the 1930s, it seems for agriculture in general, Extension brought advances in production and efficiency. For Iowans in particular, Extension, through involvement in the AAA, helped bring quicker relief to the farm economy, which in turn brought quicker relief to the economy of the state. Of greatest importance for farm families who chose to take part, economic and social rewards were abundant. For these families, Extension seemed to offer something for everyone.

It must also be recognized, however, that for some farm families Extension really made very little difference. Some did not attend the programs nor did they seek out any assistance from personnel. Perhaps it can be argued that in the broadest sense, these families were aided through programs like soil conservation, but not in immediate terms. Throughout the 1930s certain assumptions persisted which resulted in some rural people believing that Extension was not for them: the first, a misconception, was that people must belong to Farm Bureau to take part in any Extension activity; and the second, a perception, was that Extension was only interested in prosperous farm families, not in less fortunate ones.

The Depression offered opportunities to increase Extension's visibility and to show that it had some value for all rural Iowans. With programs like the AAA, Extension was provided access to almost all farmers in the state, including many who had not previously been involved with its programs. Some farmers seemed to accept the AAA and the Extension Service simultaneously, although that fact belies the important role Extension had played in creating an environment for that acceptance. Extension agents believed that the AAA experience had also taught farmers the value of cooperation and record keeping and had helped change farmers' ways of thinking about production. A long-term change was that more farmers began to feel that the organization was valuable; one study noted that after the 1933 AAA program, "The confidence of farmers in Extension surged."[84] In the thinking of some Iowans, perhaps the greatest benefit was that Extension was salvaged by its participation in the AAA.

Other changes also resulted from activities in the 1930s. As Wayne Rasmussen has pointed out, the role of county agents changed: "The county agent, in much of his work, became a promoter rather than an educator. He became an administrator rather than a teacher as he was assigned responsibility for programs that offered farmers large rewards for cooperation and imposed penalties for noncompliance as well."[85] The same changes did not affect Home Economics Extension. Within the next few years the role of county agents as well as other staff would continue to change. By 1940 with a world war underway, Extension would again urge farmers to return to full production. It seemed that once again both farmers and Extension were on a roller coaster ride, moving from the depths of a depression where government intervention had curtailed production to the dizzying heights of great prosperity brought on by the federal government's call for record production during World War II.

5

"Food Will Win the War and Write the Peace"

World War II

In 1939 when Ralph K. Bliss prepared to write his annual Extension report, the world was a far different place than it had been the year before. In September Germany invaded Poland, marking the beginning of a world war that would last for six years. To Bliss, who had served as Director of Extension during World War I, the start of another war undoubtedly signaled that Iowa farmers would soon be called upon to increase production. In 1940 Bliss devoted several pages in his annual report to a discussion of national defense. The following year he noted, "1941 brought Iowa farmers face to face with the approach of World War [II], and that year witnessed the changing over of the Extension Service from a peace-time to a war-time basis."[1] For the next five years the subject of national defense would dominate the thinking and actions of the Iowa Extension Service. During the war Extension put some of its traditional programs on hold and moved energetically toward increasing the production and preservation of food, as well as dealing with other needs brought on by America's involvement in World War II. Paramount, however, was the goal of all-out production. At the same time, on the home front, the Extension Service helped maintain good morale and healthy farm living.

On the eve of America's entry into World War II, Iowa's farm population was on the road to economic recovery. Rebounding from the early years of the Great Depression, Iowa's total cash farm income had increased $60 million from 1938 to 1939 alone. This recovery meant that by 1939 the Extension Service had returned to many of its traditional programs and was spending little time on emergency measures. In his 1939 annual report, Director Bliss underscored that fact when he wrote that the Extension Service had reached a high point by providing service to twenty-seven thousand more Iowa farm families than in the previous year.[2]

By the end of the 1930s Iowa's farm population had undergone considerable change. In spite of the difficulties of the Depression, many families had managed to purchase more farm equipment. As a result, by the end of the decade farms were becoming mechanized. As Earle Ross has pointed out, "The most determining addition was that of power—the perfected and adapted tractor." In 1939 Iowa led all states in the number of tractors with 135,000 units. That year three-fourths of the tractors had low-pressure pneumatic tires that allowed for increased speed, lower maintenance costs, and greater comfort in operation. Corn-picking machines were also becoming more abundant in Iowa; by 1940 about half of the state's corn crop was picked mechanically. Iowa farmers had witnessed the introduction of the "midget" combine in the late 1930s. In terms of production, Iowa remained the banner corn state aided considerably by the introduction of hybrid seed corn. In 1937 farmers had planted 13 percent of the state's corn acreage with hybrid seed; that percentage would increase for the next six years until by 1943 almost 100 percent of Iowa's farmers used hybrid seed.[3]

In a recent study of American agriculture historian Gilbert C. Fite, presents a prototype of the American farmer in 1940. It is instructive to note that Fite chooses to locate this imaginary person, John Johnson, in Iowa. Fite writes that in 1940 Johnson "was on his way to a fairly comfortable living." He had increased the size of his farm to 240 acres, had largely changed over from the use of horses to a tractor, and raised commercial crops rather than oats which he had formerly needed for feeding his horses. Johnson's granary was full of hybrid corn (yielding fifty-two bushels an acre in 1940). He had additional expenses for commercial fertilizer but felt the additional income offset them. Johnson's check from the government in 1940 was about $1,000. Reflecting the specialization underway throughout the country, Johnson sold all of his milk cows but one or two; these he kept to provide milk for the family.[4] Assuming that the imaginary John Johnson was typical of the Iowa farm population, by 1940 even before the state's farmers began to mobilize for war production, their industry had experienced considerable recovery.

In that same year, given the outbreak of war in Europe, greater demands were being made on America's farmers. In Iowa Director Bliss immediately set up an Extension Project Committee to study the ways that the Extension Service could be used to aid national defense. One of the first concerns was communication. Bliss quickly determined that with the assistance of Iowa State College, the U.S. Department of Agriculture, Iowa's 100 (Pottawattamie had 2) county farm bureaus, and the appointment of local cooperators, "it is possible to supply information to nearly every rural resident in Iowa within a week from the time it is started from the administration at Washington."[5] Following the same procedure used in both World War I and the 1930s, the appointment and use of the local coopera-tors provided an indispensable link in the communications network.

In the fall of 1940 the Extension Service began its campaign to urge farmers to increase production. In September Extension issued a leaflet entitled "Iowa Farm Outlook for 1941," which encouraged increased production of hogs, dairy products, poultry, and eggs. The publication stated that "good hog raisers" would probably find it profitable to raise more hogs in 1941 in "view of prospects for higher prices." Extension also issued other information during November and December of 1940 and the spring of 1941, pointing out the need for increased livestock production and livestock products. When Agricultural Secretary Claude Wickard made his appeal in April 1941 for "food to win the war and write the peace," Director Bliss believed that Iowans were already working hard to accomplish that goal. Supporting Bliss's view is the fact that Iowa farm families produced more livestock, milk, and eggs in 1941 than ever before.[6]

In the early stages of war preparedness in 1941 Bliss observed, "One of the most valuable attributes of the Iowa Extension Service in Agriculture and Home Economics is its ability to adapt its educational programs to changing conditions and to emergencies." Later in the same report, Bliss provided proof of that statement when he wrote that all educational projects had been overhauled and "priority . . . given to those directly connected with the war effort. Educational work which would help Iowa farmers in their important job—that of increasing food production—[have been] given special emphasis." In 1942 Bliss reported that all Extension projects not making a direct contribution toward winning the war "have been shelved for the duration."[7]

The same views were immediately evident at the county level where Extension directors (formerly known as county agents) discussed their concerns in the annual narrative reports, particularly in the "Outlook and Recommendations" section. Writing shortly before the Japanese attack on Pearl Harbor in December 1941, the Greene County agent explained:

> With the Government wanting more hogs produced and larger production of certain crops, the Extension and Farm Bureau Program should deal primarily with all projects along this line and give every farmer in the county an opportunity to do his share. Many of the other projects which are of lesser degree, not necessary for the production of food and defending America should be set aside for the time being at least.[8]

To emphasize that view, farm families from 1941 on frequently heard the term "The food for freedom campaign."

While county directors saw national defense in terms of increased crop and livestock production, home economists quickly saw the effect of war on the home and the necessary contributions of homemakers. In many counties the Home Project for 1942 was "Food and Health for National Defense." In keeping with that theme, home economists listed objectives for 1942:

> Focusing attention on personal health and efficiency as a means of national defense
> Stressing importance of good diets for farm families as a factor in national health
> Helping farm families make adjustments brought on by the immediate effects of the war
> Working to aid in "preparing the farm family to meet the crises which will follow the close of the war."[9]

By 1942 almost every topic discussed by county Extension directors and home economists in their annual reports was cast in light of national defense. The Fayette County Plan of Work for 1941–1942 succinctly presented its goals, and, in turn, typified the goals of all Iowa county Extension organizations.

> In this program special emphasis will be given to the following

activities which have been designated by the federal government as an important part of the national defense program: (1) the conservation of our agricultural resources and efficient production with immediate attention to adequate supplies of dairy, pork, poultry, vegetable and fruit products, and (2) nutrition as related to personal efficiency and public health.

The report added that attention would also be given to the "economic distribution of farm products, farm home improvement, youth training, effective organization and the development of democratic processes in . . . rural communities."[10]

The priority placed on each area included in the official plan or program of work varied depending on the interests of the staff and the particular resources found in each county. Beginning in the late 1930s, soil conservation had become an increasingly visible subject and that would be further emphasized during the war. Writing his Guthrie County Program of Work for 1942, the county Extension director placed soil conservation at the top of the list in regard to "Special Reference to National Defense." He explained, "Total National defense requires conservation of all soil resources." In his county two widespread types of soil depletion were evident: erosion by wind and water, and depletion of plant food by crops. He suggested the continued demonstrations of contour farming and the establishment of five or more cooperative demonstration farms in the spring of 1942 for soil conservation work.[11]

By 1942 Iowa farmers were responding to wartime demands and producing more than ever before. In the area of livestock production, Extension specialists had set down a two-fold responsibility for themselves. First, to help each Iowa farmer realize "the size of his job and the urgency of the situation so that he might set his individual production goals high enough"; and second, to assist him in reaching those goals. Extension specialists prepared the "War Emergency Livestock and Feed Budget," helping farmers determine the amount of feed needed for their individual programs. A leaflet, "Keep 'Em Eating," contained information on various aspects of livestock production. Iowa's hog farmers shared in that success, producing 17 percent more swine than in the previous year, adding up to an all-time high. Poultry producers also did well, producing 12 percent more eggs than in 1941 and hatching 20 percent more chicks than in the previous year.[12] Throughout the war, as the Extension Service continually urged Iowa farm families to produce a greater supply of food, Extension personnel formulated attention-getting slogans. In 1944 dairy specialists initiated the "More milk" campaign; the following year Extension specialists added an extra reminder with the slogan, "An extra squirt from every cow!"

Iowa farmers, no doubt, responded to the urgent requests for more food for a variety of reasons. Certainly patriotism was one, a desire to serve one's country in time of war, but other considerations were also present. Remembering the disastrous economic situation of 1920 and 1921, Iowa farmers, like farmers everywhere, initially hesitated to increase production. Their fears quickly dissipated, however, as Congress passed legislation that guaranteed a sufficient margin of profit. In May 1941 Congress passed the Bankhead Amendment, which "guaranteed prices for the five basic crops at 85 percent of parity through mandatory government nonrecourse loans." A second measure passed in 1942 guaranteed farmers price supports of 90 percent of parity for two years following the end of the war.[13]

While advice given by Extension during the war was certainly vital in increasing production, the earlier groundwork laid by Extension personnel should not be ignored. For many years county agricultural directors and Extension specialists had provided farm men and women with information and demonstrations on proper methods of feeding, vaccinating, and caring for their livestock and poultry, all of which had produced a more enlightened and informed farm population. In his 1942 annual report, Director Bliss noted, for example, several improvements in swine production in the state. He cited better balanced rations, reduction in outbreaks of diseases, widespread use of vaccinations, and better care, particularly in the form of more sanitary conditions on Iowa farms.[14] Before 1941 the annual narrative reports of county agents frequently mentioned demonstrations given to both farm adults and farm youths on the importance of clean ground in hog raising. By 1942 there was little doubt that this type of information was paying big dividends.

By 1942 farm women as well as men were responding to pleas for increased production, an increase that again underscored earlier work carried out by Extension personnel. That year Fayette County director Paul E. McElroy wrote about the success of a local farm woman, Mrs. Herbert Rummel of Maynard, in raising poultry and eggs. McElroy explained, "By keeping her flock confined to a clean poultry house, supplying a balanced ration, systematic culling, and not overcrowding her pullets or hens, Mrs. Rummel . . . obtained an average egg production of 169 in 1941 and realized a net income of $3.82 per hen." McElroy further explained that Mrs. Rummel took considerable care to raise the chickens on clean ground and feed them a balanced ration, recommending a particular ratio between protein mash and grain.[15] In effect, Extension's work in dispensing bulletins and other information, presenting culling demonstrations, and making recommendations for proper feed and facilities had paid off: Iowa women were raising greater numbers of chickens and eggs than ever before.

A major problem confronting Iowa farmers during the war was the shortage of farm labor, particularly acute in 1943 and 1944. When the United States entered the war in 1941, the Farm Security Administration was in charge of the farm labor program. In 1942, however, representatives of agricultural organizations, including the American Farm Bureau Federation, the National Grange, and the National Cotton Council, testified in Washington that under the FSA, farm labor programs had "failed to provide adequate labor and that enforcement of protections for farm laborers interfered with the farmers' ability to meet the nation's wartime food production needs." The testimony referred to the fact that during the war, the FSA hoped to continue safeguarding farm workers' living and working conditions, the same as they had done before the war. After hearing testimony, the House recommended the transfer of the farm labor program from the FSA to the federal and states' Extension Services.[16]

Following the transfer of the program, Extension had responsibility for recruiting intrastate labor and farm labor placement. In effect, county Extension directors played a central role in bringing farmers and prospective workers together. According to the directors' yearly reports, the farm labor issue was, next to Extension organization itself, the most time-consuming issue facing county staff. As more farm youths entered the military, the Extension Service found it increasingly necessary to help locate additional workers for farms all over the state. In most counties directors had help with the program from part-time field assistants and part-time secretaries. The field assistant's office was typically located in the county Extension office.[17] Also beginning in 1943 Iowa Extension personnel worked with two federal agencies, the Office of Labor and the War Manpower Commission, to secure the labor of prisoners of war and foreign nationals.

The extent and type of farm labor organizations set up by Extension directors varied considerably from county to county, as did the type of workers recruited. In some counties directors set up labor centers in local communities. In Marshall County, for example,

Extension created thirteen centers, in effect, in every community in the county. Each center then handled its local registration and placement of workers, usually day labor during the harvest season. In Emmet County Extension set up committees in each town with the arrangement that farmers should first contact their local committee for labor needs; if this proved unsatisfactory, officials forwarded requests to the county Extension director's office.[18]

While labor needs were often general in nature, there were exceptions. In Lee County local farmers had need for seasonal workers to harvest specialty crops such as strawberries, cucumbers, and tomatoes. At the end of 1943, the Lee County director recorded the following:

Number of workers requested—777
Number of people registered—814
Number of workers placed —734
Number of youths enrolled in Victory Farm Volunteers—460
Number of women enrolled in the Women's Land Army—13

The director concluded that nearly every demand for labor had been met.[19]

The Lee County director used almost every means at his disposal to publicize the need for additional workers including placing items in local newspapers and broadcasting ads over local radio stations. The Fort Madison and Keokuk Chambers of Commerce donated space and clerical help to locate and engage workers. Local manufacturing firms posted notices to employees, urging them to use vacation time to do agricultural work. Union officials repeated the process. In smaller towns in the county Extension personnel urged older men and boys to sign up for part-time work. Guards at the Fort Madison penitentiary were asked to spend their days off working on local farms.[20]

While most county directors could report at the end of the year that labor demands had been met, they typically encountered many difficulties along the way. In the view of the Lee County director, some firms just did not pay sufficient wages and had to be encouraged to raise their rates to find suitable labor. In a few cases the Lee County field assistant simply had to wait until the employer was willing to raise the wage before help could be found. The director noted that "tactful suggestions were sometimes necessary." Even after help had been secured, there was no guarantee that the employer would be satisfied. One Lee County farmer, unhappy with the workers he had been getting, responded huffily that "there ain't noth'n now, but d–n culls."[21]

The general assessment of workers' abilities varied from county to county. Some directors felt that the quality of work was good and the cooperation excellent. Others, like the Marshall County director, were not so pleased, as this director noted.

> The majority of the workers found for general farm work were of sub-standard qualities. Many of them were of transient type, willing to work only long enough to get some money to move elsewhere. A number of them were of the type not wanted by employers for industrial work and many others were dismissed from farm work elsewhere because of the poor quality of their work.[22]

At the end of 1943 the Floyd County director believed that farmers themselves needed to change their actions regarding the labor situation. He observed that many farmers had the tendency to wait "until the day they need the help to put in their requirements." Also, farmers often let help go when they had "a few days intermission" and then found themselves without workers a short time later. The director expressed concern that farmers often failed to provide time to train inexperienced help and pay sufficient wages.[23]

In many counties neighborhood cooperation played an important part in solving the farm labor shortage. In Floyd County the director reported that "the volunteer efforts of businessmen in a number of towns helped materially in supplying efficient labor." In Marble Rock approximately fifteen businessmen worked "more or less regularly" on the farms in that vicinity. The director added that there were ten businessmen from Nora Springs (and about the same number from Charles City) who worked several days each in putting up hay and shocking grain.[24]

While county Extension personnel were directly responsible for recruiting intrastate labor, Extension officials also worked with federal authorities to bring Mexican and Jamaican nationals into Iowa as farm laborers. Beginning in 1942 with Mexicans and 1943 with Jamaicans, the federal government negotiated agreements with both governments for importation of workers. Contracts included provisions for transportation, wages, and shelter. In total, 1,509 Jamaican workers and 2,645 Mexicans were hired for farm work in Iowa between 1943 and 1945. As with other labor programs, county directors served as the go-betweens for farmers needing help and foreign workers. As a result of these programs, Mexicans and

Jamaicans worked in many different locations in the state including Emmet County where they harvested potatoes and Muscatine County where 100 Mexicans worked for local truck farmers.[25]

In the spring of 1943 the federal government devised yet another plan to help solve the labor shortages of the nation's farmers. In April the federal government began plans to use prisoners of war as agricultural laborers with the first prisoners arriving in rural areas in May. The following year Iowa officials established two base camps for German prisoners of war in Algona and Clarinda, each with its own camp commander. Nine branch camps were also established to provide labor for a greater number of farmers. Federal authorities determined where the base camps would be located while the establishing of branch or subcamps was negotiated between the state directors of Extension and the commanders of the nearest prisoner base camps. The federal War Manpower Commission determined that prisoners could be used as laborers only when no other labor was available. State Extension directors were to work with camp commanders in providing housing, feeding, transportation, and security for prisoners and also record keeping for the program. Although state Extension directors had to certify the need for such labor—in effect decentralizing the program—county directors were authorized to work directly with appropriate personnel to assign prisoners to farmers and businesses in need of help. County officials also had considerable autonomy in operating the program. In Page County, for example, local authorities set up a special group, the Page County Agricultural Emergency Labor Association, to make better use of available labor from the prison camp. Prison labor made it possible to meet most demands for workers by local farmers.[26]

Most prisoners in Page County worked within a radius of fifteen miles from Clarinda. The county director estimated that during the summer, "12,491 man days of prisoner labor were used . . . by some 60 different farmer employers." Local officials had the responsibility of informing farmers about the availability of labor, the methods of obtaining and using it, and then assisting them in preparing and processing certification of needed forms. In effect, the farmer was making a contract with camp officials for the labor. Supervision of the labor also had to be provided. The Page County Extension director stated that camp officials had cooperated fully with other agencies in the county.[27]

In Kossuth County the Extension director reported that the presence of the prisoner-of-war camp took care of most labor needs there. He explained that war prisoners were used in groups of five to ten men for shocking and threshing grain, making hay, pulling weeds, and in a few cases, tilling. He observed, "With but few exceptions the work was most satisfactory and farmers found that they rather liked the idea of having a greater number of men for a few days, rather than one man for several days." He added that prisoners were not used when local people were available.[28]

Although most prisoners were utilized in Kossuth and Page counties, the branch camps also provided prisoners for work in other areas. Extension reports indicate that farmers in Pocahontas, Emmet, Dickenson, Floyd, and Fayette counties used some German prisoners. Satisfaction with the prison labor force varied. The Grundy County director estimated that about 40 percent of the prisoners "were good help and the rest were not much good." Perhaps the most meaningful assessment of the importance of prisoner labor was made by the Fremont County agent in 1945. He noted that the amount of prisoner help during 1945 "would be equivalent to every farmer in Fremont County using one prisoner for a period of about 10 days' time."[29]

In February 1945 authorities announced that Japanese prisoners would begin replacing German prisoners at Camp Clarinda. At the time it was one of only two in the country singled out for Japanese prisoners. During the months of May, June, July, and August, "3173 man days of the German P.O.W. labor" were used by local farmers. By comparison, the Japanese prisoners during the same time worked at the Shenandoah nurseries, totaling 9,609 man-hours of labor. Later in the war, federal authorities also sent a few Italian prisoners to Iowa. Officials utilized some of these men at the Pioneer Hybrid Seed Corn Company in Marengo.[30]

One type of farm labor often overlooked in World War II was that provided by farm women and children. The Franklin County director reported in 1943 that "the farm housewife and her daughter" supplied 25 percent of the labor in the county with another 15 percent supplied by high school boys. The director expressed concern that farm women were not always considered as a source of labor.

One of the major problems which seemed to handicap the labor program was the failure of county labor placement committees to recognize that women would need to have a place in filling emergency labor demands if the labor problem was to be solved. In spite of this, women of Franklin county automatically shifted into the gaps and did creditably their share toward the 1943 total crop of food and fibre production.

Many teenagers in towns and on farms responded to the calls for workers, particularly for detasseling corn. When the call went out in Johnson County in the summer of 1944 for five hundred detasslers, 70 percent of those responding were boys and girls under the age of eighteen. In the same county the director concluded in his annual report, "The farm labor problem was met the past year only by the farm family working long hours and adopting all shortcuts possible." The Fayette County director also noted the contribution of farm women and children. In his report he singled out women first, adding that seventy-three women had volunteered for work in that county. He concluded, "Farm women deserve much credit for their efforts in operating Fayette County farms."[31] In effect the directors were recognizing a condition that had long existed on Iowa farms—when extra labor was needed, women and children usually provided it. Because farming has traditionally been viewed as a male occupation, the importance of women and children as farm workers has often been obscured.

The shortage of farm labor underscored another situation highly visible during World War II—cooperation between town and country people. In Ida County during harvesttime local businessmen donned their overalls and headed into the fields alongside local farmers. The county director wrote, "The businessmen would divide up into crews with eight or nine men to a crew and go to help different farmers in the county shock their grain." Because of their own business responsibilities, these men would go out after 6 o'clock in the evening. In Johnson County several professors from the University of Iowa "spent their vacation helping out on the farms."[32]

Along with a shortage of workers, Extension personnel also helped farmers cope with the shortage of new machinery. The goal was to keep old equipment in the best shape possible. To do that Extension directors and local implement dealers set up special meetings each spring in which they presented ways to overhaul machinery so when planting started there would be fewer break-downs. As early as 1941 the Greene County Extension director wrote, "Throughout the year suggestions have been given to farmers and especially this fall, relative to repairing and fixing all their farm machinery. Much publicity and other information was given to farmers through the year." In Fayette County in November 1942, as a result of a discussion at the Fayette County War Board, plans were set in motion to hold a machinery repair school in both Oelwein and West Union. The evening before the school, implement dealers, agricultural teachers, representatives from farm organizations and

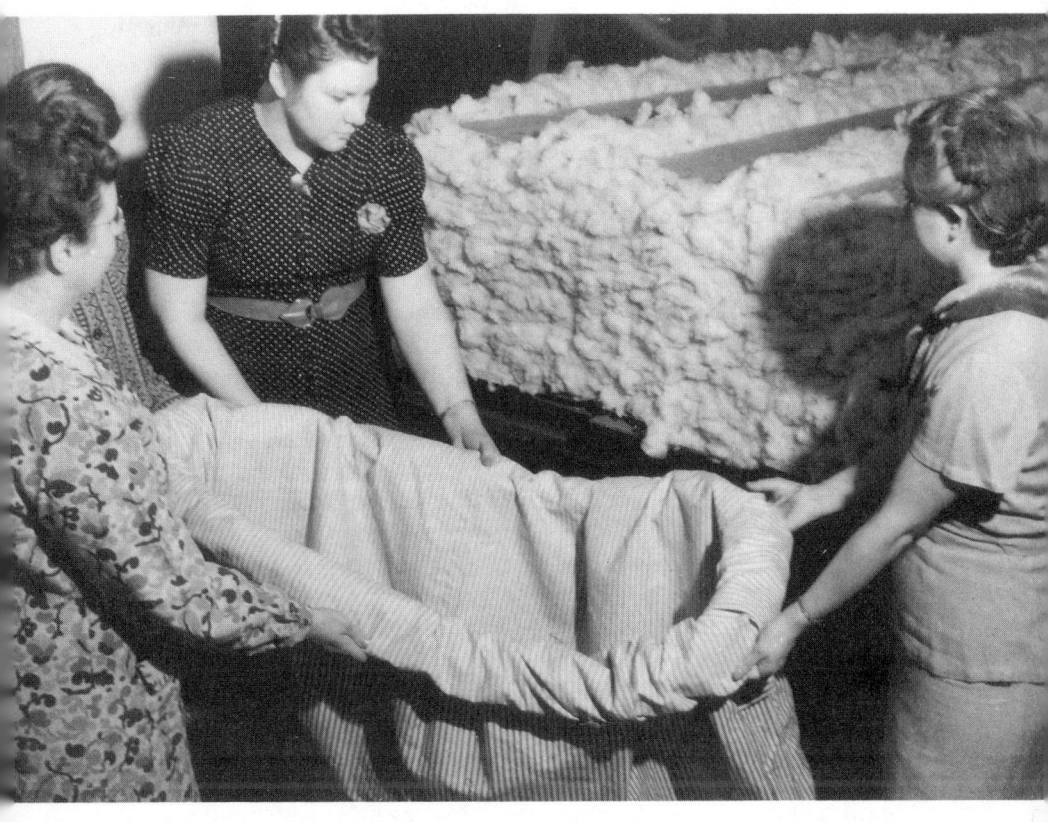

IOWA WOMEN MAKING mattresses in Morrill Hall
in 1940. The mattresses were made from surplus cotton
acquired by the Iowa Extension Service during the
1930s. Courtesy Iowa State University Library/Universi-
ty Archives.

credit unions, and blacksmiths were asked to attend a planning session. In addition, Extension staff sent a checksheet to all farmers in the county urging them to "check their machinery repair needs and order parts at once, because of the defense program, and because the ability of the farmer to produce products needed is America's first line of defense." Local officials held the machinery repair schools in January of the following year. In March engineers from a local gas firm held tractor operation and maintenance demonstrations at an implement business in Fayette County. Those in charge used slides, movies, and actual demonstrations for the more important points.[33]

Extension staff repeated the machinery repair programs annually throughout the state for the remainder of the war and with good results. Over and over, county directors wrote in their yearly reports that cooperation with implement dealers had been excellent and that contacting farmers early in the year had led to earlier placement of parts orders, which in turn led to more dependable operation of farm equipment. The Franklin County director wrote in 1943, "The success of this program was largely due to the fine cooperation and genuinely public spirited activities of the machinery dealers. They went far beyond the dollars and cents side of their business to insure that every machine possible was in shape to operate."[34]

Like their male counterparts, the work of Extension home economists varied considerably during the war. Home economists continually stressed the production of more meat, milk, and eggs, but they were also concerned with the efficient utilization of food. They advised Iowa women how to deal with rationing and food shortages, how to make up food budgets, how to grow even larger victory gardens, and how to can food with lower percentages of spoilage. In 1942 Director Bliss estimated that 80 percent of all farm families, along with many women in towns and cities, had been reached by local leaders dispensing information about home gardening and home conservation of foods. Home economists also presented programs dealing with proper nutrition. Like other programs the nutrition lessons often produced good results. One farm woman in Floyd County commented that until she attended a nutrition class, she did not realize that skim milk had any value.[35]

Extension personnel strongly emphasized victory gardens in 1942. In Jefferson in March of that year county home economist Ruth Cessna made a presentation before a countywide meeting to get the "victory garden program" underway. Following speeches that stressed their patriotic nature, Cessna presented specific information on the subject. She presented a "food budget" designed to help families figure out the quantities of vegetables and fruits to be planted, explaining that a "moderate-cost diet" for a family of four would require "a cash outlay of about $600." But, she added, a garden could greatly reduce that amount. She suggested further that if Iowans produced most of their own food that would release more commercially canned food "for the army, our allies, munitions workers and city people who cannot raise food." Cessna also explained the importance of good diets because of the physical labor required of farm people. She called the home production of food the "war work" of farm women and girls.[36]

The Greene County presentation on gardening illustrates yet another aspect of Extension work in World War II. A major concern of county staff was to cooperate with other local groups and federal agencies whenever possible. In setting up community programs during the war, this cooperation was often evident. Following Cessna's presentation in Greene County, the local REA (Rural Electric Association) manager spoke on electrical equipment designed for garden use, and the administrator for the county rationing board presented information on sugar rationing.[37]

In 1943 Dubuque County reported that a special program on food preservation and gardening had been established there with emphasis on gardening, canning, and drying foods. Extension personnel worked with the Office of Civilian Defense in Dubuque where a garden committee was set up. Officials secured vacant lots from the city, the county, and private individuals with the result that local citizens started over two thousand new gardens. Local newspapers cooperated, running daily suggestions on the care of gardens.[38]

Dubuque County home economists carried on their garden work throughout the summer and into the fall. In June and July they held a series of canning demonstrations and in August a series of meetings on the drying of foods. Both city and farm women attended. In total, Extension staffers held ninety-six meetings with a total attendance of 3,359 people. In the fall Extension personnel set up a surplus food exchange in four vacant gasoline stations and a telephone exchange in the Chamber of Commerce. After two weeks, however, officials terminated the surplus food exchange because of the lack of activity.[39] In her report the home economist wrote,

More food has been canned and preserved in Dubuque County this year than in the history of the county, much of it due to the fact that the food campaign was carried through so successfully. People had gardens who never had gardens before. Families canned vegetables and fruits who never before had any experience in canning and they did an excellent job all the way through.[40]

In other counties as well, women realized benefits from gardening and canning programs. In Greene County homemakers in six townships reported growing vegetables that they had not grown before such as kale, kohlrabi, New Zealand spinach, and broccoli. In Floyd County the home economist reported, "This fall, one woman . . . said, 'My corn is keeping for the first time since I used the method demonstrated at our canning meeting. It is delicious, too.' "[41]

Marie Bishop worked as a home economist in Monona County in World War II and recalled the efforts to increase food production and food preservation. She explained that "night, after night, after night" she and the county Extension director traveled out to the different townships to present programs to help increase production of hogs and poultry. Bishop worked with the women on poultry production while the director handled hog production. The meetings would be "in homes, church basements, and community halls and all sorts of places."[42]

At one point during the war Bishop presented programs on using meat substitutes. In a typical meeting the women assembled at 10 A.M. and spent the next five and a half hours listening and participating. Bishop explained,

> If you didn't have organization, they didn't learn it because there were a variety of kitchens with all kinds of facilities and a variety of people. . . . I think I soon learned to have them draw for the jobs so you would have two working on liver loaf, one working on carrots, and somebody setting the table. And then we'd prepare and eat the meal and then, of course, evaluate it. And then you'd go on with some of the other education work.[43]

Bishop recalled that all meetings had to end by 3:30, because many women had children coming home on the school bus. Since Monona County had twenty-four townships, Bishop gave the same presentation twenty-four times. Local leaders from elsewhere attending Bishop's presentation then presented the same material several times within their own townships.[44]

Bishop also recalled that for a time during the war Monona

County did not have a permanent county director. In fact, there were three women in an eleven-county area serving as temporary directors. Bishop related that the director in nearby Woodbury County was very helpful, but the women had to "organize the programs, have the Farm Bureau meetings and [handle] the legal material."[45]

As more health professionals went into the military, some communities experienced a shortage of nurses and doctors. As a result, home economists looked upon home health care as a topic to be promoted by the Extension Service. County home economists presented "Home Care of the Sick" meetings as a part of their professional duties. In Floyd County the home economist gave a bed bath demonstration at a township meeting attended by people of all ages. She wrote in her annual report, "There were thirty in attendance and they were a most appreciative audience. The Home Project leaders in that section asked for the demonstration on account of the nurse and doctor shortage. Their idea was that their husbands many times had to take care of them when they were ill and had no idea how to do it." One farm woman in Floyd County told the home demonstration agent, "My home nursing training saved a trip for our family doctor. I was never able to read a thermometer before. The doctor called by telephone to get the temperature of my father who was threatened with pneumonia. I was so glad to be able to take it accurately and to save the doctor a trip to our home." At the end of the training, participants received a certificate in home nursing care.[46]

Sometimes health care work had a humorous side. In Floyd County a local leader who attended a demonstration on making up a hospital bed met a local farmer who had attended the same demonstration along with his wife. He informed the leader, "Say, Mrs. Jones, you know my wife has learned something good from the nursing demonstration. She's been trying these new-fangled corners that lady showed her and the result is that my feet aren't sticking out of the bed with no covers on them. If there is anything I hate it's a messy bed!"[47]

While much of the war work of home economists had to do with food production and food conservation, there was also the matter of maintaining good morale. Louise Rosenfeld, appointed assistant state leader of Home Economics Extension in 1943, recalled that home economists viewed that as a part of their responsibilities. Rosenfeld particularly felt that recreation and music were important in boosting morale. "It helped the people get their mind away from the war and the tragedies of war. I always felt it had so much to do with people keeping their perspective in some way. And I think its influence was much greater than it would ever be possible to relate by the spoken word or to measure." Rosenfeld felt this was also the beginning of the effort to broaden home economics programs. Before that, she explained, the emphasis was to take the drudgery out of housekeeping, but later the emphasis changed to teaching management and other programs associated with the totality of family life. She recalled many administrative board meetings with Director Bliss. "We'd get together . . . sometimes just to brainstorm [or to talk about] what should we really be teaching and much more than that, how should we do it?"[48]

Rosenfeld also commented that during the war specialties in home economics were often forgotten and everyone pitched in to help in various emergencies, such as flooding. "At the state level Director Bliss or one of his associates would call us all together and identify the kinds of needs that Extension could have some input into solving. Oh, foods, for example, [or] what can you do to upholstered furniture? What about canned goods? And we had to be very careful that we did everything to keep people safe, that the things were safe for them to use."[49]

Like adult programs, 4-H activities throughout World War II reflected wartime demands. Many of the girls' programs were similar to the ones farm women selected as home projects, including nutrition, sewing, and home furnishings. In 1942 according to Extension's statewide plan, the girls' 4-H clubs in each county selected a major home economics project that lasted for two years. In Fayette County 4-Hers chose a second-year clothing project. The first year project had presented the fundamentals of sewing, while the second year offered more advanced sewing instruction. The project required girls to keep a record book, which meant they made up a clothing allowance and planned their year's wardrobe. They then had to make three garments. The Fayette County home economist noted that several new club members were from homes where living conditions were poor and where children received little encouragement in their club work. The home economist expressed considerable satisfaction that the leaders were able to help some of the new members in their projects and in their personal appearance. She commented about one young girl.

> Her dress visibly improved (personal grooming was studied in the project), she made her three required garments (which the leader

helped her choose), kept up her record book and walked to meetings. One day she came to [the leader] and asked that she might have the next club meeting. She said, "I'm really cleaning that house up and know you won't mind coming over for a meeting, now." The home economist concluded that the girl had started high school in the fall and "looks as nice and as well groomed as the other members of her class."[50]

During the war girls' 4-H clubs also included health lessons in their activities. In Fayette County every club member, which included girls from a total of twelve clubs, had a health exam. The girl receiving the highest rating in each club then went on to a county contest. The home economist noted that "Betty Yearous of the Putnam Peppy Pals received first and was awarded a pair of Health shoes."[51]

In 1944 the Kossuth home demonstration agent explained that girls' 4-H work had an effect on three groups.

> The girl develops a healthy philosophy of farm life and also learns to do her everyday tasks in an easier and more efficient manner. The leaders enjoy working with girls and seeing them grow in the abilities as well as learning more about the project and activities studied during the year. The parents . . . cooperating with their girls and the leaders . . . have attended club meetings so that they could learn more about what was expected of their girl. The success of a club and the possibility of having a leader stay with a club for longer than one year depends very materially on the attitude and interest of the parents.

The agent might have added that the girls' work also had an economic benefit. At the local Kossuth County achievement day in 1944, the home economist proudly announced that the 4-H girls in the county had made a total of 496 new garments, 240 made-over garments, and 1,297 garments repaired with a total store valuation of $2,559.92 or an average of $18.90 per girl.[52]

As an Extension home economist Marie Bishop worked with girls' 4-H clubs in Monona County during World War II. She particularly remembered one night when she and the director had traveled together to the northern part of the county to organize both a boys' and a girls' 4-H club. She reported, "I met with the girls and women in one room and Cal met with the boys in the other." Bishop soon discovered, however, that when farrowing time arrived, that event took precedence over the meeting.[53] She explained:

> To get somebody to be leader took top priority. The mother of the
> family where we were meeting that night would take her turn out
> in the hog barn when the sows were farrowing and that was their
> priority then, it wasn't these youngsters. So that was one of my first
> experiences with priorities that were not with your children. . . .
> And their hog facilities were heated![54]

Bishop added, "It really made a dent on me how they thought so
much of their hogs."[55]

While the girls' 4-H clubs pursued many traditional projects, they
also did work that directly affected the war effort. A major activity
was promoting the sale of war bonds and stamps. In some cases girls
assisted with local bond rallies, while at other times they canvassed
their rural neighborhoods securing pledges from their neighbors to
buy bonds. The girls themselves also purchased war bonds and
stamps. In Kossuth County in 1944 out of 136 girls involved in 4-H
work, 126 reported buying war bonds and stamps. The local vice-
president of each club served as club bond chairman and sent reports
to the county vice-chairman, who in turn served as county war bond
chairman. From July 1 to September 1, 1944, the Kossuth County 4-
H girls bought a total of $3,948.35 in war bonds; they also pledged
to buy at least $10,000 in bonds and stamps the following year. In Ida
County in 1944 three clubs conducted community programs at which
members sold a total of $8,530 worth of bonds and stamps. To
further promote the sale of war bonds, in July 1944 Ida County
officials held a bond queen contest (patterned after a similar state
contest) at which a total of $39,925 worth of war bonds were sold by
eighteen girls.[56]

It remained for the Johnson County girls' 4-H clubs, however, to
receive recognition for selling the highest number of war bonds and
stamps. In 1944 the girls' clubs there held an auction in which they
sold a total of eighty articles including pies, cakes, and dressed
poultry. Iowa City businesspeople purchased most of the items and
turned them over to the local USO. Eleven different clubs participated in the auction receiving a total credit of $503,925 in bond sales.
The same clubs also held a war bond pledge campaign in their local
communities. The True Blue 4-H Girls Club of North Liberty won
the contest with pledges totaling $15,725.[57]

While girls' 4-H club projects often were focused more toward
group or community activities, boys' 4-H club projects remained

more individual in nature. During World War II, however, boys' clubs had the same interest in helping the war effort as did the girls. Traditional projects such as baby beef, purebred beef heifer, market pig, and dairy were cast in light of producing more for the war effort. In Jones County in 1944, for example, six boys' 4-H clubs were organized with seven basic projects. All were production of livestock with the exception of poultry and garden projects. Swine proved to be the most popular project. According to the county director's yearly report, the projects claimed more success than the previous year primarily because the pigs were raised on clean ground and were vaccinated and castrated.[58]

Throughout the war as county Extension directors and home economists formed the front line in mobilizing Iowa's population to deal with wartime emergencies, they faced two major problems: first, determining how to deal with special problems and needs brought on by the war; and second, determining how to keep the Extension organization intact and to pursue most of the existing programs. Although Extension personnel often lamented that certain groups were languishing, it seems that most programs which existed in the late 1930s were carried on throughout the war.

The county Extension director, as the senior Extension official in each of Iowa's ninety-nine counties, wore a multitude of hats. In at least a few cases, the service was still personal in nature, as when county directors helped farmers with their income taxes. In Plymouth County in 1944, in addition to his regular duties, county director Bruce Clampett took part in a fire prevention campaign; he also gave assistance to a number of farmers in filling out their applications for gasoline. The same individual was asked by the local Red Cross chapter to help with their fund drive. As a result, he spent two days soliciting and collected about $500 from businessmen in LeMars.[59]

In Franklin County the Extension director was also involved in many different organizations. Within the community he served on numerous boards including the county war board (as secretary), the local draft board, the farm labor board, and the county stamp and bond committee. In 1942 the same director listed the community events with which he was directly associated: secretary of the Hampton Forum Club; member of the Franklin County Institute Committees and secretary of the Program Committee; member of the Franklin County Civilian Defense Committee; member of the Franklin County School Garden Project Committee; and advisory member of the Franklin County Fair Board. In effect, the county

Extension office served as the clearinghouse for many activities within that county, in towns as well as in the countryside. In September 1943 Franklin County director Ross L. Huntsinger reflected on the wartime demands.

> Probably the greatest test that must be met is involved in the need for maintaining the long time program while carrying out the many projects which war has brought up. This question in the main will have to be decided on a month-to-month or almost day-to-day basis as shifts are too rapid to make any fixed plan very useful.[60]

During the war good planning was essential as staff was often reduced and travel had to be curtailed. Meetings still needed to be held, but staff always had to be mindful of ways to minimize the number considering the rationing of rubber tires and gasoline. For example, in some counties directors and home economists traveled together throughout the county. Often boys' and girls' 4-H clubs met at the same time and same place so parents needed to make only one trip.[61]

In addition, cooperation with other agencies, which had always been a hallmark of Extension, continued throughout the war. Particularly evident was the cooperation between soil conservation officials and Extension personnel. In Dickinson County the two groups cooperated in developing a permanent soil conservation program. This included conducting contour demonstrations, testing soil, and assisting with soil management problems. The county director helped set up a county soil conservation committee consisting of farmers in each township. He saw it as his responsibility to promote soil conservation work continually among farmers and other area landowners.[62]

Wartime production needs also created additional work for county directors in other ways. Given certain production needs, the county director found himself urging farmers to forego corn production and move into other areas. In the early 1940s, Iowa farmers raised only small amounts of soybeans but because they provided oil for the war effort, the federal government urged greater production of the crop. Each county had a soybean quota, and it was often up to the county director to convince farmers to make the transition from corn to soybeans. In Grundy County, for example, in 1942 farmers increased their soybean production by nearly 200 percent. Throughout the war, county agents also promoted four new varieties of oats.[63]

Sometimes the county director needed to ask farmers to change their traditional views on production. In Hamilton County, where many livestock farmers had become known for "de luxe beef," the county director found it necessary to tell them that "it was not a wise use of food, particularly corn." He noted, "The army type of beef is good beef but does not have the extreme finish and can be made with less corn." He added, "It meant quite a change in [the farmers'] plans to produce this beef known as the army type of beef."[64]

In promoting the production of different crops or in encouraging farmers to adopt new methods of farming, the county director needed to always keep his finger on the pulse of his constituents. In 1943 the Dickinson director wrote in his yearly report that "some of the farmers showed an interest in the contour work but most of them were indifferent to the program or took the attitude of 'let the other fellow try it first.'" Knowing which farmers would be more disposed to try new methods undoubtedly had an effect on the success rate of any program.[65]

As well as working with other groups, keeping up with changes in agricultural production and sometimes urging farmers to change production plans, county directors also needed to keep up with changes in farm technology. In Kossuth County in 1944, the director noted this problem in his yearly report. "The Program Committee contends that we have dealt with generalities too much and need more information that is up to date. The machinery program is a good example. We should advance ourselves from adjusting the knotter on the binder to uses and problems of the combine, baler, and other new pieces of machinery."[66]

Extension home economists also faced difficulties in carrying out necessary programs. Although farm people typically responded favorably to wartime demands, there were exceptions. Frequently home economists found themselves unable to locate an adequate number of local leaders who were essential to carrying out the Home Project activities. In Franklin County in 1942 the home economist wrote in her annual report that some townships had not been active in Home Project work.

All townships except West Fork participated in the program. In this township, a chairman who refused to serve had unfortunately been elected. Thus the group became inactive through lack of leadership. The Grant Township group . . . had only one training school in the township. Another meeting with Reeve Township was attended by one woman.[67]

The home economist, attempting to explain the lack of interest, wrote, "Contentment in . . . [their] own plan of living seemed to be the main cause for their indifference. One man expressed his sentiments in this way—'Mary can cook good enough for me. If more women would stay at home and attend to their business in place of running around getting new fangled ideas about how to raise their children, we would be better off.' . . . this in reference to neighbors who had taken part in the extension program the previous year."[68]

The following year the Floyd County home economist indicated concern over the apathy of farm women. She noted that farm women did not always respond enthusiastically to their roles as local leaders.

> The need is great for effective publicity to convince the public that the extension program is developed according to the recommendations and needs of the people. They must be made aware of their needs for more satisfying family living, more efficient, and greater food production with increased gains, financially. The financial appeal might be the wedge which would serve to interest certain families in the broader program.[69]

Throughout their wartime work, county directors and home economists found themselves frequently cast in the booster or cheerleader role. Implicit in much of what they did was the promoting of projects, the persuading that projects were worthwhile, and the sustaining of enthusiasm to carry participants through to the end of the project. The annual reports of Extension personnel from 1941 to 1945 provide continual examples of the cheerleading role. In the fall of 1943, the Dubuque County agricultural director provided evidence of that activity when he wrote,

> Every farmer should consider it his Patriotic duty to produce livestock to the maximum in the year 1944. To do this he must have the greatest production possible of the various feeds. In order to get the best production of feeds and grains, he must attack the problem of soil management in an intelligent way, must conserve soil and moisture to the utmost, and must use machinery and labor efficiently.[70]

With the end of the war in August of 1945, Iowa's Extension Service could congratulate itself on a job well done. Extension's goal for the war was all-out production and Iowa farmers had measured up to the task. In many ways that success served as testimony to the good work of Extension personnel even before the war. In 1942, when Mrs. Rummel of Maynard experienced a banner year in raising poultry, the procedures she followed ran like a litany of the advice Extension specialists had been dispersing throughout the 1930s. When 4-H youths raised more pigs than ever before, they were, in effect, following the advice that county directors had been preaching for years. In other words, the work of Extension specialists, county agricultural directors, and home economists through the 1920s and 1930s had a highly visible payoff in higher farm production in World War II.

The matter of farm production can also be viewed in a more general way. During each war year Iowa's farm families produced higher numbers of livestock and poultry and more bushels of grain than in the previous year. In 1942 Bliss recorded that Iowa's hog farmers had produced 17 percent more swine than in 1941 while Iowa's farm women had produced 12 percent more eggs. In the following year, Bliss wrote in his annual report, "The fields and feedlots of Iowa produced 640 million bushels of corn, 39 million bushels of soybeans, 21 million head of hogs, 7 million pounds of milk, 70 million chickens and 326 million dozens of eggs; all new production records set in 1943." The same production patterns continued through 1944.[71]

Yet another way of assessing Extension's involvement and contribution to the war effort was through the many different organizations that Extension had helped establish during the inter-war years. That list would include 4-H clubs, rural youth groups, and farm women's township organizations. During the 1930s some counties had even organized a group for newlyweds, appropriately called Recent Weds. These groups were all involved in helping the war effort, from promoting the sale of war bonds to collecting scrap metal. The organizing of these groups during the 1920s and 1930s resulted in far greater involvement of farm people in all phases of war work during the 1940s.

Throughout the war the Iowa Extension Service had at the helm a very experienced director. Ralph K. Bliss became head of Extension in 1914 and continued in that position until 1946. That meant that during World War II, Iowa's Director of Extension could call on his own personal history of setting up programs during World War

I. Because of the director's background, Extension could move more rapidly in converting to wartime work in 1940 and 1941, a fact that paid dividends throughout the entire war. Bliss's experience was perhaps most visible with the quick reestablishing of the local cooperator township system and the rapid transition of Iowa farmers to wartime production.

As a result of Extension programs and activities of its personnel, other changes had also taken place. Cooperation between Extension and other agencies had never been better. During the war Extension personnel had cooperated in every way with town and city agencies. The latter groups had also reciprocated. Businessmen, for example, had provided temporary labor on farms and town women had raised hundreds of victory gardens. Townspeople "shared in the glow of success" that came from those endeavors.

Cooperation between farm and town residents also improved as a result of wartime activities. The home economists' reports contain numerous comments from both town and farm women about the pleasures of getting to know each other. Town women felt that working with Home Projects was personally satisfying and economically worthwhile. The distance between farm and town families seemed to have narrowed as a result of wartime cooperation.

While much attention had been given to emergency measures, many prewar programs had been continued throughout the war. In effect, this meant that Extension in 1945 still provided something for almost everyone in rural Iowa. Frequently county staffers lamented the fact that some programs were not doing well because of wartime demands. Yet it does not appear that many programs were eliminated. The Rural Youth group, for example, had fewer members in 1945 than in 1940, but it still existed in many counties. Some counties had fewer 4-H clubs than before the war, but it remained a healthy institution for both boys and girls throughout the duration. No doubt the energy needed to maintain traditional programs along with responding to special needs meant that Extension staffers worked even longer hours each week.

Finally, it is instructive to note that although the demands of war brought a great many additional responsibilities and pressures to its personnel, the Extension Service seemed to be doing what it did best: dispensing educational materials, solving production problems, making use of the township method of organization, and in general marshaling the forces of the farm sector to reach a specific goal. All the resources of Extension were called into play to reach the goal of record production. It is a paradox, perhaps, that when the goal was pulling out all the stops and pushing for total production that the Extension system was at its best. The difficulties would come when full production did not solve all problems. That situation, however, lay in the future.

6

Post–World War II

The 1940s and 1950s

During the second world war, the Iowa State College Cooperative Extension Service experienced one of its finest hours. Called upon to help bring about record production of food and fiber, Extension assisted Iowa's farm families in accomplishing that goal, thus bringing prosperity to the farm sector. For a few years after the war, demand for the nation's farm products remained high and prosperity continued. By the early 1950s, however, farmers began to experience an economic downturn. For the remainder of the decade Extension sought to cope with a contradictory situation. On one hand, Extension's successful transmission of scientific and technological information to Iowa farmers had paid dividends as agricultural yields increased considerably. But on the other hand, largely because of this success, surpluses were accumulating, thus driving farm prices down.

Extension continued, nevertheless, to carry out its traditional mandate of providing the farm population with the latest developments in research; the emphasis on agricultural technology continued to be the "basic core" of Extension education. At the same time Extension experimented with different approaches, seeking ways to make farming a more personally profitable venture and to make farm living more rewarding. An influential national Extension study published in 1948, known as the Kepner Report, helped promote both the Farm and Home Development Program and public policy education. In the first program, Extension increasingly placed

126

emphasis on working with farm families as a unit rather than providing separate services to farm men, women, and children. In the second, Extension specialists set up programs to help inform Iowans of public policy issues on all levels. By mid-decade a major change took place in the organizational structure of Extension as the close relationship between Extension and the Farm Bureau ended.[1] By the end of the 1950s, however, after almost a decade of searching for new approaches and solutions to the economic difficulties facing Iowa's farm families—and initiating an extensive reexamination of its own programs—one thing was clear: coping with production profitability in peacetime was far more difficult than dealing with record production in time of war.[2]

As a war weary nation entered the final year of the second world war, the Iowa Extension Service continued its efforts to help Iowans produce even greater quantities of food and fiber. At the same time Extension began to plan for the postwar world that lay ahead. Extension officials believed that countywide planning was necessary to ensure a smooth transition from wartime to peacetime conditions.

Beginning in 1944 county Extension personnel played an important role in setting up organizations composed of community leaders from all parts of each county to discuss postwar needs. A major part of the planning concerned returning service people and their roles in their home communities. In Hamilton County the agricultural director was deeply immersed in carrying out an ambitious postwar planning program that involved sending out surveys to both county residents and service people. The surveys asked farm families about "the amount of building and rebuilding that needed to be done, the amount of farm and home equipment expected to be purchased, the amount of farm labor needed and whether or not veterans of the war [would] take over many of these farms." County directors sent surveys to local service people, wherever they might be in late 1944, asking them about their postwar plans: Did they intend to return to school or did they intend to come back to the county? In Palo Alto County the Extension director attended a 1944 postwar planning committee meeting with representatives from all parts of the county to "consider methods of giving work to returning veterans."[3]

There is considerable evidence that county Extension personnel viewed postwar planning as an effort to bring about greater cooperation between rural and urban people. The Hamilton County director H. M. Nichols described it as an "outstanding example of rural-urban relations for the past year." In Jackson County, county director E. D. Stout wrote, "Every attempt was made to seek out the interests and problems of town and country women, and to develop a mutual understanding of the shifting problems during the period of Reconversion. The interdependence of town and country women has been proven."[4] Throughout the remainder of the 1940s emphasis continued on developing good rural-urban relations. In his memoirs longtime Extension staff member E. F. Graff wrote, "Much has been said from time to time with respect to the need for the Extension Service to work in other areas than the open country. . . . In all counties [in the late 1940s] the Extension Service was increasingly cooperating with the people of the towns."[5]

Before postwar living became a reality, however, one more task remained. In 1946 Secretary of Agriculture Clinton P. Anderson made yet another appeal to the nation's farmers: "The end of the war has not brought an end to the almost unlimited need for American food." Clinton observed that civilian Americans still had to be fed as well as the military forces. At the same time Clinton explained, "We are not forgetting our allies who now face hunger because war destroyed or damaged their normal food production."[6] In effect, the federal government was asking America's farmers to continue wartime production through 1946. Iowa's Extension Service retained its wartime educational program to achieve that goal. County home economists took charge of the program to save food, much as they had done during the war. Home economists explained that "to meet the government request . . . it would be necessary for a family of five to save two-thirds of a loaf of wheat bread each day, or enough cakes, pies and pastries to make the equivalent of two-thirds of a loaf of wheat bread a day." The Extension Service urged hotels, restaurants, and other public eating houses "not to put bread on the table before a meal was served, to serve only one slice of bread with each meal, to cut down on cakes, pies and pastries and to save as much fat as possible."[7]

While postwar planning continued, Extension resumed traditional programs set aside during the war. Even with the disruptions brought on by a global war, there was still considerable continuity in Extension work between the late 1930s and the immediate postwar period. Dubuque provides a good case study of a county in the period right after World War II and allows for a more in-depth look at the programs and work of Iowa's Extension personnel.

Since Dubuque County has a rolling topography, the Extension director had long been working to interest farmers in soil conservation practices. In 1946 that emphasis continued as the county director reported that thirty-three contouring demonstrations had been held and fifteen farm plans had been developed in cooperation with the Soil Conservation Service. The agent observed that local farmers were receptive to this work and had made great strides in establishing good soil conservation measures on their farms, many for a period of twenty-five years. He noted in particular the Ernsdorf brothers farm, where "they probably haven't lost a bucketful of soil off of their farm in a year." The agent rightfully added, "All of this did not come suddenly, but is a result of years of constant effort, constant demonstration, proper kinds of publicity, [so] that today in Dubuque County a real constructive program is being carried on as a result of many years of honest to goodness effort."[8]

Continuity of programs and projects was also visible in other areas of the county. In 1946 the director assisted farmers with locating additional labor during harvest, obtaining both short- and long-term credit, and helping them with rental leases. Extension personnel held schools to train local leaders so they might, in turn, present material in their townships on rural family relationships, school conditions, road problems, and inflation control. This cooperator system, which functioned so well in both world wars, was continued after 1945. One new development for many farm families, however, was electricity. The county director noted that in 1946, 152 farms "had hooked up during the year to the R.E.A," while information was given to at least another 350 additional farmers on how to secure electric current. The director also stressed the repair of farm machinery.[9]

Immediately after the war Dubuque County 4-H clubs resumed their policy of having separate programs for boys and girls. Girls' 4-H often had the same programs of study as their mothers, including nutrition, first- and second-year clothing, and health and safety. In 1946 the county home economist wrote that all 4-H girls "pledge themselves to have their teeth cleaned by a dentist every year."[10] Boys' 4-H projects continued to include baby beeves, dairy calves, pigs, and poultry. As before the war Extension personnel recognized that it was necessary to include 4-H clubs in adult projects, since 4-H contained the future farmers of the state. The Dubuque County director noted the boys' 4-H clubs "also gave valued assistance in carrying on [soil conservation demonstrations]. . . . These boys were especially helpful in doing contouring. They were a little bit quicker than their parents in catching on how to do the work and gave material help not only on the farms of their parents, but helped neighbors as well."[11]

Continuity was also apparent for Dubuque County home economists as they dealt with many of the same topics as before the war. Helping farm women "make do" with what they had was a longtime interest of Extension personnel. In 1946 Dubuque County farm women decided that reconditioning and reupholstering old furniture would be their major project for the year; other home improvements were also stressed. At the end of the year the home economist reported that "362 women refinished furniture, 117 refinished floors, and 998 women made kitchen improvements. 231 have made plans to remodel when materials are available."[12]

Even while carrying out traditional responsibilities, the Dubuque Extension staff had considerable latitude in their day-to-day activities, a pattern reflected throughout the state. While the Dubuque County director emphasized soil conservation, other directors often had greater interest in crop production, public policy education, or youth club work. In Delaware County Extension director Bob Hall had a different concern. Soon after arriving there in 1948 (where he remained for thirty years), Hall perceived that his major challenge was leadership. Hall remembered the situation in Buchanan County, where he had previously worked. "One person was trying to do so many things." Hall determined that when he got his own county, "I would want to try to figure out how I could teach leaders to do some of the things that professionals were doing."[13] Hall explained that within six months in Delaware County, he had established the ground rules.

> The County Agent would not necessarily go to every township meeting or every 4-H meeting and so in order to get that job done they set one night for Farm Bureau and that meant I could only go to one Farm Bureau meeting a week. And 4-H night, I could only go to one 4-H meeting a week. And so that left three other nights to work on ideas for training 4-H leaders, and training township Farm Bureau program people so they would plan their own programs. So I got that going right off the bat. Luckily it was accepted.[14]

Dan Merrick, who started as a county agricultural director in Cass County in 1957, also developed strong views regarding the importance of leadership. He quickly realized that "to be an effective Extension agent, you need to try to get people to organize, to get that organization started, [and to] teach leadership. Once they

IOWA 4-H MEMBERS taking part in a bread-making demonstration at a state meeting at Iowa State College in 1951. Courtesy Iowa State University Library/ University Archives.

assume leadership, then back out the door and go to another project. That's primarily what Extension has done through the years." Merrick recalled that in the 1950s, livestock producers in Cass County expressed interest in organizing a cattlemen's association. He and another individual decided to hold an organizational meeting by inviting over 150 people to a steak dinner. Merrick explained that the planning was not without some anxiety as shortly after the invitations were mailed out, his friend came to the Extension office to voice a concern: "You know what my wife told me? Do you think those people are going to come and expect you to buy those steak dinners?" Merrick admitted that he hadn't thought of that. The guests paid for their own dinners, however, and by the end of the evening, seventy-five men had joined the newly organized Cass County Cattlemen's Association. Although he helped the group organize, Merrick related that in later years he seldom attended their meetings unless he was to present an educational program.[15]

Publicity constituted another responsibility for county staff and again directors had latitude in carrying out that duty. During his early years in Delaware County, Bob Hall started putting together a farm page for the local newspaper. In the early 1950s he started writing a weekly column, "Just Browsing Around," which he continued for about twenty-seven years. Once a week Hall and his staff sent out news releases to all media in northeast Iowa. Hall explained that the purpose was to build up the identity of Delaware County: "Public relations. Delaware County, Delaware County." At the same time Hall noted the importance of publicity for individuals. Hall typically carried a camera around in his work as director. He explained that it was part of the recognition process. "[You would] recognize people wherever you went, something popped out, you mentioned their names, you got them, you got their pictures in the paper and they got so they expected that. . . . People like to be recognized and if you can get that going your way in your program [its an asset]."[16]

For Extension personnel in northeast Iowa as elsewhere in the state, the postwar period brought considerable change in state leadership. On July 1, 1946, Extension Director R. K. Bliss retired after thirty-two years of heading Iowa Cooperative Extension. During his tenure Extension had helped rural Iowans survive some of the most catastrophic events of the twentieth century including two world wars, a worldwide depression, and two devastating droughts. Herbert H. Kildee, Dean of the ISC Agriculture Division, was named as Director of Extension; three years later he retired from both posts.

CLAYTON COUNTY FARM WOMEN attending a basket-weaving demonstration sponsored by Home Economics Extension in 1956. Courtesy ISU Photo Service.

College officials then named Floyd Andre, a graduate of Iowa State College, as Kildee's replacement. Andre had worked for the USDA and since 1949 had been assistant dean of agriculture at the University of Wisconsin. He also owned an Iowa farm and therefore had some familiarity with rural Iowa.[17] Marvin Anderson was named associate director of Extension in 1952.

Although Dean Andre and his staff would soon face a wide array of problems, in 1950 the future looked bright for both the Extension Service and its main constituency, the Iowa farm family. By any assessment the Iowa State Cooperative Extension Service was by midcentury a highly successful program. By 1951 the central Extension staff included more than one hundred people trained in the various phases of Extension activities. County Extension staffs included more than two hundred workers with all counties having agricultural directors, approximately seventy counties having home economists, and thirty-three counties having youth assistants.[18] At the same time Iowa farm families appeared to be in a highly favorable position. The prosperity of the war years had continued, and families had money to spend on needed consumer goods such as new farm machinery as well as modern household equipment. Many were remodeling kitchens for the first time, landscaping farmyards, or even building new homes.

Apparently sensing that the stable, prosperous times might not continue, Dean Andre wrote in his first annual report in 1950 that uncertainty pervaded the agriculture scene. He cautioned that demand for some farm products would fall as European countries began to recover from the war and that it was not clear what path the federal government might follow in regard to farm policy. Andre also indicated that "people who had made an all-out production effort for almost eight years were beginning to think in terms of adjusting their operations to a more normal basis. Instead of striving for maximum output they were thinking in terms of increased efficiency."[19] In other words, Andre was telling his organization and his constituents, be prepared for possible difficult times ahead.

By 1953 Andre's premonition had become a reality: Iowa's farm income began to drop, signaling the beginning of difficult times for the state's farm population. In fact, a slump in food exports took place even earlier in 1950, but the Korean conflict provided a "temporary solution." As one economic report put it, "By 1953, 'the farm problem' began to take shape again—surpluses, lower farm prices, lower farm incomes, higher farm costs." At the same time there was increasing evidence that agriculture was out of step with the rest of the economy. Other sectors were earning higher returns while returns to resources in agriculture were decreasing. Though the national economy as a whole was growing, "agriculture was not sharing fully in the fruits of a progressive economy."[20]

At the same time that the "farm problem" began to appear, however, Extension was experiencing the fruits of its past labors. As a result of research done by the USDA, state Experiment Stations, and private firms—and delivered to rural people by Extension personnel—farmers were utilizing a "package of practices" that involved looking at all aspects of the farm operation and then working to improve each part. The result was greatly increased production. These gains were so substantial that historian Wayne Rasmussen has referred to them as "the second American agricultural revolution." Rasmussen described this procedure in the following way. "These experiments [combined] the application of the most productive levels of nitrogen fertilizer, the use of hybrid seed, adherence to suitable conservation practices, use of appropriate mechanical power, and the effective control of pests and disease."[21]

While the changes such as Rasmussen described certainly aided farmers and the economy in terms of total production, they also presented problems: as production rose in the 1950s so did surpluses. And as ISC economists pointed out, lower farm prices, lower farm incomes, and higher farm costs then became a reality. Given these economic difficulties, there appeared to be much soul-searching by all levels of Extension as to what future direction the institution should take. Veteran Extension staff member Ed Graff wrote in his memoirs that even as early as 1952 "much concern was evident during the year with the role of the Extension Service."[22]

Before Extension officials had time to respond to the economic downturn, they faced a major organizational change. In 1954 Secretary of Agriculture Ezra Taft Benson ordered that "extension could no longer accept funds from private organizations or submit to the direction of a private organization in the conduct of its responsibilities." In effect, this order required that Extension and the Iowa Farm Bureau Federation sever their longtime relationship. The next year the Iowa General Assembly responded to Benson's directive by repealing the Farm Aid Association Law passed in 1913. This law had called for the creation of county farm aid associations to act as sponsoring agencies for Extension. Over time these associations became known as farm bureaus. In 1955 the legislature replaced the Farm Aid bill with the County Agricultural Extension Law, which provided for the creation of county councils to assist with the administration of Extension in every county. County councils would then carry out the work previously done by the Farm Bureau county boards.[23] It is instructive to note that if the sponsoring associations (the county farm bureaus) had remained just that—sponsoring associations—later conflict would have been avoided. The Iowa county farm bureaus, however, soon formed the Iowa Farm Bureau Federation, which in turn helped organize the American Farm Bureau Federation in 1920. The organization then developed its own staff and programs. In short, the Farm Bureau took on a life of its own, in addition to serving as a sponsoring agency for Extension.

The new law ended a relationship that had long been the center of controversy and one that had often been misunderstood. Since 1913 many Iowans had criticized the close tie between county farm bureaus and county Extension staffs. Farmers who did not belong to Farm Bureau often charged that Extension personnel gave special consideration to those who did. Confusion existed in the minds of many Iowans about the actual relationship and whether one had to become a member of Farm Bureau to take part in Extension programs. Membership was not a prerequisite to participation in any Extension program, but many Iowans were under that impression, a misconception that lasted into the 1960s. According to a history of the Iowa Farm Bureau Federation, if the membership workers (including county agents) were questioned as to whether families had to belong to Farm Bureau to take part in Extension programs, particularly 4-H, the workers would obviously say no. If no one asked, however, workers "would not be unduly concerned if a farmer assumed that he had to join Farm Bureau for his children to participate in 4-H."[24]

It is easy to see why Iowans were confused about the relationship between the two organizations. Although the county agent formally wore only one hat, that of Extension agent, he actually had a joint employer: Iowa State College (the parent organization for Extension) and the Farm Bureau (the sponsoring farm aid society), represented by a Farm Bureau county board. In his daily interactions with farm people—passing along scientific and technical information, helping to solve production problems, and cooperating with dozens of local organizations—the county agent (later known as the county agricultural director) represented Iowa State College. Yet the agent often sold Farm Bureau memberships to county residents, thus closely identifying himself with the bureau in the minds of farm people. In effect, the agent had a vested interest in memberships as the 1913 law required that at least two hundred memberships in the farm aid association be sold before Extension qualified for county tax money. In many counties the Extension agent and the county Farm Bureau representative shared the same office and the same secretary. When a county needed to hire a new agent, a district Extension official brought the candidates (previously interviewed by state Extension officials in Ames) to be interviewed by the Farm Bureau county board. Once the board and Extension officials agreed upon a particular candidate, the county board helped negotiate the new agent's salary. Each county's annual Extension program was also strongly influenced by the Farm Bureau county board.[25]

During the 1940s Farm Bureau began establishing various business interests such as the sale of farm supplies and insurance. Sometimes farm supplies, like serum, were kept in the shared Extension–Farm Bureau office where the sales were then made. Farm Bureau representatives also sold insurance from the same office. Even earlier Farm Bureau began political activity by lobbying state legislators. These actions brought even stronger responses from some Iowans who believed the arrangement between Extension and Farm Bureau gave the bureau an unfair economic advantage.[26]

Outsiders voiced criticism about the close relationship between Extension and Farm Bureau and so did the staff. As early as 1942 Farm Bureau had started developing a county organization director plan that would provide for a part-time person to head the membership work. After World War II the Farm Bureau expanded this position into a full-time county fieldman plan. Farm Bureau officials reasoned that "membership was really only preparation for building a program. If a C.O.D. [county organizational director] was needed for membership, surely it would pay to have a full time fieldman to implement a program after the year's membership had been acquired." But as the plan expanded, Extension agricultural directors feared that the fieldmen were intruding into the directors' domain and that they were being "relieved of a portion of their rightful responsibilities." Some Farm Bureau members believed that the Extension staff "resented the fieldman program from the beginning."[27]

According to a study of the Iowa Farm Bureau, as the fieldman plan expanded to more counties, a heavier and heavier financial burden was placed on the county Farm Bureaus resulting in competition for funds between Extension directors and the fieldmen. It became "so keen" that state Farm Bureau President Howard Hill and Extension Director Floyd Andre recommended a clear separation of budgets and a specific division of funds and responsibilities between the two county agencies. Officials then established separate bank accounts in each county and outlined separate responsibilities. The Extension agricultural director "was requested to work with the county Farm Bureau treasurer on records, budgets and reports dealing with extension" while the fieldman was to work with the county Farm Bureau treasurer on the remaining Farm Bureau financial accounts.[28]

The County Agricultural Extension Law passed in 1955 called for the establishment of County Agricultural Extension Districts; in effect, each county constituted a district. The law also called for the organization of an Extension council in each district or county "to cooperate with the Iowa State College and the United States Department of Agriculture, in conducting educational programs in agriculture, home economics, and 4-H club work in the counties of the state." The councils would consist of township representatives, in effect, one person elected from each township. To replace the money previously obtained from Farm Bureau memberships, the law provided for the levy of an annual tax to carry out these programs and for the appointment and supervision of county Extension personnel.[29]

The new law gave county agriculture Extension councils major responsibility to see that an Extension staff was in place in each county and that programs were carried out. According to Extension Director Andre, under the new law, "Extension work in the various counties should be under the control of a local governing body, elected by the people and having the responsibility for planning, guiding and directing the program according to the needs of the people in the county." That principle of the new law translated into major areas of supervision for Extension councils. As well as securing staff, council members were to make an annual budget; prepare and adopt educational programs on Extension work in the three divisions of agriculture, home economics, and 4-H club work; and review the yearly programs.[30]

At the same time the state legislature made clear its intent to prevent any repetition of the close relationship that Extension had experienced with Farm Bureau for so many years. Limitations of powers under the law included the provisions that Extension staff or Extension council members would not engage in commercial or private enterprises, or legislative programs; would not attempt to influence legislation or other activities not specified in the legislation; and would not give preferred services to any individual, group, or organization. Extension councils, moreover, were not to collect any dues.[31]

In his yearly report at the end of 1955, Andre noted that "despite the gigantic size of the task, the reorganization of extension work in each county . . . has been accomplished." Andre praised both the Extension staff and the Farm Bureau membership for making a "smooth transition" possible. For the most part county agricultural directors echoed Andre's sentiments that the separation had gone smoothly although directors had faced far more practical matters than the central staff. In Crawford County the director noted in his annual report that the "divorce" meant spending money for office equipment since the current equipment had belonged to Farm Bureau. Delaware County director Bob Hall explained that because Extension and the Farm Bureau had their offices side by side, "All that really had to happen to make that legal in our county was to just change the division walls and to make two entrances into the building. And it was wholeheartedly accepted." Former Extension director Eldon Hans observed, "It was the best thing that ever happened to us."[32]

While Extension developed numerous new programs during the 1950s, Farm and Home Development marked a different approach to the needs of farm families. The program apparently developed out of a sense that specialists' work, which had become visible in all states by the latter 1940s, had its limitations. In a report issued by the USDA and the Association of Land-Grant Colleges and Universities—known among Extension personnel as the Kepner Report—officials observed,

> [The farmer] wants to profit from what he hears [from the specialists]. But the more specialists there are to serve him, the more complicated becomes the job of fitting together their varied recommendations into a workable whole suited to his soil, his financial situation, his preferences and abilities, his family needs, his market outlets, and all other significant factors bearing upon the most practical course to follow. . . . This committee would point out that farm life itself is not lived in segments or projects. It is lived as a whole. The operator faces a multitude of problems of which production is one, marketing another, conservation of soil resources another, and so on. The end objective of solving all these problems is a better life for the farm family and the insurance of an adequate supply of agricultural products for the general public. . . . The

average farm family needs the help of more generalists rather than of more specialists. They need a competent interpreter and integrator of usable facts.[33]

In effect, the joint committee was saying that by the latter 1940s the American farmer, overwhelmed by an ever-growing avalanche of scientific and technical information, needed help in processing that information and applying it to his own particular situation. And, as the joint committee noted, this was a task for generalists, not specialists.[34]

Following the publication of the *Joint Committee Report on Extension Programs, Policies, and Goals,* some states began developing methods of carrying out Extension work in terms of "the totality of farm and home problems" rather than by unrelated, specific projects. Some state Extension Services set up training schools for both county directors and specialists, frequently using demonstration farms to illustrate the new concept. Officials described this program as the "balanced farming" or the "family unit plan."[35]

In a textbook published in 1949 for graduate Extension education, authors Lincoln David Kelsey and Cannon Chiles Hearne wrote that "Extension programs in individual farm and home planning currently are among the most advanced developments with great possibilities for the future." The authors believed that the development of this program marked an advancement in Extension work from the days when staff members thought in terms of projects rather than programs. The staff provided information and guidance that allowed the family to prepare a new or revised plan for operating the farm on a more productive, satisfying basis.[36]

When Iowa began to implement a farm and family development program in the early 1950s, the state's Extension personnel, like its counterparts elsewhere, had previously thought in terms of projects for its clients. Each county staff member expected to serve one part of the farm family through the promotion of projects. Although each area of work—agriculture, home economics, and youth—had clearly become more sophisticated since the 1920s and 1930s, for the most part county personnel still worked in only one of these areas. This family approach meant promoting the same general projects in all three areas. In the early 1950s, however, Iowa Extension began to provide, through its Farm and Home Development Program (FHDP), a new, integrative approach to programs for the farm population.

At first the Iowa Extension staff opted to design it primarily for young families, often those just getting started in farming. In his annual report for 1952–1953, Director Andre acknowledged that Extension had begun a pilot program that he described as an "intensive program" in farm and home planning and related subjects for younger farm families. Iowa officials selected two counties, Hardin and Wayne, for initiating the program, expanding it in 1954 and 1955 to farm families in thirty-four counties. As before, most of these families were just beginning a farming career.[37]

Iowa officials apparently modeled Farm and Home Development after earlier programs such as one established in Illinois. According to Andre, the program was designed to help each farm family "with its own special problems. [The program was to help] them see more clearly what they want to try to accomplish in farming, homemaking and family living. It teaches them how to do a good job of organizing the ability of family members, their own resources and those available to them in the community." Extension personnel provided participants with "ideas, information and counsel," but the family made and implemented its own decisions. As Iowa's program developed, it differed somewhat from those of other states. Iowa's Extension staff seemed to put more emphasis on teaching economic principles and restricting the program to younger families.[38]

By 1957 more than half of Iowa's counties had instigated Farm and Home Development Programs with 1,455 young farm families participating; this marked an increase of 607 families from 1956. While overall participation was high, the numbers varied widely between counties. Wapello County had 100 families enrolled while the adjacent counties of Monroe and Jefferson had only 6 and none respectively. Undoubtedly, the staff's interest in the program had a good deal to do with the number of couples involved within a given county. Like so many programs in Extension, if the director or home economist was particularly interested, that interest was reflected in the overall rate of participation.[39]

Decisions made by farm families in the program were often far reaching. In 1957 Director Andre noted in his annual report that as a result of the information provided by Extension personnel and the meetings attended by farm couples (individually with Extension personnel as well as jointly with other farm couples), many families opted for significant changes in their farm operations. Andre explained that 144 families obtained larger farming units, 38 through the purchase of additional land and 105 by renting more land; an additional 100 families decided to enlarge their farming operation. Andre also reported the following: 390 families made major reorganizations within their farming enterprises, 178 in the cropping area and 212 in livestock practices, which contributed to an increased income or improved efficiency; and 258 farmers intensified existing enterprises. At the same time 44 families "left the farm for other employment." In effect, the message seemed to be clear: if the family could not expand their operation or increase their profits, then perhaps it was best to consider another line of work.[40]

The influence of Farm and Home Development was soon visible in different counties. In Hardin, for example, the annual report for 1955 clearly reflects the change in emphasis brought about by the new program. In describing staff objectives and planning, the agricultural director wrote, "A concept running through the objectives is that the farm family is really the important unit in the farm business. How the plans for the cropping and livestock program effect the family living and the satisfactions they get out of farming were a major concern." The director further explained that decisions made regarding the farm should be a family affair and that the farm wife, as well as the farm husband, should understand the farm business.[41]

The 1955 Hardin County annual report indicates that the principle of "the farm as a family affair" was to be interpreted broadly and to be applied to each of the areas of production. The Extension staff first assisted the family in making an appraisal of their general situation and background, their desires and goals, and what they wished to accomplish in these areas, taking into account the "human, physical, financial and community resources they have or can call upon." Once through these processes, the staff then asked the family to consider what changes in their farming operation or family living patterns they might be willing to make. Throughout the program it was emphasized that Extension personnel were not to make decisions. Rather they were to provide the clients with sufficient information and procedural guidance so clients themselves could make intelligent decisions. Extension personnel, moreover, stressed record keeping, particularly convincing farm families of its importance in helping make informed decisions and developing proper skills. Yet another aspect of the program was to encourage participating couples to take a greater role in community affairs. Extension personnel seemed to view the program as one that would produce future community leaders.[42]

Extension workers used a variety of techniques throughout the program. In the Eldora area participants took part in small-group meetings but also held individual meetings with Extension personnel.

IOWA FARM men and women attending an Extension-sponsored farm tour in Hardin County in 1955. Courtesy ISU Photo Service.

Extension staff quickly perceived the need to respond to personal differences. The Hardin County director noted in 1955 that above all, the program must be flexible because individuals varied greatly in the amount of assistance that they required. He observed that because of these differences "some couples may require individual [counseling] over a two- or three-year period while others will grasp the ideas presented and progress without individual attention." Some farm couples were obviously more predisposed to accept new ideas than others. Social considerations were also important. The director observed that "many wives are reluctant to come to meetings because of feelings of inferiority and the inability to meet people. These things have been noted during individual home visits." Further, the agent stated, "It is also important not to let the program of Farm and Home Development get a reputation of being for down-and-outers, or couples will be reluctant to take part." As a later study also pointed out, "The stigma of an educational program to assist low income farmers has purposely been avoided in Iowa."[43]

By decade's end the Farm and Home Development Program was still in effect but had undergone some change. In 1959 the Hardin County agricultural director devoted attention to the program but cast it primarily in terms of farm business analysis. In that year fifteen farm families were taking part in the county program. In his 1958–1959 annual report, Director Andre still emphasized the fact that the long-range concerns of farm people had not changed much and that all concerns were still family-oriented. "Extension must be geared to help the family." At the same time, however, he included much less material on Farm and Home Development than in previous reports. Andre observed that many of the families, about two thousand in total, "fall within the 'low income' bracket and nearly a third have had no previous experience of participating in Extension programs." While Andre explained that it was too early for a complete assessment he did observe that the 1958 annual income of farm families participating in the program showed an increase of 44 percent over the previous year, while that of all Iowa farmers increased only 24 percent.[44]

Elsie Van Wert worked with the FHDP when she served as an Extension home economist in Hancock and Winnebago counties during the 1950s. Van Wert recalled the "human development" aspect of the program, which she believed brought husbands and wives together to discuss mutual problems. In regard to management, Van Wert explained that in certain situations, "Women could see why the men had to have the tractors. [And why] they couldn't have

JIM GOODE, county Extension director, discussing a
blueprint with an Iowa farm family in 1955, probably as
a part of the Home and Farm Development Program.
Courtesy ISU Photo Service.

the piano. . . . And it brought them together and they realized what they needed to do, what their priorities had to be in order to get them where they wanted to be. [Before] they weren't looking ahead far enough, planning ahead." Van Wert added that after participation in the program, farm women said, " 'You know, we didn't realize all this was necessary.' And the men would say, 'Why I didn't realize my wife felt like this.' It was human development."[45]

Van Wert's comments underscore a significant shift in Extension policy. Before 1950 Extension had followed a sex-segregated approach in regard to clients. County agents served male farmers while home economists worked with farm women. Farm men and women did attend social and educational programs together, particularly those developed by rural sociologists, but the main work of county staff resulted in different projects for each sex. In the FHDP Extension personnel viewed the family as an integrated unit whereby agricultural directors, home economists, and specialists such as agricultural economists all worked with both husbands and wives and sometimes even with children. With the assistance of staff, farm couples made decisions together regarding many farm practices. As Van Wert pointed out, joint decision making led to better understanding by each spouse of the needs and concerns of the other.[46]

The FHDP represented greater change for farm women than for farm men. Although the term family farm had been used for some time to describe farming operations in the Midwest, in reality male farmers typically made critical farm decisions. Most farm women earned money through sale of eggs, cream, and butter, but decisions to make major nondomestic purchases were viewed as a man's job. Usually investments in farm buildings, additional livestock, and new machinery seemed more sensible than household improvements. With the inception of the FHDP, for those participating families, decisions were to be discussed and equal weight given to all family needs. While it is doubtful that this mutuality took place in every case, nevertheless the interests and desires of farm women were being considered, not only concerning domestic concerns but in regard to the entire farming operation. For perhaps the first time Extension officials had established programs that provided for shared decisions and elevated domestic work and concerns to the same level as agricultural concerns.[47]

A second Extension program of importance during the 1950s was public policy education. Interest in this area was evident as early as the 1920s when agricultural economists observed that events off the farm significantly affected farmers' welfare. As Leon Thompson has written in his study, however, Extension officials were then "reluctant to take up the kinds of problems that involved group action and often led to controversy." Given Extension's main concern of greater production for the Iowa farmer, involvement in social or public policy was then viewed as perhaps not legitimate or safe for Extension.[48]

In 1944, however, federal Extension officials began to discuss the need for public policy work with state Extension staff. Federal authorities believed that farm people needed a better understanding of federal agricultural programs, tariffs, foreign trade, and economic issues. In the same year the Association of Land-Grant Colleges and Universities issued a report, *Postwar Agricultural Policy,* which singled out three issues that federal Extension officials believed should be emphasized in most state postwar public policy educational programs: foreign trade, fiscal and credit policies, and agricultural adjustment. Described as "an articulation of land grant college thinking," the report helped legitimize Extension's implementation of public policy. Further, the report defined the policy role of land-grant colleges as one of presenting citizens with information affecting policy (enabling them to make recommendations based on this information) rather than determining policy. According to one study, the report guided state Extension personnel by clarifying "the value position of extension" on public policy and by identifying some "major issues on which extension specialists in public affairs could develop educational programs."[49]

The fact that federal officials began to push for public policy programs in the 1940s is understandable given the national and international events of the period. It was clear by 1944 that the United States would play a critical international role in the postwar era, far different from the position that the country had taken after World War I. Given the emergence of internationalism, Extension officials at all levels sensed the need to help the nation's farm population understand both political and economic issues more thoroughly. In response to these as well as local needs, Extension officials began postwar planning in 1944. Public policy education carried out Extension's most basic mandate: Extension was (and continues to be) an educational agency. It had always tried to inform Iowans about a multitude of issues. The educational process was often extremely specialized, as when county agents provided information on the treatment of hog cholera. But in the post–World War II era, Extension leaders believed farm people needed broad understanding of "federal agricultural programs, tariffs, foreign trade, and economic issues."[50]

In 1948 another influential report, the *Joint Committee Report on Extension Programs, Policies and Goals,* followed. It stated that public affairs education programs should be initiated by state Extension Services. Although the report recognized that some issues would be "less tangible and more controversial," it argued that Extension must accept its educational responsibility. In regard to presenting public affairs programs, the discussion group technique was recommended and it was suggested that for successful discussions, an informed resource person was necessary or that reliable, impartial educational material be available. The person or materials should present all sides of the issue under discussion and raise pertinent questions. According to one authority, this report was "considered a landmark by many workers in extension public affairs education" and it responded to reservations that had blocked state Extension Services from moving into the area of public policy education earlier.[51]

The federal Extension Service with M. L. Wilson as director was also influential in moving state Extension personnel along the road toward public affairs education. In 1949 Director Wilson brought together personnel from eighteen state Extension Services that had experience in public affairs work. The conference identified some guiding principles for conducting this education as well as bringing about the commitment of the Farm Foundation—an organization concerned with improving the economic, social, and educational welfare of farm people—to support the first public policy education conferences.[52]

A survey taken in 1949 indicated that public affairs work had already begun in Iowa, Montana, Vermont, California, Michigan, Tennessee, and Wisconsin. At a conference held for Extension workers of the north central states in 1950, the keynote speaker observed that in the early days of Extension, farmers "had been trained to think in terms of personal interests rather than public interests." Presently, he observed, agriculture was just one phase of the total economy and there was a need for understanding broader issues and the relationship between agriculture and the rest of society.[53]

Iowa's Cooperative Extension first began specific action on public affairs education in January 1946, when Extension agricultural economists Wallace Ogg and Carl Malone held two informational meetings in northwest Iowa on fiscal and monetary policy for full employment. Enthusiastic reactions to the two meetings, attended mainly by farm leaders, prompted Ogg and Malone to request a statewide series of similar meetings. From 1946 to 1948 Malone carried out most of the work. In 1948 the Extension Service created a new position, Extension Economist in Public Affairs and hired Wallace Ogg for the post. For the next several years Ogg and Malone worked together in conducting public policy meetings organized around the theme Peace and World Progress. The two men also covered subtopics such as Understanding Europe, Understanding Asia, Understanding Russia, and American Foreign Policy. A part of their responsibilities dealt with training field staff to work with the program.[54]

Ogg and Malone presented twelve half-hour programs on public policy—four on farm policy, four on fiscal and monetary policy for full employment, and four on foreign policy. In the winter of 1953–54, the two men began to develop a public affairs program combining television presentations with discussions to be held in private homes. This approach was possible because of the location of WOI in Ames, the only television station operating in central Iowa at the time. Extension officials urged county agricultural directors to organize groups of farm men and women who would meet in private homes to watch the television presentation and discuss the issues. Materials would be distributed to certain participants who would serve as discussion leaders at each gathering. Extension officials estimated that from 2,500 to 5,000 people took part in these programs. By 1955, in response to the state's increasing agricultural difficulties, Ogg and Malone concentrated their public policy presentations on farm policy.[55]

A year later county Extension staff were conducting public policy meetings on their own. Iowa's program differed from other states in that Ogg and Malone, as specialists, had trained county staff to carry on presentations themselves. Other states apparently held the view that only specialists were qualified to do this work. In Franklin County Extension personnel developed a team presentation on farm policy that received both state and national attention. County officials made the presentation to 1,500 Franklin County residents as well as over four area television stations. Eventually the secretary of agriculture invited the team to appear before the National Agricultural Advisory Commission. The USDA produced a motion picture of the presentation, making it available to other states. The USDA cited the effort as an example of what could be done by a county Extension staff in public affairs education.[56]

By late 1955, given the fact that the state's agricultural economy had not improved, the Iowa Extension Service began an "intensive self-analysis." In effect, Extension began a thorough review of the current agricultural situation as well as its own programs and organizations. The staff quickly concluded that traditional approaches taken earlier were not always successful and that the organization needed to search for new approaches. At the same time Extension made clear that it was not abandoning its "fundamental obligation" to provide technical services to agriculture. As part of what was later called a "transition period" between 1956 and 1960, Extension took numerous steps to help Iowans better understand the economic difficulties they faced. Efforts to accomplish that goal included sponsoring a seminar for the College of Agriculture staff to study Adjustment of Agriculture to Economic Change and holding conferences for county Extension councils to inform them of current economic conditions. In addition in 1956 Extension officials created the Center for Agricultural and Economic Adjustment at Iowa State College, described as an agency "to provide information to help farm families achieve incomes on a par with those received in other industries and occupations." Extension also published the papers presented at the College of Agriculture seminars in three basebooks that provided the basis for much discussion and analysis by Extension personnel. Extension's major response, however, was to emphasize public policy education to better inform Iowans of the economic and social problems confronting them.[57]

Before working out long-range plans, however, Extension's immediate response to the worsening agricultural situation was twofold: first, to issue a leaflet entitled "Cutting Costs in Today's Farming," which provided suggestions and checklists that farmers could use to study their operation; and second, to initiate quickly programs on agricultural policy. At a hurriedly called meeting of county staff members in late 1955, public affairs specialists presented material on the "price and income crisis." Several counties then developed similar programs of their own.[58]

Throughout 1956 the Extension staff carried out "extensive discussions" on their responsibility for expanded research and ways to improve public education dealing with the state's basic economic and social problems. By the end of that year, according to Extension officials, the organization was placing "unprecedented emphasis on long-range problems in agricultural policy." As a way to underscore that fact, Extension officials selected as the theme for the annual conference "a 10-year forecast of broad state and world-wide policy problems . . . in an agricultural setting."[59]

The following year, Extension strongly emphasized programs in the area of public policy referring to them as a "bold move." They were Extension's major response to the economic difficulties of the 1950s. It is instructive to note, however, that these programs did not represent a totally new approach. Extension had been involved with public policy education since 1946. Rather it was emphasized much more than before.[60]

While the farm problems of that time undoubtedly influenced the decision of Extension to promote public policy issues, the recent separation from Farm Bureau might also be considered as a factor for change. Before 1955 public policy programs had been less formal than those developed later. The topics selected frequently dealt with foreign policy issues like Understanding Europe, Understanding Asia, and American Foreign Policy. Since Farm Bureau had been influential in all matters effecting Extension, it is logical to assume that they were also a factor in the selection of public policy topics. The separation from Farm Bureau opened the door for Extension officials to select a wider array of topics and also to chose ones that had previously been considered too controversial. Leon Thompson's study of public policy education indicates that the Iowa Extension Service approached public policy education in a cautious, tentative manner. When the 1957 program, Our Changing Agriculture, proved successful, however, Extension officials were encouraged to initiate another program, Challenge to Iowa. Participation in this program greatly exceeded Extension's expectations: administrators had hoped that forty counties would participate; instead ninety-six of Iowa's ninety-nine counties participated "to some degree." In effect, Challenge to Iowa made it possible for some fifty thousand Iowans to study the farm problems of the 1950s. According to Extension officials, "Substantial time was spent in examining, not just 'alternatives,' but opportunities for action which might open up wholly new alternatives at individual, family or community levels." By 1960, having put together two successful programs, officials acknowledged that their fear that Iowans might resent "Extension's invasion of highly sensitive and controversial issues" was unfounded.[61]

Extension officials followed Challenge to Iowa with a series of three, one-day conference-workshops for 1,500 selected community leaders throughout the state. The intent was to involve them in the effort to determine new approaches to social and economic problems as well as to measure reactions to the public policy program. Given a positive response by community leaders, plus the one by Iowans in general, Extension officials felt that the emphasis on public policy education was justified.[62]

Even though programs like Farm and Home Development and public policy education proved successful in the 1950s, one hard fact remained. Economic conditions had not improved in rural Iowa. While many plans of action were considered, one theme was reiterated by Extension administrators and Extension agricultural economists. Open country Iowa had a surplus of population and some of these people should perhaps look elsewhere for employment. Every year the central Extension staff prepared a Plan of Work for the following year which included an assessment of the state's current economic situation. The Plan of Work for 1957 noted that "farm income is decidedly unsatisfactory and is falling further and further behind that of the rest of the economy." The report also noted that more and more farm men and women were holding off-farm jobs to supplement their farm income. For many families, this work arrangement was becoming permanent.[63]

The 1957 Plan of Work singled out what the Extension administration believed were the two basic problems faced by the state's agricultural population. First, they cited the need to bring "total farm output into balance with total demand. An unprecedented slowing down of farm output growth must take place if demand is to catch up with output." In turn, the report noted, an even greater slowdown in production must take place if "excess farm stocks are to be liquidated." The second basic problem was "the adjustment that will permit each farm family to have an adequate economic base for their farming operation. The direction needed is to spread the labor and capital over the larger acreage of land; thus, larger farms and more extensive farming methods rather than more intensive ones." Extension officials were stating explicitly what staff members had been implying for some time: Iowa had simply too many farmers and some might think about leaving the farm permanently.[64]

In applying these basic problems to Extension, the report stressed two basic points. First, young people needed to understand the current "limited nature of good opportunities in farming" and that this situation would likely persist for some time. In effect, Extension officials believed that this understanding would cause some young people to decide against farming as a career, thus further decreasing the farm population. Second, established farm families needed to "reappraise their income potential in farming." This would mean that some families might conclude that they could do better economically in other occupations. If Extension could encourage some less productive individuals to move into another line of work, there would be opportunities for the more efficient ones to enlarge their acreages. That would enable the more productive farmers to make a greater profit and would relieve them of some pressure to farm as intensively as before. One agricultural economist wrote, "These data indicate that as size of farms increase we can expect a less intensive agricultural production."[65]

Not all decisions to leave the farm turned out happily, however, as Wallace Ogg relates in his memoirs.

> I distinctly remember the meeting of a series on "Agricultural Adjustment to Farm Size and Equipment." A janitor in the Memorial Union came up to me after the meeting. With intense anger in his voice and his facial expression he said, "I am an example of this agricultural adjustment. I used to be a farmer and enjoyed it. Now I am a janitor here in the Union."[66]

By the end of the decade Iowa indeed had fewer farmers than in 1950. Director Andre wrote in his annual report for 1960, following the availability of census data for that year, that Iowa's farm population had dropped a little more than 5 percent between 1949 and 1954 and an additional 9 percent between 1954 and 1960. The Director also pointed out, however, that the matter of agricultural surpluses remained: contrary to the thinking of some agricultural economists, fewer farmers were producing an ever-increasing supply of food.[67]

By the end of the 1950s, Iowa's Extension Service had undergone almost a decade of frustration in regard to the difficult situation within the state's agricultural sector. The economic problems of the 1950s were complex and frustrating. As the first report of the *Iowa Basebook for Agricultural Adjustment* pointed out, many people were "puzzled" when farm incomes began to go down in 1953. Certainly agriculture had been in trouble before but other segments of the economy had also suffered. In 1953, however, agriculture faced a downturn when the general economy was growing. The report continued that there was increasing evidence that "agriculture was out of adjustment with the rest of the national economy; resources elsewhere in the economy were earning increasing returns while returns to resources in agriculture were decreasing. Though the national economy as a whole was growing, agriculture was not sharing fully in the fruits of a progressive economy." This situation would persist at least until the end of the decade. In 1959 in the Iowa Extension Service's Plan of Work, the authors noted, "Iowa as a state is no longer fully in the main stream of economic growth—it has drifted into the slower-moving eddies."[68]

In effect, Iowa farmers were caught up in the same current as farmers elsewhere in the nation. As agricultural historian Gilbert Fite has pointed out, "Since 1940 the expansion of farm production has taken place at a phenomenal rate. Considering farm output in 1957–1959 as an index of 100, total agricultural production rose from 70 in 1940 to 108 in 1962, or an increase of nearly 60 percent." And, Fite continues, this increase was carried out on some 30 million fewer acres. Several other factors should also be considered: farms became larger and better managed during this time period; technological developments, especially the internal-combustion engine tractor, led to greater production; and (as noted earlier) higher yields of crops and livestock had been important. As Ralph K. Bliss also noted in his history of the Iowa Extension Service, not only did output per man-hour increase during the 1940s and 1950s, but also output per acre.[69]

The continually increasing productivity of the Iowa (and the American) farmer and Extension's original mission of helping them achieve increased production created a double bind for the institution. If Iowa farmers were to do well, both to provide sufficient income for themselves and to fit Extension's implicit definition of success, they must continue to produce ever-increasing amounts of agricultural products. A corollary of this formula for success was that farmers should also adopt new technology and new scientific procedures, which would help them produce even more. The result of that success then meant an increase in agricultural production, which continued to produce surpluses. The surpluses, in turn, helped drive down agricultural prices, meaning that farmers would then make less even though they were producing more.

In response to these trying times, Extension had developed new programs and approaches. Through public policy education, Extension helped move Iowa's farm population along the path toward developing an appreciation and understanding of public policies and international issues. Extension also underwent change in terms of its philosophy of service and its delivery system. During the 1920s and 1930s Extension personnel concerned themselves primarily with greater agricultural production, spending considerable time helping farmers solve specific problems. In effect, the county agent or the home demonstration agent often prescribed a solution for a problem based on information obtained from central staff, the state Experiment Station, or from the agent's own considerable experience. Through the 1940s individual projects dominated the work of all county staff and subject matter specialists. But during the following decade Extension placed emphasis on programs that might encompass the entire family or an entire community rather than individuals or gender-specific groups. Farm and Home Development provided an excellent example of this transition in philosophy and approach, which was, as former Extension official Eldon Hans put it, a change from practices to principles. The FHDP gave young farm couples pertinent information and assistance in analyzing problems, thus enabling them to make informed decisions. No doubt this change in roles was difficult for some older Extension personnel to accept. After years of prescribing solutions for specific problems—whereby they played an active role—county staffers were being asked to abstain from making the actual decision, thereby casting staff in a passive rather than an active mode.

By 1958, as the Iowa Extension Service clearly showed signs of an institution "in transition," the national Extension Committee on Organization and Policy issued a report signaling the direction in which state Extension Services ought to be moving in the immediate future. The report, entitled "The Cooperative Extension Service . . . Today: A Statement of Scope and Responsibility," stated that there were certain areas of program emphasis that should be receiving "high-priority attention." The 1958 report, usually referred to as the Scope Report, identified these as efficiency in agricultural production; conservation, development, and use of natural resources; management on the farm and in the home; family living; youth development; leadership development; community improvement and resource development; and public affairs.[70]

It is instructive to note that the Iowa Extension Service had been stressing most of these areas throughout the entire decade. The Scope Report stated, for example, that treating the family as a whole "is the course of action being intensified in the unit approach to farm families' problems."[71] In Iowa this was the approach followed in Farm and Home Development. The Scope Report singled out leadership development as a distinct area of concern, while in Iowa this emphasis had been integrated into many of the earlier projects for men, women, and youth. By 1958 the two newest additions to Extension programming were community improvement, and resource development and public affairs. In Iowa the community improvement area had been gradually formed throughout the decade with the assistance of subject matter specialists in sociology and economics. The Extension Service believed that it had a responsibility to help people understand such principles as adequate standards for community services and efficient methods of providing them; and methods of improving conditions and available services offered by health, educational, recreational, and other governmental and private institutions. Before the 1950s Extension employed rural sociologists who were primarily concerned with open country institutions such as churches and schools. By the end of the decade this interest had broadened to include both towns and cities. It seems that the Scope Report was more a blueprint for what the Iowa Extension had been doing rather than what it was urged to do in the future.

While the services provided by Extension were enlarged during the 1950s, one fundamental aspect of the organization remained the same: Iowa Extension was (and is) tied to the fortunes of agriculture. If farm families were doing well economically, there was not much cause for concern; indeed, everyone could assume that Extension was successfully carrying out its mission. But if the agricultural sector was not doing well, as throughout most of the decade, then doubts continually surfaced—both inside and outside the organization—as to Extension's efficiency, effectiveness, and even as to its continued usefulness.

Even in light of the difficulties of that time as Extension personnel looked forward to a new decade, they had reason to be at least guardedly optimistic. Extension programs were clearly providing many needed services for Iowa's rural people and Extension had obviously won a large and faithful following. At the same time the organization had indicated a willingness to recognize new problems and respond accordingly. A fundamental objective of the 1948 Kepner Report was "the development of people through education so that they could identify and resolve problems that affect them."[72] Without question, the programs sponsored by the Iowa Extension Service were in line with that directive. Moreover, a fundamental aspect of the Extension Service from its beginning was flexibility. That characteristic would continue to be alive and well into the 1960s as Extension expanded its services to meet the problems of urban as well as rural Iowans.

CLAYTON COUNTY farm women attend a traditional township meeting sponsored by Home Economics Extension in 1956. Courtesy ISU Photo Service.

7

A Decade of Continuity and Change

The 1960s

While the Iowa Extension Service experienced considerable change in every decade of its existence, in the 1960s change seemed more accelerated than before. It is difficult, in fact, to find any area of Extension that did not experience reorganization or some reorientation during that period. Expansion took place in the numbers and types of programs Extension carried out and changes began with Extension's major client. In 1960 Extension Director Floyd Andre observed that a "new farmer" was making an appearance in the state. Much of the response to this development came in the form of new technical information as well as a new deliverance system. The 1960s also brought a revision in the organization of Extension: in the field, Extension officials phased out districts and implemented an area plan; in central administration, ISU officials created the office of Dean of Extension. The Iowa Extension Service also began to reach out to a new urban clientele with programs such as Expanded Nutrition. Even though the 1960s brought a new day to Extension, some of the old rules still applied, particularly concerning economic well-being: as long as Iowa agriculture did well, Extension did well.

Fortunately for both, the 1960s was generally a prosperous decade.

While Iowa farmers had for some time been moving toward greater specialization and a stronger business orientation, by 1960 those tendencies seemed more pronounced. Extension Director Floyd Andre underscored that change when he wrote in his report to the *Iowa Yearbook of Agriculture* in 1960 that a new farmer had made an appearance in Iowa.

> [Keen observers] describe him as a professionally oriented man who sees his farm as a business, rather than solely as a "way of life," and who sees himself as a manager. He operates a highly capitalized business; he is increasingly in the cash market buying production items; his income is from sales on the market; and his family buys rather than produces goods used in family living.[1]

Andre explained that these farmers had "new kinds of needs for education," particularly for unit technology which Andre described as the "bundle of individual practices [or the package of practices] which are fitted together for modern, high efficiency [crop production such as corn]." He emphasized that Extension was concerned with four main clusters of educational needs including technology, management, human resource development, and community resource development.[2]

By the early 1960s it was clear that new technologies and new knowledge were being developed at an ever-increasing rate. Decisions as to how this mass of new information was to be passed on to Iowa's farm families were becoming more and more difficult. In effect, virtually an explosion of knowledge was taking place related to all aspects of farm life. Throughout the decade, the Extension director's reports referred to the problems inherent in finding better ways to keep the Extension staff updated and to find better ways to continue delivering the new information to the Iowa farmer, still Extension's main client.

Even in spite of major change, however, an old saying still applied: "The more things change, the more they stay the same." Many of its programs continued to deal with problems visible since Extension's inception such as the need for record keeping. As David May, a former CED (county Extension director) in Adams County, explained, "I think farmers always historically have been poor record keepers and even in the 1950s this was rudimentary."[3] Many programs throughout the 1960s continued to emphasize record keeping and, in turn, better management practices. May recalled that through the FHDP (Farm and Home Development Program) in his county, record keeping was a number one priority for participating farm couples. May noted that this practice was "an absolute must for a husband and wife to be involved in sound record keeping and business planning."[4]

The situation in Adams County also underscored another longtime characteristic of Extension: all counties were not equal in terms of economic resources and needs. David May began work in Adams County in 1956 as the county Extension director and quickly perceived the differences between his former place of residence, Grundy County, and his new home. Adams County, the smallest county in the state, had far greater needs for low income families. In fact, in Adams County low income farm couples were singled out for the FHDP. By contrast, in some northern counties Extension officials had expressed concern that low income families not be selected for the FHDP to avoid the perception that the program was established mainly for that group.

In 1964 May wrote an article for *Extension Service Review* in which he described programs offered to low income residents in his county. Noting that these families were reached for the first time in that year, May explained the preparation and use of commodity foods. He observed that the participating residents responded enthusiastically. May wrote that it also quickly became apparent that some county homemakers were interested in lessons on make-over clothing. With the cooperation of a state specialist in textiles and clothing and a local public welfare worker, a clothing workshop of six lessons was quickly set up for the low income families. As interest in the project grew, May and other Extension personnel worked to involve a wider group of people. Five Farm Bureau women volunteered to help with the organization of the workshops and to give personal assistance in teaching sewing skills while the local Singer Sewing Machine Center at Creston loaned portable machines for the project. The Adams County Farm Bureau donated space for the workshops and local churches donated old coats and suits for remodeling purposes.[5]

When the six clothing workshops had been completed, Adams County officials agreed they had been highly successful. Twenty-two women had taken part, making many articles of children's clothing for both school and church. As a project finale, the participants held a potluck dinner and style review where the children modeled their new clothing. As May observed, benefits extended beyond the sewing skills themselves. The workshops brought "a feeling of new friendships and understanding and a realization that someone really did care what happened to [the participants]. They needed status in their community just as much as anyone else does. They wanted their children properly dressed for school and Sunday School." May concluded: "This has been a most rewarding experience for the Adams County Extension staff because these people appreciate so much what the Extension Service has done for them."[6]

One major program carried over from the previous decade was the Farm and Home Development Program. Started in the mid-1950s, it had been introduced in a few counties and then expanded. Like all programs, support and promotion by Extension officials varied from county to county. Initially it appeared that the FHDP would encompass all farm activities including household management and family expenditures as well as decisions about agriculture. In Boone County in 1961 CED Truman N. Nelson listed five goals for the FHDP, all of which included consideration of farming, homemaking, and family living. By that date in many counties, however, it appeared that most FHDPs focused on the economic aspects of production, which in effect meant maximizing agricultural production, or making other decisions related to production. In Adams County CED David May reported in 1960 the following regarding the program:

> Several families are maximizing crop income through continuous corn on their best soils. Many families used fertilizer to maximize corn yields in 1960. . . . One young farmer disposed of his dairy herd after making changes in his land use and swine program. This family used the decision making process to make this major decision. Several farmers have enlarged the size of their land unit.[7]

By 1962 and 1963 county Extension directors were commenting less and less on FHDP in their annual reports. Franklin County's CED noted in 1962 that it was becoming increasingly difficult to find time to carry out the program. In Floyd County in 1963 the director started what was to be a three-year FHDP, but the following year dropped it for lack of interest.[8] By mid-decade it seems that the program had been de-emphasized in many counties although some annual reports still mentioned it briefly as late as 1968. Apparently the upturn in economic conditions for Iowa farm families made it easier to put aside concerns about management and formulation of long-range goals.

Everett Stoneberg worked with the FHDP for several years as a farm management specialist. He typically worked with families first to produce better records and then to analyze their records in regard to future economic decisions. According to Stoneberg, a major role of the farm management specialist was to point out economic alternatives and their possible consequences. Sometimes that decision called for the family to leave the farm. Stoneberg explained,

> Many decisions such as "should I expand, should I try to rent additional land" and looking back there were an amazing number of these families [to whom] we pointed out . . . that they did not have management resources with adequate income potential and after several years . . . they got the message. They realized from studying their farm records that probably they didn't have adequate resources to make a very good living on the farm.

Stoneberg added that he was amazed at the number of people who left the farm (especially in the 1950s) but added, "I think every one of those I have run across since has probably done better by leaving the farm than by staying there."[9]

Stoneberg's experiences touch on another aspect of Extension work, relationships between county staff and state specialists. Stoneberg noted that the FHDP was a county program. "We wouldn't go in and service the program over the heads of the county staff so you had to have the cooperation of the county staff." Stoneberg's comment underscores the fact that not all CEDs were interested in every program. Stoneberg tried to make two visits to each farm annually at least the first several years, accompanied by either the CED or the county home economist. He hoped that later in the year either the CED or the home economist would visit the farm again. He felt that "where we had an active home economist and she was interested in this . . . [it] made an ideal arrangement. Especially if you had a home economist with a farm background." Stoneberg estimated that he worked with a total of 150 farm families and when closing the farm couples' records for the year, tried to handle 10 to 12 a day. Again, the relationship between the farm management specialist and the CED was crucial. Stoneberg believed that FHDP was not only time-consuming, but it also required scheduling and some "county staff just didn't feel all that comfortable with a lot of this." Also some CEDs and home economists did not feel comfortable in advising farm families on economic matters;

moreover, many felt they had enough work without that required by FHDP.[10]

Stoneberg's experience with FHDP points out a critical factor in Extension work: the clients' attitude toward programs and the need to share financial information. Stoneberg explained that some farm couples were reluctant to open financial records for him and other Extension personnel. "But many times by the second or third visit, I knew what their net worth was. How [many] loans they had at the bank and what investments they had." Stoneberg felt that some couples were more concerned about sharing information with the CEDs who lived in the same community, while Stoneberg did not. He concluded, however, that records were confidential and he felt that most Extension personnel did a good job of respecting that fact.[11]

While FHDP was a carryover from the 1950s, in 1961 Extension began moving in a different direction with a pilot program in area development known as TENCO. Extension officials, ISU faculty, and business and community leaders in ten southern counties pioneered an approach to area problem solving based on what economists called the "functional economic area." In effect, TENCO was a multicounty area where residents shared economic and social interests and activities. The area included a hub city, in this case, Ottumwa. In describing the project, ISU economist Karl A. Fox, a key participant in TENCO, wrote, "By definition, a labor market area is relatively closed or bounded with respect to income-producing activities of its residents. It is also relatively closed or bounded with respect to a cluster of consumer-oriented or 'residentiary' activities. Almost all of the labor resident in the area is sold within it and almost all of the goods consumed in the area are bought within it."[12]

Former Extension official Ronald Powers described Karl Fox as the person who really had a tremendous impact on putting the concept of a functional economic area in place and getting acceptance of it.

> Karl did some of the very early work, really demonstrating the fact that people were no longer obtaining their goods and services within a single population center or community but, in fact, they were getting it around a central city. . . . Eventually he put the concept together and drew what everybody referred to as "Fox's box," a kind of diamond shape around the [cities] which said that given our square grid system, and the people's willingness to travel about an hour, if you went out 50 miles in any direction from that

center you . . . captured the social-economic drainage basin for economic activity.

Fox then demonstrated this concept with data in regard to commuting patterns, people's workplaces, and sites selected for medical services.[13]

Powers, who in 1961 worked as an Extension sociologist, recalled that he and Darrel Hobbs were part of the first TENCO effort. The two sociologists started training field staff in the ten counties so that the program could be officially started on September 1. Powers explained, "We spent the night before in a motel in Ottumwa putting [the finishing touches on] the presentation on how [one identifies] the key influentials, the power actors so we could go to that set of people, present the concept of an area development idea, get their support and get an area wide committee."[14]

TENCO was launched after residents of ten southern Iowa counties met in November 1961 to examine area economic problems and search for solutions. The Ottumwa area seemed a logical place to begin a program on economic development as business activities there had declined dramatically by 1961. Coal mining had declined 50 percent since 1950; agricultural employment by 35 percent; and business repair services by 33 percent. It also appeared that school enrollment in the ten counties would decline by over four thousand during the decade of the 1960s. By January 1962 a steering committee had formed and the group decided to accept an offer from ISU Extension to arrange for a staff member, Mahaska County Extension Director Arthur Johnson, to work with the program.[15]

With Johnson's involvement, the steering committee decided that four areas should be emphasized: agriculture, industry, education, and recreation. The Extension Service provided four specialists to work with local individuals in conducting studies in the four problem areas. One result was the publishing of several booklets such as "TENCO of Iowa," which informed people of historical and recreational attractions in the ten-county region. A second booklet, "Agriculture in TENCO," identified area economic problems, such as the fact that the agricultural work force had declined considerably, going from 26 percent in 1942 to 12 percent by the mid-1960s. The agricultural publication also offered recommendations related to improving livestock production, exploring possibilities for providing technical training for people interested in agriculture, improving land use, and conducting a study of the area's tax structure. In education local individuals, with assistance from Extension specialists, carried out an evaluation of the thirty-one high school districts in TENCO. As a result of the evaluation and the decline in area population, officials suggested that ten or twelve school districts would be adequate to provide quality education to area young people.[16]

TENCO quickly became visible as one of the first programs in the nation to put rural development on a regional basis. In 1967 Secretary of Agriculture Orville Freeman visited the ten-county area as the first stop on a four-state tour to determine what the government "is doing—and still needs to do—about improving the economic status of rural citizens." Freeman made clear that TENCO was the reason for his visit to Iowa. Wilson Ervin, a Centerville banker, told the visiting delegation how his community had "bounced back" from a severe economic slump. Ervin explained that "we've gone from gloom and doom to boom and zoom," adding that the average family income of Appanoose County had doubled in the previous six years, thus removing the county from the government's list of depressed areas. At the end of the day Freeman summed up his tour by saying that although more long-range planning and coordination were necessary, he believed that TENCO had significantly improved living conditions in south-central Iowa.[17]

While Extension increased its involvement in areas such as economic development, the organization had always concerned itself primarily with agricultural production. The 1960s would be no exception. The CED was no longer regarded as "the crop doctor" as in the 1910s and 1920s, but he still spent much of his time dealing directly with production issues. The CED also continued to be concerned with community relations, coordination of community events, and promotion of Extension's work in community and public affairs. Even in the 1960s, the CED still served as a booster of his community. All of these responsibilities led David May to observe that one of the difficulties of being a CED "was having to spread oneself too thin."[18]

Although the work of CEDs dealt primarily with agricultural matters, it covered a wide range of subjects and presentations. In 1961, the Fayette County CED supervised experiments on the maturity rates of various corn hybrids, arranged for a three-day short course on agronomy, helped with a fall tour for corn club members, held a county-wide meeting on weed control, assisted with a field day on erosion control, and held two meetings on small fruits and shrubbery. Additionally, the CED worked with two dairy herd improvement associations, assisted with a June Dairy Month promotion, worked with groups participating in mastitis control, and assisted with a series of five training sessions for poultry producers. As well, he was expected to help with clients' management decisions such as "Can I afford to invest in more dairy equipment?" Typically, the CED worked with other groups or individuals in carrying out many of the programs.[19] CEDs also held outlook meetings in livestock or other production areas.

Each CED's work obviously depended heavily on the needs of his particular clients. In northeastern counties farmers were more interested in dairy production, while in northwest Iowa, a concern was more efficient arrangement of feedlots. In 1961 the Des Moines County Extension Director, located in the southeastern part of the state, provided spraying information to clients, informing people when and how spraying of orchards should take place. In the same year in Floyd County in northern Iowa, the Extension director noted that a major emphasis had been on a soil fertility program whereby Extension urged farmers to have their soil tested and then follow recommendations for use of fertilizer.[20]

At the same time the CEDs' own interests and expertise were involved in determining work schedules. The statistical reports attached to each annual county report indicate the time spent on different programs. In 1961, Franklin County's CED spent a total of ninety days on community development and public affairs while Fayette County's CED devoted ten days to the program. Throughout the 1960s the CEDs also spent considerable time on Extension organization and program planning. The work of the Franklin County CED was undoubtedly affected by the fact that the county employed an Extension associate for the full year.[21]

Since the beginning of Iowa Extension in the first decade of the twentieth century, the number and type of support staff had been increasing. For twenty years some specialists had resided away from the campus in the district that they served. The first specialists were in agronomy and farm management, but in the 1960s, Extension added specialists in 4-H and youth programs, consumer education, area economic development, and livestock production. In his annual report to the *Iowa Yearbook of Agriculture,* Director Andre noted that by 1965 the organization included twenty-three specialists working with a field staff of 275.[22]

While every county had a CED, not every county employed a home economist. Sometimes two home economists served two or three counties jointly with a specific division of subject matter responsibilities. Although home economics programs had been a part of Extension since the 1910s, public confusion still existed as to who could take part in the program. The Adair County home economist wrote in 1961: "There are still many people who do not understand how they may take part in the Extension Family Living program." In Dubuque County the home economist made a similar comment: "Gradually more and more people are learning about the educational services Extension has to offer." The Dubuque County agent also noted that confusion still existed over the relationship between Farm Bureau and Extension. "Many farm people thought that one could not participate in the Family Living Program unless they belonged to a Farm Bureau Township Group. Many urban people thought one could not participate in the Extension Family Living Program, unless they lived on a farm."[23]

The Family Living Program represented the main interest of county Extension home economists in the 1960s. Within that area the home economics program was moving toward studying topics that affected the whole family rather than concentrating on subjects of interest only to the farm homemaker. This move from studying projects to more broadly based programs was going on throughout the state.[24]

While overall emphasis centered on family living, within that area county participants could select from a wide variety of specific topics. In some counties Extension personnel distributed questionnaires to solicit areas of interest. In Allamakee County, for example, the Family Living Program consisted of programs on the following: Cheese and Its Uses; Sandwich Meals; Hobby Fair; Vegetable Cookery; What's New in Wall Finishes; and Sewing on New Fabrics. In Des Moines County, the Family Living Program called for four lessons: Fashions for Fall; Foods for the Holidays; Building Responsibility for Children; and Whistle While You Work (program in principles of time and energy management). The Extension office also started a young homemakers newsletter. County Extension personnel worked with an appointed Family Living Program Committee to determine a specific Plan of Work. Although selected topics varied from county to county, all generally fell within the six major areas of mental and physical health, management, housing, consumer information, human development, and community and public programs. In turn, this Plan of Work had to be approved by the county Extension council. Some counties selected programs reflecting specific interests such as Fayette, a leading dairy county, which selected a program entitled Milk.[25]

During the first half of the decade, Extension personnel also started nutrition education for low income families. In 1962–1963 this program was carried out in thirty-six counties. The work, conducted in cooperation with the State Department of Social Welfare and county welfare units, particularly emphasized the use and storage of foods available through food donation programs.[26]

Home Economics Extension still relied heavily on the local leader training program whereby volunteer farm women attended sessions presented by district or state specialists and then returned home to their own rural neighborhoods to present the programs. In this way the number of people benefiting from the information was greatly increased. At the same time county Extension staffs had a large number of specialists to call upon for assistance. The six Extension districts had specialists residing within the districts as well as some specialists housed at Iowa State University. Many Extension programs were training sessions for volunteers, while some were presented for direct consumer information or entertainment.

While Extension home economists had the same clientele through the years, by the 1960s there was indication of change regarding programs. In the 1961 annual report, home economist Mary Lou Evans wrote that women in Guthrie County "have several different and conflicting values." She observed that many women were working outside the home, which meant that fewer women participated in educational meetings. Those who remained at home fell into two groups: "retired people or those whose families are grown and left home; those mothers with several small children." While the program described for that year did not appear to deviate from previous years, Evans certainly identified a growing trend throughout the state: an increasing number of rural women working outside the home. Home economists also noted that more urban women were taking part in Extension programs. In Dubuque County especially, the home economist emphasized that urban women who had never been involved before had attended some Extension programs on fashion.[27]

The third major Extension area, 4-H and youth activities, also witnessed change in the 1960s, but less than the areas of agriculture or home economics. In his annual report in the *Iowa Yearbook of Agriculture* in 1961, Extension Director Andre wrote, "Both youth and their adult leaders and parents respond heartily to shifts of emphasis from largely project-oriented education to developmental education and experience." Andre added that the project had been

COOPERATIVE EXTENSION STAFF work in school classrooms with Extension's Expanded Food and Nutrition Program. The focus is on choosing more nutritious foods, food preparation at home, and understanding the connection between diet and health. Courtesy of the ISU Extension Communication Services.

a "distinctive contribution of 4-H to youth" and remained as an important focus. He added, "As youth leaders put it, 'the 4-H program is more interested in the boy who holds the lead strap than in the animal at the other end.' "[28]

Andre's comments in 1960 seemed perhaps a bit premature, as in looking at the CEDs' annual reports filed throughout that decade, it does not seem that such shifts always took place. In effect, state officials were urging county Extension personnel to merge programs for boys and girls. That meant, at least partially, moving away from projects such as beef cattle and corn production for boys and sewing and home decoration for girls and placing more emphasis on developmental skills such as program planning and leadership. But this change was often difficult to accomplish. In 1961 the Dubuque County CED noted that although many joint activities were planned, the 4-H program in Dubuque County continued to operate primarily as a boys' 4-H program and a girls' 4-H program. As in previous decades, more girls than boys took part. Individual clubs still held Dad's Night Out for boys and the Mother-Daughter Tea for girls. Girls in some counties held rally days and boys held basketball tournaments. In effect, the state contained some county staff who held more traditional views while others opted for change. In 1960, for example, the Adair County home economist wrote that an objective of girls' 4-H was "to learn skills which will prepare girls for their adulthood responsibilities of home making." In contrast, a number of county staff members lamented the lack of leadership training for 4-H youths.[29]

At the same time some county Extension officials began to promote combined programs for boys and girls. In 1960 all 4-H clubs in Allamakee County worked together to raise money for equipping a room in a local hospital. In Appanoose County Extension staff planned a special activity, clothing and grooming for both boys and girls. In 1965 the Franklin County CED wrote in his annual report, "Whenever possible, subject matter materials are prepared that can be used by both boys and girls either jointly or separately."[30] More and more, recreational activities for boys and girls were combined, both at the county and state levels. By the end of the decade CEDs were making three entries in their annual reports: girls' 4-H activities, boys' 4-H activities, and joint activities.

While it is clear that state Extension officials did not accomplish all they might have hoped for in moving 4-Hers from projects to programs, it should be noted that their task was sizeable. It is always difficult to change longtime, successful programs, particularly where

Have a Healthy Heart

Avoid SMOKING	High Blood PRESSURE	High Blood CHOLESTEROL	Lack of EXERCISE
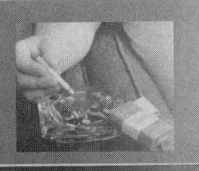			

Problem:
- Doubles risk of heart attack
- Constricts small arteries which leads to high blood pressure
- Increases risk of emphysema by 2000%
- Increases heart rate 15-25 beats per cigarette
- Reduces bloods ability to carry oxygen

Solution:
- Quit smoking

Problem:
- Triples risk of stroke
- Doubles risk of heart attack
- Increases risk of kidney disease

Solution:
- Use less salt
- Maintain ideal weight
- Check blood pressure often

Problem:
- Increases risk of heart attack by 500%
- Increases fatty deposits in arteries

Solution:
- Avoid too many fatty foods and saturated fats
- Maintain ideal weight
- Check blood cholesterol level

Problem:
- Contributes to heart disease
- Increases body fat
- Weakens bones

Solution:
- Do aerobic-type exercises regularly

LOSE POUNDS		STOP SMOKING		MAINTAIN NORMAL CHOLESTEROL

POSTER EXHIBITED at the Iowa State Fair by Extension Home Economic specialists entitled "Have a Healthy Heart." Circa 1970. Courtesy ISU Photo Service.

the leadership (in this case, volunteer) does not change. 4-H had been highly rated by Iowa's farm youths, and many families (and probably county Extension personnel as well) felt that it was the projects that drew youths to the program and brought the greatest rewards. In one sense the lack of success in restructuring programs underscored the enduring success of Iowa 4-H programs. Iowans seemed to be saying, "We like things the way they are."

Other developments tended to mitigate a change of emphasis within 4-H. In his 1968–1969 report in the *Iowa Yearbook of Agriculture,* Dean Marvin Anderson wrote, "The last half of the 1960s has seen some revolutionary change in thinking and practices relative to market beef type and performance." He went on to explain that "innovative work" by ISU scientists had affected the 4-H beef program. "Youth leaders, extension livestock specialists and leaders in the beef industry put emphasis on bringing the 4-H market beef project into line with the reality of practices and profit in the beef industry." These individuals, in effect, were urging 4-H youths to think of their beef projects in terms of marketability and profitability as well as the ribbons that they hoped to win at the local fair. While this change in emphasis made good sense in terms of training the future farmers of Iowa, it did little to support the earlier goal of 4-H to move from projects to programs.[31]

Iowa 4-Hers in the 1960s, however, continued to enjoy the program started a decade earlier — the development of the Iowa 4-H Camping Center. Camps for farm youths had been held as early as 1909 on various fairgrounds throughout the state, but in April 1945 the State Extension 4-H Club Committee set about investigating the possibility of a permanent camp. Paul Taff, chair of the committee, and Edith Barker, state girls' club leader, solicited material from other states that had also considered establishing 4-H camps. The committee determined that the camp location must meet four requirements: (1) be near the center of the state; (2) preferably be located on a body of water; (3) be situated in a wooded area so campers could study nature; and (4) if possible include 160 to 200 acres of land. Four years later the committee agreed to establish the Iowa 4-H Club Foundation, which "would handle any funds that Iowa 4-Hers may have" for the construction of the camp. Plans moved along rapidly and in 1952 the camp was ready for its first occupants. The resulting location, a wooded, 556-acre site along the Des Moines River near Madrid, closely approximated the committee's original requirements.[32]

While always an integral part of Iowa Extension, 4-H has

A 4-H STATE LEADERSHIP CONFERENCE in 1970. The adult male leader is Arthur Johnson, Extension sociologist. Courtesy Iowa State University Library/University Archives.

occupied an interesting and special niche. The program was (and is) the most visible part of Extension. Even today, ask any group of people around the country about various Extension programs, and the majority will likely be most familiar with the activities of 4-H. Still, not all Extension staff seemed to rank 4-H programs as highly as outsiders. In a national study of Extension, Thomas and Marilyn Wessell point out that some 4-H officials believe that their programs do not get "a fair share of the funds" that CEDs allocate each year to the various Extension programs.[33]

In Iowa, the 4-H professional staff has traditionally experienced a higher turnover rate than either the CEDs or the home economists. While all counties had CEDs, fewer counties had home economists and even fewer counties had youth workers. Commenting on that fact, the Wessells write, "While the growth of the 4-H agents' association was fundamental to expanded programs and increased professional status for youth work, most agents retained the lingering suspicion that advancement in their careers required moving to adult programs." Several retired Extension staff members remarked that in Iowa it was generally accepted that the position of youth leader was looked upon as the training ground for the CEDs. Given the lower number of 4-H professionals, it is not surprising that the program has relied most heavily on volunteer leaders. In the 1960s finding 4-H leaders became increasingly difficult as more women began working outside the home. Innumerable annual reports indicated that leaders for 4-H clubs were getting harder to find.

With the many changes in American society by 1960 and the need for new programs, Thomas and Marilyn Wessel feel that across the country Extension 4-H leaders did not quickly respond to these needs. Rather than looking at "critical issues" such as civil rights, urban migration, and the search for equality for women, the focus remained on local issues such as helping "rural youth adapt to nonfarm employment opportunities" and determining how 4-H might work "more closely with the agribusiness sector of the economy." By the end of the decade, however, 4-H had become involved in wider issues. Congress appropriated money in 1969 to give $4.5 million of the Expanded Food and Nutrition Education Program to 4-H nutrition education. Extension staff also placed more emphasis on developing 4-H programs in urban areas. Throughout the 1960s Iowa 4-H clubs took part in the International Farm Youth Exchange Program. It allowed for better understanding of agriculture and culture of foreign countries as well as providing for some American students to live abroad.[34]

Like 4-H, other areas of Extension had also become involved in wider issues (as well as responding to the needs of more Iowans) during the 1960s. These changes were not always noticed by the public at large or by public officials, however. In December 1963 the *Des Moines Register* published the results of the Iowa Poll that asked Iowans about their perceptions of the ISU Cooperative Extension Service, particularly the work of the "county agent." The poll indicated that many farm people had only "vague ideas" about the work of this individual. When asked "What kind of job would you say your county agent is doing? Would you say he is doing an excellent, good, fair, or poor job?" 17 percent of the respondents rated the county agent excellent while 40 percent expressed "No opinion." When asked: "Do you feel that the duties of a county agent should also include assistance to city and town people as well as farmers?" 54 percent answered yes.[35]

On the same day the *Register* carried an editorial entitled, "The New County Agent," in which it called for Extension to become "a general educational service more than a technical farm service." The editorial stated that a need existed in Iowa "for education on industrial development, land zoning in growing communities, recreational uses of farmland, public schools, taxation, problems and many more 'new' subjects." Further, the editorial called for the Board of Regents to consider "the practicality" of a merger of Extension Services at the University of Iowa, Iowa State University, and the University of Northern Iowa. The editorial concluded, "Extension in the old pattern is dying on the vine. It will take further bold and dramatic changes to stop the decay and start a new university-wide public education service."[36]

During the following month, probably influenced by the *Register's* poll and editorial, Governor Harold Hughes publicly expressed the same view that the ISU Extension Service be used for purposes other than agriculture. The *Knoxville Journal,* like other newspapers around the state, quickly responded to the governor's suggestion.

It is difficult to tell whether the recent suggestion of Governor Harold Hughes that the activity of the Extension Service of Iowa State University could be more useful to the state if switched in greater degree toward non-agricultural education stems from lack of up to date information on his part or a deliberate attempt to down grade and belittle the Service. Actually all the specific suggestions that the Governor made regarding community development, zoning, industrial development, schools, taxation and public affairs are fields that the [ISU] Extension Service is already emphasizing and has been for several years, in addition to its purely agricultural technology phases of off-campus instruction.[37]

It seems clear from newspaper editorials around the state that many Iowans were aware of Extension's move into areas outside of production agriculture even if the governor and the *Register* were not.[38] The 1960s, in fact, would include a multitude of new programs. TENCO had already involved Extension in all of the areas singled out by the *Register* and Governor Hughes. In February 1964, several weeks after Hughes's statement, Extension began the first of a series of public service finance workshops in Sioux City. The workshops had obviously been in the planning stage for some time before either the *Register* editorial or Hughes's public statement. The workshops followed a "fact-finding and research phase" in which officials brought together data on public revenues and expenditures. The workshops, presented in twenty-three locations in the state, were attended by local leaders for the purpose of helping Iowa's community leaders gain a better understanding of public financing. The third phase was a self-administered discussion series in the winter of 1965 in which more than sixty thousand Iowans met in homes to hear about and discuss the issues related to public financing.[39]

A second educational program on local government affairs was started by Extension in 1967. John M. Whitmer, Jr., a city government expert, was hired to begin the program. Whitmer first developed a survey to determine specific problems of local governments. Results of the survey were then used to "reveal problems and . . . point out short course topics that would shed light on the specific problems mentioned." The short courses consisted primarily of off-campus education programs. By 1970 Extension Dean Anderson reported that some "7,740 government leaders, community influentials and citizens studied and discussed present-day problems of local government for about 15 hours."[40]

The 1960s would not only result in new Extension programs, but also would bring major organizational changes in Extension's administration, both on and off campus. In 1966, shortly after assuming the presidency of Iowa State University, W. Robert Parks reorganized the Extension Service, creating University Extension and the position of Dean of Extension. University Extension brought together four different areas: the ISU Cooperative Extension Service; the Engineering Extension Service; the Center for Industrial

Research and Service (CIRAS); and the Agriculture Short Course Office, later renamed the Office of Continuing Education. Reflecting on that period, former Dean of Extension Robert Crom recalled Parks's motivation for making the change. In effect the President was saying, "We ought to have an outreach function that [is] as broad as the University and ought to deliver the investment [and] benefits of the investment . . . whether it be in agriculture or engineering or in one of the other colleges."[41] Parks then appointed Marvin A. Anderson as the first Dean of Extension. Anderson, who had served as associate director of Extension since 1952, was an Iowa native who had previously been a youth worker in Wayne County, a soils specialist in Creston, and later an Extension agronomist.[42]

The second change concerned the state's division into Extension supervisory areas. This move phased out the existing six districts and created twelve areas, the first set up in Ottumwa in 1965. Ottumwa seemed the logical choice for that designation, as work on TENCO in the early 1960s had already created a ten-county area organization centered there. In the next few years eleven more area offices would be created, the last being Des Moines in 1969.

Russ Swenson, a former district and area supervisor, recalled that Extension officials began to think about this change as early as 1963 or 1964. He explained that state leaders "could see . . . especially in agriculture, the technology was such that it was getting harder and harder for the county Extension director to handle all the questions, to really provide all the leadership that was needed because of technology." He explained that much planning went on before the changeover actually occurred. As a district supervisor, he had been asked to develop a new staffing plan for part of his district; about eighteen months later he was asked to do the same for the other half of the district. In 1965 state Extension officials set up a staffing committee to examine reorganization possibilities. According to Swenson, even though much planning and discussion had been going on regarding reorganization, the actual plan—especially the idea of resident area directors—still came as a surprise to district supervisors. He recalled that even though he had been on the staffing committee, and had been "intimately involved on this thing all the way through," he had "never dreamt of that." Six months later Swenson was setting up an area office in Cedar Rapids.[43]

Following implementation of the area plan, Extension Dean Anderson gave two major reasons to explain the change. "The explosion of knowledge in technology and the sharpening demand for specialization by those dealing with educational services." Anderson went on to say that "expansion of knowledge has brought volume beyond the capacity of one person to keep abreast across several fields." To illustrate his point, Anderson pointed to the Iowa corn farmer. In looking for all pertinent, up-to-date information, the corn farmer needed "to apply the best known practices in at least nine fields of scientific study—soils, fertilizers, genetics, conservation, machinery, weed control, insect control, disease control, and management." Anderson also pointed out that farmers in other production areas wanted information of the same quality. "One person in a county extension office," Anderson explained, "cannot hope to keep up to date in that many fields of knowledge." In short, in order to respond to these needs, the Extension Service needed more specialization among its staff.[44]

Extension officials designed the area organization to bring more specialized Extension educators into closer contact with clients. A small group of specialists, such as crop production experts, would be located in each area office. Typically, they had completed graduate work in their areas. The number and types of specialists would not necessarily be the same in each area because agriculture and farming operations differed throughout the state. They would be assigned based on the particular needs of an area. Six areas out of twelve, for example, included specialists in resource development programs. In addition, Extension officials implemented what they called the multicounty approach; most permanent county staff members had an area of specialization that could then be utilized. The home economist, for example, who specialized in clothing and textiles would teach that subject matter in two or three counties while another with a specialty in food and nutrition would do the same. Throughout, the effort was to bring more specialized knowledge to the citizens of the state.[45]

David May provides another perspective on the area plan. May believed the change benefited him as a CED considerably as well as making it easier for state specialists.

> [With the area plan] I had an agronomist and if I ran into difficulty I had him almost at my fingertips. And the same with an Animal Husbandry specialist. And an agricultural economist. . . . [The change to the area plan] was certainly a change at that time that was very necessary. We had gentlemen like Tiny Gunderson, Entomology, and Dr. Sylwester in Botany and Plant Pathology. . . . They were just run ragged. They were state specialists and they were expected to carry 99 counties.[46]

As an area director, Russ Swenson viewed the restructuring as highly beneficial. "I absolutely loved it because you were so much closer to your staff. My, my, I knew what was going on. I knew how staff were developing, I knew where problems were. To me . . . it was very, very desirable." Swenson also believed there were more program options under the area arrangement, noting "we did things on an area setup that we never did on a county basis. Real heavy utilization of TV. [Previously] we weren't using TV hardly at all. . . . There's a lot of things that you can do in this day and age on an area basis that you just can't do on a county basis." Swenson concluded, however, that some aspects of the change did produce difficulties: "There was a lot of anguish [for] some people who had to move out of Ames."[47]

At the same time that Extension officials were establishing the area plan of organization, Extension itself was responding to the needs of a new clientele. In the late 1960s with increasing emphasis on good nutrition for low income Americans, the Extension Service began to develop nutrition programs for low income Iowans. In 1965 Extension completed the first stage of planning for a statewide research and educational program on poverty and welfare, *Dimensions of Iowa Welfare.* Approved by the Iowa Board of Regents, it was to involve not only Iowa State University but also the University of Iowa and the University of Northern Iowa. According to Wallace Ogg, Extension economist, results of the welfare study became available in 1967 and 1968 for educational programs. Recalling that the program was new and controversial, Ogg believed that Iowa was the only state that "tried to research poverty and welfare in depth and teach what was learned." He added, "People don't like to study about failure and poverty, its causes and results."[48]

The welfare study brought out startling information about a state where many people associated poverty with urban, not rural areas. Officials estimated that based on the sample, 460,000 people in 180,000 households in Iowa were disadvantaged. The dimensions or guidelines identified for people in this category included children under eighteen not living with both parents; males twenty-five years of age and older who did not have an eighth grade education; men with unskilled occupations; families with less than $3,000 income; and dilapidated housing units or units lacking some plumbing. Once available, Extension personnel spent considerable effort disseminating the information. Ogg recalled that Extension staff members held three-day conference-workshops in forty-four locations with 3,700 people taking part. Three two-person teams managed each set of meetings. Following the practice earlier established by community and public program specialists, statewide discussions were held in private homes. Participants (having previously received materials on the subject) viewed a videotape and then took part in discussions. *Dimensions of Iowa Welfare* was the last major program in public affairs in the decade.[49]

The completion of the Iowa welfare study coincided with action in Washington that provided federal funds for developing nutritional programs for low income Americans. In 1968 the USDA received $10 million from Congress to initiate the Expanded Food and Nutrition Education Program (EFNEP). Earlier the USDA had been involved in supplying food to the needy, particularly with its donated food and food stamp program. The department acknowledged, however, that many people did not have extensive knowledge about nutrition and further did not have access to that information. In the early 1960s the USDA carried out pilot studies in five states. Paraprofessional nutrition aides worked on a one-to-one basis with low income families to increase their knowledge of nutrition and use of donated foods. The pilot studies led to two conclusions: such studies, if tailored to the needs of low income homemakers, could be effective in changing families' eating habits; and the use of paraprofessionals, under the supervision of trained home economists, could be effective in reaching these homemakers. Two basic rules guided the work: information must be based on the latest research findings; and the teaching must be focused "to produce measurable behavior change in the target population." The initial funding permitted every state to have several program sites but later allocations were based on the number of people in each state below the poverty level.[50]

Iowa's involvement in the EFNEP started in 1969 in twelve locations with twelve home economists supervising the program. Officials selected sites in both urban and rural areas. By the end of the year more than sixty family food aides worked with the program. The USDA advocated that the paraprofessional workers be recruited from the ranks of the very groups that the program was to benefit. Iowa officials generally followed this suggestion.[51]

Josephine LaFrance Pickett, an African American woman from Des Moines, exemplifies the type of paraprofessional selected for the program. In 1967 Pickett, a widow with four children to support, was seeking employment. Pickett related that Extension officials sought her out to work with the project. She remembered, "I don't know to this day where they got my name. I think the reason might have been that I had good communication with the people I worked with, because I was in the same kind of situation. So I understood. I knew what they were talking about." For the next twenty-two years Pickett worked with the program, recalling that it changed considerably through the years. Originally Pickett and other aides "used to do demonstrations in supermarkets, and we did more group work. I worked in homes for the physically handicapped and with the elderly, but as the funding became less, we had to cut our audiences." Later she worked directly with young, low income homemakers using twelve lessons prepared by ISU home economists. Pickett explained that she never talked about the "contents of the cupboard" on the first visit. "Sometimes it was quite a while before we got into that, because we listened to what some of their problems were. It was our way of getting them to trust us. We listened a lot."[52]

County Extension staff also carried out other programs for economically disadvantaged people. In Boone County in 1968, the home economist estimated that about 20 percent of the county's total population was in the low income group. In their Plan of Work for 1968, the county staff determined to make food and nutrition lessons available for this group designed to help the women better understand the basics of good nutrition, ways to stretch their food dollars, ways to make food more appealing, and methods of food preservation. This material would be presented in five lessons, each one and one-half hour long, with Extension officials providing participants with transportation and babysitting. In addition, plans called for the home economist to help set up and train homemaker health aides and be available as a resource for the Headstart program and mothers of Headstart pupils.[53]

Extension staff also set up programs for the elderly. In Madison County in 1968 the home economist helped develop the program Food for Senior Years. The object was to help older people increase their understanding of basic nutrition, become more informed shoppers in regard to nutrition, and plan meals for one or two people. Twenty-seven people took part in the program.[54]

Some county staff also gave assistance to the Headstart program. In Humboldt County in 1967 the home economist spent almost a month helping to set up the Headstart program in the town of Humboldt. She recorded in the annual report for that year that she had obtained prices of needed equipment, such as kitchen ranges and refrigerators, and then helped purchase these items. She also helped interview potential employees. Once the program was underway, she assisted in making up menus and helped shop for the needed food items. She then worked with mothers of the Headstart children regarding nutrition. On one occasion the home economist and Headstart mothers visited an area grocery store where they talked about the food content of packages, nutritional value of food, and what constituted economical purchases. The same home economist also discussed the use of food stamps with Headstart mothers.[55]

The 1960s represented both change and continuity for Iowa's Cooperative Extension Service. Change came in many forms including TENCO initiated in 1961 when Extension personnel helped pioneer an approach to area problem solving based on what economists called the "functional economic area." This same model was later used with nine counties in northern Iowa, called NIAD, as well as contributing to the concept of area offices.[56] Major reorganization took place within Extension itself as ISU President Parks created University Extension and the office of Dean of Extension, thus removing the leadership of Extension from the College of Agriculture and creating an independent position. Even within subject matter areas, such as home economics, considerable change had taken place. While home economists still presented material on sewing and cooking, staff people had also developed countless programs on other aspects of family living. The term "family and home living" was an appropriate one as home economists looked at all aspects of the family, including problems of low income Iowans. It should be noted that these changes were possible, at least in part, because Iowa farm families in the 1960s had rebounded economically from the dark days of the previous decade.

At the same time the basic purpose of the organization remained unchanged. In his annual report to the *Iowa Yearbook of Agriculture* for 1970, Dean Anderson reiterated the general goal of Cooperative Extension. "Its task is to 'disseminate to the people . . . useful and practical information on agriculture, home economics and rural and community life.' " Anderson noted the following about the use of professional time: 38 percent devoted to agricultural production and conservation; 20 percent to home and family subjects; 30 percent to 4-H and youth programs; and 12 percent to community resource development and public affairs.[57] One area not visible in the years before 1960 was assistance to low income families, which in 1970 accounted for about 10 percent of Extension's total effort.[58]

While not explicitly stated in Anderson's report but evident in annual reports and other Extension material, is the fact that all Extension personnel were being asked to know more and do more in responding to clients' needs. Throughout the 1960s—as well as throughout earlier decades—new programs were carried out alongside older, more traditional programs, thus increasing the total amount of work for staff. It seemed, moreover, that Extension people, both county personnel and specialists, were always "on call." Everett Stoneberg related that one Sunday evening he went to the wedding of a county Extension director and hoped that he would be able to relax. "Four guys cornered me and wanted to know when they should sell their cattle, etc. at a wedding on Sunday night!"[59]

In his history of the Cooperative Extension Service, Wayne Rasmussen has noted that expansion in American agriculture peaked in the 1960s and "then gave way to evolutionary rather than revolutionary change."[60] For Extension's main clientele—the Iowa farm family—the next two decades would bring both great prosperity and great hardship as they began to experience that evolutionary change.

8

The Best of Times,
The Worst of Times

The 1970s and 1980s

In a national assessment of the Cooperative Extension Service published in 1984, Paul D. Warner and James A. Christensen write that as an organization, Extension is "unique in structure and function." They explain that Extension has not been restricted to one program or one activity, but rather "has been allowed to adjust to changing needs." The authors note that few organizations have been permitted this flexibility; rather, organizations tend to be created for a single purpose. These comments, included in *The Cooperative Extension Service: A National Assessment,* are particularly appropriate when examining the Iowa Cooperative Extension Service in the 1970s and 1980s. During most of the former decade farm families did well, but by the late 1970s prosperity faded. With the coming of the farm crisis of the 1980s it was imperative that Extension "be allowed to adjust to changing needs."[1]

In the 1970s, although programs in agriculture remained much the same, changes were taking place in other areas of Extension, particularly home economics and 4-H. These changes would continue into the 1980s. Moreover, it was clear by the 1970s that Extension had come to serve a much wider circle of clients than the traditional farm population. Iowa Extension workers at all levels were dealing with an ever-expanding range of issues including problems of the elderly, inner-city youths, low income urban families, and small town businesspeople. It is interesting to note, however, that the public's perception of Extension, as revealed through opinion polls, had not changed. Most Americans still viewed Extension as an "agency that [served] agricultural producers."[2]

In 1970 there was little evidence that by the end of the decade the state would be facing a serious depression. Although 1970 was not a banner year for agriculture, by 1972 significant changes had taken place. Because of a poor harvest, the Soviet Union in the summer of 1972 purchased roughly $750 million worth of wheat and feed grains. As historian Gilbert Fite has observed, "Prices began to rise sharply in the fall of 1972, exports shot up, and by early 1973, the American grain cupboard was almost bare." Given the depletion of surpluses, the USDA switched its position from production restrictions to recommendations that farmers grow more. Secretary of Agriculture Earl Butz reverted to the advice heard during World War I when agricultural officials urged farmers to plant from fencerow to fencerow. By the summer of 1973 prices had risen even more. Farmers received $10 for soybeans and almost $3 for corn. As Fite pointed out, "For hundreds of thousands of productive commercial farmers, 1973 and 1974 were a bonanza." In 1973, for the first time since records were kept, per capita farm income exceeded that of people off the farm.[3]

Given the agricultural prosperity of the early and mid-1970s, it is not surprising that no major policy changes occurred in this area of Extension. The emphasis was clearly on greater and greater production. In commenting on this time period, former Extension official W. John Johnson stated that Extension continued to do "what it had always done so well, only more of it." An area director in northwest Iowa at the time, Johnson noted, "The emphasis really was on being efficient and producing all you [could] because prices were high and the more you could produce, the [more money] you would get."[4]

The prosperity also carried over into the day-to-day operations of Extension. Area director Johnson recalled the effect of good times.

> In the early and mid-seventies as you met with . . . the County Extension Councils, to negotiate a salary sharing schedule for staff

or whatever it was, or a new position, or this or that, it was very easy to negotiate. There was money and they thought that that would be endless and there would always be more money . . . they were very agreeable.[5]

During the 1970s the ISU Cooperative Extension continued its four major areas of service: agriculture, home economics, youth work, and community resource development and public affairs. Extension continued to give a first priority to agriculture. In 1970 agricultural programs accounted for 38 percent of the organization's total resources. Within that 38 percent, approximately one-third was devoted to agricultural production and another one-third to livestock concerns; 40 percent was devoted to production problems, mainly corn and soybeans. Extension personnel allowed a small percentage for facilities, equipment, and management.[6]

In his biennial report in 1971, Extension Director Marvin Anderson noted that even in spite of fairly prosperous times on the farm, Iowa farmers still faced some difficulties. In 1970 and 1971 farmers suffered an invasion of southern corn leaf blight. It was soon evident that this was a major threat to the state's corn crop. Extension personnel provided assistance. Twenty-five specialists held meetings with farmers to keep them informed of the situation. Extension also distributed literature helping farmers to consider their individual courses of action. In 1971 a group of specialists met every Friday morning from late May into August to "pool observations and interpret those facts into suggestions for corn producers."[7]

The decade of the 1970s made clear that both Extension and the Iowa farm family had joined the computer age. In 1973 Director Anderson reported that a new educational program, Crop-opt, was available to farmers who wished help with their cropping program. Anderson described the program this way.

> The cooperating farmer lists his inventory of inputs—the time, energy, capital that he is willing to invest in his cropping program. His inputs are then fed into the computer at Iowa State. His personal printout gives five alternative optimum programs over input situations ranging from no additional land to land enlargement.[8]

In the first half of the 1970s Extension personnel also turned their attention to environmental issues. In 1970 and 1971 Extension held a series of forums throughout the state (in each of Extension's twelve areas) where specialists discussed the topics of health, soils and water, wildlife, waste disposal, and public decision making. About the same time pesticide control became a concern. After World War II the pesticide DDT had come into use along with other chemicals. Following the publication of Rachel Carson's *Silent Spring* in 1962, Americans became increasingly concerned about the long-term effects of farm chemicals. In 1976 the Environmental Protection Agency (EPA) allotted $5 million for Extension to provide training programs in each state. Iowa, then, was to develop its own certification program according to standards set by EPA and train applicators to meet these standards. At Iowa State, specialists in entomology, botany and plant pathology, and agricultural engineering educated county and area staff on safe, efficient use of pesticides as well as users' legal responsibilities. Area crop production specialists then helped develop a pesticide applicator training program in each of Iowa's twelve Extension areas.[9]

By the 1970s programs in community resource development (CRD) and public affairs had become an integral part of Cooperative Extension. Throughout the 1960s public affairs seemed to be more heavily emphasized than CRD. In fact, in 1971 Extension Director Marvin Anderson noted that Iowa had been a "trendsetter" in public affairs programming. One year earlier the three regents' institutions had worked together to produce a major public affairs program, "Government by the People," which focused on contemporary problems of local government. Participants were helped in identifying goals for local governments, improving understanding of ways to achieve these goals, and learning how to measure the effectiveness of local government. The producers utilized an interdisciplinary approach involving political scientists, economists, sociologists, educators, and journalists. The Extension Service, mainly responsible for the delivery of the program, arranged to have it presented in forty locations throughout the state. This program differed from previous ones in that the Extension Service also made the materials available to high school social studies teachers, who responded enthusiastically as they typically had few resources available on the subject.[10]

While rural and community development obtained higher visibility in the 1960s and 1970s, the program had roots that reached back to the Country Life Commission report in 1909. One of the first federal Extension publications on the topic was the 1915 *Community Development: Making the Small Town a Better Place To Live and a Better Place in Which To Do Business.* According to historian Wayne

Rasmussen, specific programs in rural development in the 1970s actually began in 1954 when rural poverty persisted even though the country was experiencing prosperity and agricultural abundance. In 1962 Congress authorized a rural renewal program, hoping to decrease the number of rural poor moving to the cities. Under this authority, Congress gave Cooperative Extension responsibility for assuming organizational and educational leadership. In 1972 Congress passed the Rural Development Act, which then became the "charter" for the work with Title V of the act defining Extension's responsibilities. A part of the mandate called for Extension to carry out research and development programs that would benefit small farmers. Since 1954, Extension studies have emphasized expansion of programs for rural community development.[11]

In addition to existing Extension facilities, officials also established regional centers for rural development. In 1971 the Cooperative State Research Service funded the first Regional Rural Development Center (for the north central region) at Iowa State University. Before long, Extension also contributed to the funding and the center became a joint effort between Cooperative Extension and the Cooperative State Research Service. Later, officials established rural development centers in the northeast region, the western region, and the southern region. At Iowa State Ronald Powers became head of the North Central Regional Rural Development Center in 1974, remaining until 1981.[12]

In 1974 the Center decided to focus on a nine-county area around Fort Dodge that could be used as a demonstration model. Powers related, "We involved a wide, cross section of citizens from within the area, key leaders, to help us identify what they thought the most pressing issue was and then [we] began to do both research and applied projects in a number of areas." The projects included comprehensive attitude surveys that identified concerns of local citizens. Powers explained that an early focus centered on recruitment and retention of business and industry in the area. Local citizens wondered whether, in terms of longevity, it was better to recruit outside businesses or try to start their own. According to Powers, the research showed, "If you want to get sustained rural development you better concentrate on the people who are already there rather than trying to make it by just going out and buying or stealing plants from somebody else." If companies were willing to leave one locality, they might be just as apt to leave the Fort Dodge area. Among other projects the Regional Rural Development Center worked with Iowans to get a better understanding about the cost of

CROP RESIDUE REMAINING in the field from last year's crop. The practice aids in water and soil conservation. Picture by Dan Burkhart, Fayette County Cooperative Extension Education Director. Courtesy of the ISU Extension Communication Services.

rural government.[13]

Extension has always been an educational agency and in the 1970s, perhaps no program better illustrated that fact than rural and community development. In 1970, for example, Extension community resource specialists were called upon to provide information for western Iowans when a large firm announced plans to build several one-stop agribusiness centers in that part of the state. Since local people had expressed concern that the new developments would have a negative impact on local businesses, Extension personnel met with these citizens to help them understand the advantages and disadvantages of the new centers. Extension staff members made it clear, however, that they would not advise people what to do; rather, they would offer materials related to the potential sales of the new businesses, its impact on local businesses, and discussion of alternatives available to communities. Then members of each community would need to make their own decision whether or not to encourage the development of the new business. Following one meeting, businesspeople decided to put out the "welcome sign." In another community the local development group retreated from an earlier decision to welcome the new business. Extension specialists also presented educational programs in business management and resource development in other parts of the state. In 1970 Extension personnel sensed that across the state interest in these programs greatly increased. According to one source, "Now that [programs in business management and resource development] had revealed that Extension had something to offer to businessmen as well as to 'traditional' clientele, the Main Streeters wanted more."[14]

In the late 1960s and early 1970s Extension community resource development specialists provided information and assistance to residents of Fenton, a town of 440 people in northwest Iowa. Like many small towns that had earlier depended on farm jobs for their well-being, Fenton saw those jobs slipping away. With the help of Extension specialists, residents formed the Fenton Community Development Corporation with a membership of about a hundred rural and town residents. The development group became the "nucleus of a new optimism" for the town and led to the establishment of the community's first library, a community youth center, and a senior citizens' center.[15]

Along with changes in programs, University Extension would also undergo considerable change in leadership during the 1970s and 1980s. In 1966 ISU officials had appointed Marvin Anderson as Dean of University Extension and Director of the Cooperative Extension

Service; in 1974 Charles Donhowe replaced Anderson. Donhowe had served as a longtime Extension staff member and since 1971 had been assistant dean of University Extension and assistant director of Cooperative Extension. In 1981 Donhowe retired and was replaced by Robert Crom, who like Donhowe had earlier served as assistant dean of extension and assistant director of Cooperative Extension. Following Crom's resignation in 1988, Ronald Powers served as interim dean and director from 1988 to 1989, when he resigned to take a position with the Missouri Cooperative Extension Service. State leader of Home Economics Extension, Elizabeth Elliott, then replaced Powers as interim dean and director.

While agricultural programs continued much the same as in the 1960s, home economics underwent major change in the 1970s and 1980s. Previously Home Economics Extension followed what one specialist called a "recipe book approach." State specialists put together a manual containing fifty different programs, covering all subject matter traditionally handled by home economists. People around the state were then free to choose from these topics when putting together their annual Plan of Work, asking state specialists to assist them in carrying out the selected programs.[16]

During the 1970s, Home Economics Extension began moving toward a program of issues approach and away from emphasis on subject matter. A harbinger of change appeared when in 1975 and 1976, the state staff put together a program called Accents for Home Economics Programming. Along with specific programs, the publication also included a one-page statement entitled, "The Time Has Come." This statement cited six instances where perhaps the time had come to think differently about home economics. The first case stated, "Perhaps the time has come to develop programs that assist families in anticipating problems rather than reacting to a crisis situation. Sometimes program efforts are in effect dealing with 'brush fires' rather than the anticipated." Other suggestions for change dealt with shifting to "a creative decision-making process rather than a problem-solving situation"; focusing on the total family rather than women; giving serious attention to interdisciplinary programming; and assisting "persons in thinking of the self as a growing, changing, and adapting individual."[17]

Elizabeth Elliott, who became head of Home Economics Extension in 1977, explained that up to the mid-1970s, the home economics program was "intended to address a very specific problem and to address that problem with the subject matter that [a particular] specialist had to bring to it." Elliott used microwave ovens as an example, noting that home economists demonstrated microwave cooking. The home economists "always got a crowd and they'd demonstrate how to make candy in the microwave and how to do this and how to do that." Elliott believed a new approach was needed.

> One of the things we did early on [in the latter 1970s] was to look at our role in different kinds of programming. What's our role in terms of food preparation? What was our role in terms of household appliances? In terms of sewing skills? . . . It seemed to me that we were at the point where we had to look at—are we going to be doing skills or are we going to be doing something else? And if you are always doing skills when something new comes out then you have to go back and teach that skill. If you are teaching concepts you can hope that they will be able to transfer that. So we started teaching what do you need to know before you buy a microwave oven?

In other words, home economists began to move toward emphasizing what consumers should consider before buying any appliance. Elliott acknowledged that there were, by the 1970s, other places such as community colleges and adult education classes where people could acquire specific skills such as clothing construction and microwave cooking.[18]

When Extension began to look at issues that typically affected a large number of people, it was clear that most were not limited to one or even two disciplines; rather, they were multidisciplinary, multiprogram areas. The pesticide program was such an issue. While entomologists, botanists, plant pathologists, and agricultural engineers were involved, so were textile specialists. Elliott explained that pesticide-contaminated clothing was (and is) a big problem.

> Families [who take] the coveralls that the man has worn [while applying pesticides] and wash them in the family washing machine and then do a load of diapers or dish towels or whatever, that residue [from pesticides] stays in the machine and is being picked up along the way. So when we have a pesticide applicator training program, there's a portion of that program that talks about how you care for the clothes.[19]

Elliott added that even seed corn caps were affected by pesticides,

COOPERATIVE EXTENSION helps with community day care facilities by offering training in child care and nutrition areas. Courtesy of the ISU Extension Communication Services.

noting that studies have shown that "the bands of those caps have collected high levels of pesticides."[20]

The 1970s also included program changes in Home Economics Extension brought about by a reduction in resources. In the early 1970s a highly popular service was provided by a state housing specialist who presented home planning and remodeling workshops to persons planning to build homes. Sometimes the specialist went into homes and worked out an individual kitchen plan based on that family's specific needs. In effect, this was a one-on-one service. While this approach produced a high level of client satisfaction, it also represented an inordinate amount of time devoted to a single client. As resources became more limited, a change in perception took place as to what the Extension housing program should be. Extension staff eventually replaced the one-on-one approach with a one-day monthly workshop (held in Ames) that people around the state could attend. Five state specialists from forestry, agricultural engineering, art and design, energy extension, and family environment presented the workshops. In the morning each specialist made a short presentation in his or her area, and in the afternoon specialists provided personal consultations to clients.[21] In this way, limited Extension resources were being stretched even further and what had become a service framework reverted back to an educational one.

In the 1970s and 1980s Home Economics Extension continued to find itself short of staff. Many counties had only a half-time worker. As in earlier times, they turned to volunteers for assistance. In the early 1980s Home Economics Extension started the Master Volunteer Programs, which according to Elizabeth Elliott, "really flowered in the last half of the eighties." Officials began the program in the area of clothing construction and later applied it to food preservation, as Elliott explained.

> We had master food preservers. We would give them a very intensive workshop and then they'd have to give us back forty hours during the course of the summer. And they'd give those forty hours by being in the office and taking questions on the phone which there are hundreds of. Or by going to a mall and having a booth and answering questions. [They were] doing the things that the home economist didn't have time to do.[22]

Elliott added that the master volunteers had "a very high level of experience and skill, more than the level of the young home economist coming out of the university now. You ask her about canning tomatoes and she'll say, 'I have to go to the book.' "[23]

While county home economists had long been responsible for dispensing specific information on topics such as home canning and nutrition, in 1975 Extension moved to lessen that burden. In that year Extension created a toll-free information line available to people all over the state. Individuals could call a home economist for information on many of the subject areas such as food and nutrition. The creation of the information line underscores the change that was taking place within the discipline as it moved away from an association with more technical expertise to a more broadly oriented, interdisciplinary approach to all family problems.[24]

In reflecting on her tenure as both assistant and later associate dean for Extension in the College of Home Economics, Elliott commented on changes in the way that programs were selected. She acknowledged that Extension has always "prided itself" on being a grass roots organization and getting input from local people regarding programs; in fact, at one time Home Economics Extension worked only "on problems that local people thought we should work on." But during the decade of the 1980s "we've tried to do a blend of things" and involve Extension staff, particularly subject matter specialists in program planning. Elliott explained that specialists are a part of a subject matter department, such as child development, and that they have national contacts. In this way, they communicate with their counterparts all over the country and are aware of current developments in their fields. Given this knowledge, specialists would then suggest timely programs which would be taken out to local groups for their reaction. At the same time local groups would make their own suggestions for program changes. Those responses would then be forwarded to the area level and staff would look for "matches" of similar interests. For example, how many groups were interested in a program on water quality? The various responses and suggestions would then be forwarded to the state level where a committee of area and county staff members as well as specialists would make the final decisions on programming. Elliott described this approach as one where specialists were being "proactive rather than always reactive." Elliott admitted that this approach sometimes produces a "friendly tension." County staff would say, "We need this," and state specialists might say, "But you have this and we think you need this."[25]

While some programs resulted from consultation between staff and clients, other programs were of a more immediate nature. In the 1970s when the nation faced an energy crisis, home economics specialists at Iowa State developed a computerized home energy audit to show homeowners how the installation of proper storm doors and windows and the use of insulation would help conserve energy, and in turn save money. They introduced the program at the Farm Progress Show held at the Amana Colonies in 1977. Before the show, specialists prepared a form to be printed in *Wallaces' Farmer* that had basic questions about individual homes such as square footage and the numbers of doors and windows. When the home-owners arrived at the Progress Show, Extension staff fed the information into a computer housed on the ISU campus, immediately receiving individualized printouts showing how many BTUs and dollars families would save if they made the proper changes. The data showed a direct comparison between current costs without changes and what the family could save if they added extra insulation and proper storm doors and windows. Mary Yearns, Extension housing specialist, recalled that the program was a huge success. "People were lined up all around our tent from the moment we opened to the time we closed. It was the hit of the whole show because here was computer technology." Later, Extension hired an assistant to take the program around the state, setting up displays and doing individual audits in malls and home shows.[26]

In the 1970s and 1980s, Home Economics Extension also devoted more time to working with limited resource families. The Expanded Food and Nutrition Program, first set up in 1968, continued to be a major concern of county home economists and state and area specialists. Other programs for low income Iowans, as well, seemed a natural outgrowth of President Lyndon Johnson's War on Poverty initiated in the 1960s. One Extension program dealt with the housing needs of low income families. Here, the state housing specialist presented information to area specialists about available programs, such as government-assisted housing, specifically focusing on what could be done about the needs of low income people in the locality.

One program, Operation Ship Shape, proved to be particularly popular with low income Iowans. In 1974 housing specialist Yearns and forest products specialist Dean Prestemon, developed the program to teach people to handle their own home repairs. Yearns explained, "We got an old van here on campus and we trained a [family environment] student or graduate to go out and teach simple home repairs to low income families and targeted inner city neigh-borhoods." The program began with the first aide working in the Cedar Rapids area in May 1974. Later, officials repeated it in Fort Dodge and Davenport. Some aides had especially equipped vans but one housing aide in Davenport, Joan Zelle, simply packed her tool kits in her car and began "doing a lot of door knocking."[27]

Reflecting on Operation Ship Shape, Yearns explained that she was particularly concerned with concentrating on women. "It was really an empowerment notion at that time. If we teach women—I mean it's still bad today but then it was just terrible—oh, that's a man's job. And here we have single parents and oh, that's a man's job to fix a lamp, fix the leaky faucets." Yearns explained that she wrote "a simple little publication" that covered many of these repairs. She added, "We made a point of teaching women to reach other women." The message was clear: "You need to do it. You can learn it. If you can read a recipe book, you can do it."[28]

An important program carried over from the 1960s by Home Economics Extension was the EFNEP (Expanded Food and Nutrition Educational Program). In 1970, Congress appropriated $48 million for the program, an increase of $28 million from the previous year. By 1971 nationally, the program was employing 7,300 full-time food aides and serving a total of 293,000 families. In Iowa in 1972 and 1973, it was active in twenty-five locations with more than 3,000 families participating. Programs to involve food aides and limited resource homemakers took many forms. At Friendly House, a community center in Davenport, Extension held a day-long event where people could sample ethnic foods and obtain information on good nutrition. At the same time community agencies had an opportunity to publicize their services and homemakers could display some of their crafts. Planners provided a nursery for much of the day.[29]

Sometimes EFNEP led to other types of programs. In the summer of 1972 Jane Cornelius, an Iowa State University undergraduate and a summer aide for EFNEP in Waterloo, helped set up an exchange program between farm and city youths. Earlier that summer Waterloo had been plagued by racial strife. Cornelius explained, "This [was] one way to dissolve fears and prejudices people have about each other." A major challenge was finding parents willing to participate; eventually Cornelius helped set up eight exchanges. She reported that "after the exchanges the parents had fewer fears about the other's place of residence and were happy that their youngsters got along so well with different kinds of people." She added, "Most of the rural boys and girls had never known a black child before."[30]

Although few people might have questioned the need for such programs as EFNEP, that was no guarantee that people agreed on

Extension's involvement. Extension Dean Robert Crom related that the move to deal with such urban problems was "not without its stresses." He added that "there were some who felt well, you're stealing our Extension Service . . . because you used to spend all your time with us and now you're dividing your time." The move proved difficult both because it included a new area for Extension and also because officials found it necessary to "bring along the people who had felt a high degree of ownership and direction on this system to help them understand."[31]

Along with home economics, important changes were also under way in 4-H during the 1970s. The 4-H project, whether it was a baby beef or a piece of refinished furniture, became less important. Instead 4-Hers, both male and female, began to look more frequently at programs that emphasized the development in personal growth or the development in citizenship. C. J. Gauger, who became state leader of 4-H programs in Iowa in 1959 (and remained in that position for twenty years), recalled that during the 1960s and 1970s more emphasis was placed "on human development . . . living skills . . . citizenship . . . leadership." He added that his staff moved to "more nearly individualize the curriculum through which [young people] could learn and grow."[32] At the same time 4-Hers had a wider choice of projects. In his biennial report for 1975–1977, Extension Director Donhowe underscored that change when he listed projects such as creative arts, dog care, aerospace engineering, and photography along with the more traditional projects such as beef, horticulture, and food and nutrition.[33]

Paul C. Taff, reflecting in 1972 on many years of work with Iowa Extension, also commented that there was "increased emphasis on developing the total individual 4-H member rather than emphasizing the project." Taff observed that the scope of 4-H projects had been broadened "beyond the early ones, which were oriented to livestock and crops for boys and to food preservation and clothing for girls." He added, "Not only have we added projects in new and advanced areas for the 4-H member today, but we have also added educational depth. For example, livestock projects now include more on nutrition, breeding, management, and marketing than they did in the early years." Taff observed that there had also been change for girl 4-Hers as home economics projects included money management, consumer education, and nutrition. He noted that some girls were designing their own clothes rather than using patterns. As if to emphasize these changes, a young woman at the fiftieth National 4-H Congress in

Chicago was selling buttons that proclaimed, "4-H Ain't All Cows and Cooking."[34]

In his report to the 1975–1977 *Iowa Book of Agriculture,* Extension Director Charles Donhowe referred to the philosophy behind some of these changes in 4-H.

> The purpose of 4-H is to help young people become self-directing, productive, and contributing members of society. To accomplish the purpose stated above, subject matter knowledge alone is not enough. Youth need to know how to apply knowledge in different situations that confront them. There is a constant challenge to develop new materials that identify and stress combining subject matter with relevant life skills. Learners not only assimilate information, but are learning how to use it.[35]

There was also recognition in the 1970s that even though youngsters lived on farms or in small towns, they were not immune to problems such as drug and alcohol abuse, child abuse, and crime.

In the 1970s 4-H widened its membership net to include more youth in urban areas. As Wayne Rasmussen has pointed out, some urban areas had always been involved in 4-H but these would be expanded in the 1970s and 1980s. In 1972 4-H nationally had a total enrollment of 4,080,000 young people. Of that number, approximately 35 percent lived on farms, 42 percent in towns under ten thousand population, 13 percent in cities between ten thousand and fifty thousand population, 5 percent in suburbs of cities with more than fifty thousand, and 5 percent in cities with populations over fifty thousand. One of the first major efforts to increase the number of 4-H clubs in urban areas came in the 1950s when Russell Mawby, in cooperation with Michigan 4-H, established programs in Detroit, Flint, Grand Rapids, and Kalamazoo. Congress earmarked $5 million for 4-H work in urban communities in 1973, resulting in even more 4-H work in those areas. That money provided a supplement to $4.5 million Congress appropriated for 4-H nutrition education under the Expanded Food and Nutrition Education Program in 1969.[36]

The outreach of Iowa 4-H was also expanded during the 1970s. C. J. Gauger explained, "We broadened the outreach to other youth, ones who were not members of the organized 4-H clubs. [This was what] we called an inter-organizations approach." On one occasion, for example, FFA members, church groups, and students from Ames High School joined 4-Hers for a leadership conference at the 4-H Camp near Madrid.[37]

In the 1970s African American youths also took part in leadership training while attending 4-H camp. Gauger related that Willis Bright, an African American who worked as a summer employee in the dean of students office, suggested the idea. During the summer of 1975, forty-two campers came from seven Iowa cities to attend a week-long session where all campers and all staff but one were African American. Workshops presented sessions on a variety of topics ranging from tips on multimedia presentations to assertiveness training; the emphasis, however, was on developing leadership potential and leadership training. Gauger recalled that during the week leaders, such as the city manager from Des Moines and the Ames mayor, came to speak to the group. Gauger explained, "We wanted to, in a sense, help build a little different image of what Extension and 4-H leadership programs could do."[38]

Extension 4-H staff also provided a follow-up experience for the African American youths. After the workshops ended, agencies such as the YMCA, the Neighborhood Youth Corps, and Extension agreed to hire some campers for the remainder of the summer. Willis Bright, who served as camp co-director, explained: "We wanted specific groups the youth could attach to when they went home. We tried to get jobs for them in human services, but not just the jobs young people usually get. We wanted them to get in on the planning and organizational areas of an agency." Campers from each community selected a community problem on which to work: One group worked toward getting courses on the history of African Americans into their school; another group worked on setting up a better program at the youth center in Sioux City.[39]

Reflecting on his twenty years as state 4-H leader, Gauger believed that many positive changes had taken place in the 4-H programs. He also expressed a basic disappointment.

> We failed to find ways and means of programming effectively throughout all of the areas of Extension. . . . I think there was a tendency years ago to think of 4-H as a junior agriculture, junior home economics . . . basically oriented towards teaching of skills, cows and cooking. We tried to point out that there were some learnings that go in the other direction—that really . . . are more nearly process skills or living skills. . . . But when you start talking about these, some of the old guard have real trouble. They say, "Hey, you're against steers, you're against subject matter." That's not what it is at all.

Basically, he concluded, the purpose is to provide opportunities for "kids to grow into their full potential."[40]

By the latter half of the 1970s the "giddy years" or the "glory years" of the 1970s had begun to fade. Rural Iowans found themselves experiencing major economic difficulties. Prices began to drop in 1976 and in just one year, 1977, production costs rose between 7 and 10 percent. Underscoring those concerns, farmers organized a new group, the American Agricultural Movement. Farmers certainly had faced difficult times before, but as Gilbert Fite points out the prosperous years of 1973 and 1974 had a "disruptive effect" on American agriculture as farmers "mistakenly concluded that these unusual conditions would become the norm in future years." Given the prosperity, many farmers purchased additional land, new machinery, and generally upgraded their living standard. Younger farmers especially went into heavy debt, which could only be supported if prices remained high.[41]

During the 1970s and early 1980s American farmers experienced a roller coaster effect regarding land prices. Between 1970 and 1981 an acre of farmland rose nationally from $300 to $1,700. As land increased in value, the change affected both lenders and borrowers. As historian Mark Friedberger has pointed out in his study of the 1980s farm crisis, "Lenders looked at soaring land values and rushed to lend, just as farmers looked at tax breaks and low real interest rates and stampeded to borrow, fearing that if they waited too long, they would lose their big chance." By the early 1980s, however, farmers witnessed major changes in the nation's economy as land prices fell dramatically and farm prices also declined. In turn, a substantial number of farm families found themselves in dire financial straits.[42]

In his study of the farm crisis, Friedberger writes that between 1982 and 1984, traditional farm support organizations, such as Cooperative Extension, did little to deal with the emerging farm crisis, preferring to minimize its severity. During that time, other groups, such as the Iowa Farm Unity Coalition, formed in January 1982, and Prairiefire, provided support for farm families. The latter group provided much of the impetus for advocacy work with Iowa farmers. Friedberger sees the Iowa Farm Unity Coalition as being "alone in its monitoring of the condition of farm families at a personal level" between 1982 and 1984 when Coalition counselors assisted farm people with legal, financial, and emotional problems.[43]

The farm crisis of the 1980s received wide coverage in state newspapers and on radio and television. The *Des Moines Register* in particular kept its readers well informed of the traumatic conditions facing the farm population. The media documented the many bankruptcies, foreclosures, and even suicides. The nightly television news frequently showed an array of crosses erected around the state to show the increasing number of families who had lost their land. The movie, *Country,* filmed in Iowa also focused national attention on the crisis. Even legal authorities noted the devastating effect on Iowans. An Iowa bankruptcy judge, Richard Stageman, testified at a federal hearing in Denver dealing with a possible change in the bankruptcy law for farmers.

> I cannot count the instances when I have witnessed adult, self-contained, weathered men give testimony punctuated with despairing sobs. . . . There have been too many nights that I have laid awake at night with tears in my own eyes reflecting on the day's proceedings.[44]

While the "congenital optimism of farmers" had affected many individuals as well as farm organizations even during the early 1980s, by the spring of 1985 the harsh reality could no longer be ignored. Iowa farm families and subsequently the state's economy were in a bad way. Between 1981 and 1985 Iowa land had lost 55 percent of its value. More specifically, between 1984 and 1985 the value of an average Iowa farm had fallen 25 percent. Although 40 percent of Iowa farmers would indicate in 1986 that they "were making a comfortable living," the situation by mid-decade had all Iowans concerned.[45]

By 1984 the Iowa Extension Service began to implement programs designed to deal with the emergency. In that year with a $200,000 appropriation from the General Assembly and other state funds, Extension initiated a program called ASSIST. It consisted of four parts: general awareness, FarmAid, community resource committees, and agricultural credit short courses. The first part, general awareness, called for county Extension directors to hold meetings for community leaders and local officials to inform them of the "scope and severity of the farm financial problems."[46]

The second part of ASSIST consisted of the program's financial management component, FarmAid, which provided financial analysis and counseling to farm families. Under this focus area, approximately thirty ASSIST associates were hired part time; all had four-year college degrees and some had master's degrees. Trained and supervised by the seven area farm management specialists, the associates, in cooperation with the county Extension staff, visited with farm families to find out who really needed help. A part of their job was to gather financial information from the participating families and feed that information into a computer-generated program. Farmers then received free confidential computer analyses of their financial situations. In 1985 and 1986 almost 3,500 farm families took advantage of the service. Former Extension official W. John Johnson remembered, as an interesting sidelight of the ASSIST program, that lender institutions had great confidence in the computer-generated information and in fact, some required that information before making a final decision on loans.[47]

The remaining two parts of the program dealt with community resources and classroom training. The first focus helped local citizens set up community resource committees to deal with farm stress situations. Often the first move was to put together a community resource directory. The last part of the ASSIST program offered short courses for agricultural lenders, professional farm managers, attorneys, and farm financial advisers who worked with stressed farm families. Courses dealt with financial planning and analysis, tax and legal concerns in financial restructuring, and communication and counseling techniques.[48]

A few months later Extension, in cooperation with the Iowa Department of Human Services and the United Way of Central Iowa, set up a toll-free telephone hotline referral service known as the Iowa Rural Concern Hotline. Originally officials financed this service through donations from the Farm Bureau, FmHA, and the Farm Credit System. In 1986 the General Assembly appropriated money to continue the service. The hotline served as a referral agency helping callers locate legal, financial, emotional, and educational assistance. The Extension Service hired nine counselors including several exfarmers, a minister, and a nurse. All received special training in dealing with stressful situations. W. John Johnson remembered interviewing some of the prospective employees.

> The people we hired were people who had been through trauma themselves. We hired several farmers who had lost their farms but who had a bent toward working with people, they cared a lot and were fairly good communicators. . . . Occasionally someone would call in and say, "I'm just ready to commit suicide." And then of course, we worked out systems so that when that message came the signal would go out, the location where they [were], and we had

systems worked out to try to cope with that.

According to information tabulated by Extension, between the time the hotline was established in February 1985 and May 1986, 15,544 calls were taken.[49]

In other areas of Extension, dealing with the farm crisis also became a priority. Virginia Olsen Molgaard began work as an individual and family specialist in family environment in 1985. Extension programs in this area were a part of the ASSIST programming effort. According to the Home Economics Extension Annual Report for 1985, "The major efforts for maximizing individual and family strengths were directed at farm families in financial crisis. Programming focused on individual and family stress management, helping schoolchildren under stress, and dealing with blame in the current rural crisis." Along with other specialists, Molgaard conducted in-service programs that dealt with stress management programming for field staff and conducted training groups for self-help groups. Home economics staff also conducted workshops with other professionals who worked with farm families such as farm management staff, mental health workers, and ministers. Schoolchildren represented another focal group for Extension specialists like Molgaard. They helped teachers deal more effectively with children whose families were undergoing stress. Molgaard also prepared "a help sheet" for farm wives seeking off-farm employment.[50]

It soon became apparent that during the 1980s helping to solve farm families' economic problems called for involvement of all Extension staff members, including home economists as well as agriculturalists and agricultural economists. Elizabeth Elliott related that agricultural specialists began to report, "I go into this family to run this computer program on their finances and we never really get it done because they are talking about how they're worried about what's happening with their kids or they haven't been able to take care of the medical needs because their income has dropped." Elliott recalled that even as late as May 1990 a group of agriculturalists and home economists were talking about "what we need to do to be ready because we see another crunch period coming with families this spring and fall. And there were two or three of those men saying you can't just talk about production agriculture, you've got to talk about what is happening with families." Elliott added, "And that is just a revelation to hear."[51]

Another family environment specialist, Cynthia Needles Fletcher, worked in the area of family financial management. Like her specialist colleagues, Fletcher also devoted time to problems engendered by the farm crisis. Among the different programs offered were in-service education for Extension staff working with ASSIST and helping to plan and teach workshops for volunteer budget counselors. Given the poor economic conditions that affected many parts of Iowa in the mid-1980s, Fletcher also taught a variety of workshops for the general public on financial management including Savings and Investment Basics.[52]

During times of economic stress Iowa families were not typically going to build new homes, so Extension specialists put together a program that allowed families to improve their current housing at no cost. In 1985 housing specialist Mary Yearns and Lois Warme, Extension specialist in art and design, put together the Modest Home Makeover program. Recognizing that a home "is intimately tied to a family's emotional and physical well-being," Extension specialists started by going into a few homes and working with families to analyze family activities "to see whether rooms could be put to different uses." Extension staff moved furniture from room to room to create more useful groupings and to improve traffic patterns. In one home in northeast Iowa, a delighted farm couple watched one room being divided into several activity areas. The farm wife exclaimed, "It's the same room but we have more space. . . . She [the specialist] moved every piece of furniture in the house except the dining room table." The first year Extension specialists offered the program in one county, in two counties the next year, and seventeen counties the third year. The initial participating families took part in open houses where the results were shown to other interested parties.[53]

Extension and other organizations would sometimes discover that providing the right kind of assistance was difficult. Farmers have historically been recognized as being independent and self-sufficient, preferring to handle their own personal problems rather than seeking outside help. As Mark Friedberger points out, when people admitted they needed help, they were looked upon as being weak or being failures. Not all community resource personnel, moreover, were capable of providing assistance. Small town lawyers often had had little experience dealing with agricultural bankruptcy. Local ministers sometimes refrained from seeking out needy farm families, feeling that their ministerial training had not prepared them for that situation. Even some social and mental health workers did not feel comfortable dealing with farm people.[54]

In the opinion of one longtime Extension official, some personnel were able to respond to the traumatic conditions, while others were not. W. John Johnson recalled, "Some were able to do this; they had empathy; they cared, but there were others of our own staff . . . who couldn't handle it very well. It was so traumatic to them and they just couldn't really figure out what to do with this." For many Extension personnel, however, Johnson had high praise, noting that many did a superb job. He added, "Some of our staff, as you might guess they would, some of them took this burden upon themselves and they became depressed. Some of them became almost ill and they would work ungodly hours. Now, the staff didn't all respond in this way, of course." Johnson concluded that some Extension workers would never be the same because of it. Most Extension personnel had not been trained to deal with emotional or psychological needs. As Johnson explained, "Remember, we just came through some of the best times in agriculture. That's how we were acclimated to think and all at once this fell upon the people we worked with. And upon our staff."[55]

Dan Merrick also recalled difficult times as county director and agriculturist in Cass County. "We did have a lot of counseling there, a lot of stress with people not knowing whether they were going to be able to buy feed for the livestock, etc." On one occasion, Merrick got a call at 3:30 A.M. from a farmer he had not talked to in five years. Merrick explained, "The more I talked the more I became concerned about just what was taking place. Here again, he could not sleep. He wanted somebody to talk to. So that was a very stressful period, I would say, [especially] 83, 84, and 85." Merrick also recalled a farmer coming into the Extension office and confiding, "As I cultivated my corn, I thought three or four times about killing myself. But then I also knew that I would be leaving that burden on my wife and children." Merrick added that the farmer was no longer in farming but was progressing well in a business. Although Merrick conceded that most Extension staff were not trained to handle emotional problems, he noted that they did participate in in-service training sessions that helped them to interpret behavior and respond to the crisis.[56]

While programs like ASSIST dealt with financial matters, publicizing community resources, and family stress, it was felt that even more emphasis was needed on the emotional distress of rural families. In 1985 a new federal program made funds available to provide help for farm families "in real distress to work through their difficult dilemmas." Determining that many Iowa farm families needed more help than could be provided through the Rural

Concern Hotline and ASSIST, Iowa Extension staff submitted a proposal to USDA outlining a program that would offer more intensive, long-term assistance to distressed families. That program was known as Taking Charge in Changing Times.[57]

Once they received the grant, the staff created what Don Broshar—a major participant in the project—called a case management approach. Staff went out to work intensively with distressed families for six to eight weeks to link them with resources in the community and help them deal with transitions in their lives. The staff quickly discovered, however, that six to eight weeks was not sufficient, and were thus spending even more time with each family. Broshar described the approach as using an empowerment model that "was very important in the sense that for the first time I think in the recent history of Extension, we were not going out as Extension employees and saying, 'We're here with the solution to your problem.' Instead, we were going out and saying, 'Okay, tell us . . . about your problems.' " Broshar explained that in this way the families could identify their problems and decide what they wanted to work on first. Broshar added that "the empowerment model came in the sense [that] we had no guidelines for the families, or very few guidelines. The first year of the program the guideline was distressed farm families—economically and emotionally distressed farm families." The second year staff expanded the program to include some families in small rural communities. Throughout the first four years of the program, Broshar estimated that between 2,500 and 3,500 families took part.[58]

Broshar also related another aspect of the program. Staff did not "spend a lot of time concentrating on the fact that we were from Extension" since the family may have had negative feelings about Extension or perhaps was not familiar with the organization. Rather, Extension personnel concentrated on developing good rapport with the families, developing a relationship that allowed them to talk about their problems. Broshar felt it was important that staff members went into clients' homes, talking to them on their own turf, being very careful not to be judgmental. This permitted the families "to vent their anger and their frustration and then [the Extension staff could] help them identify small increments of what [could] be done." Broshar explained that many of the families involved were "extremely immobilized." They were "so emotionally distraught and so economically strapped that they really [didn't] know where to go and what to do to get started."[59]

Broshar viewed the program as helping families deal with

changes and transitions in their lives. In some cases this involved helping families find a new occupation; at other times it involved finding off-farm employment for the farmer to supplement farm income; sometimes it involved helping farm women find jobs off the farm. These changes could be traumatic. If a woman went to work off the farm, "that created lots of confusion and change for the male in the family who would take over some of the household duties and child rearing kinds of things." If both the husband and wife would begin working off the farm, that meant that the children had to do more work at home. Broshar believes that the 1980s farm crisis has actually restructured family life in terms of rural management. Families with "a traditional rural view, who believe that the father takes care of the farm operation and the wife takes care of the house and children, that's not going to cut it anymore. And that creates lots of distress." Broshar added that as a result, more farm couples are divorcing and more social problems are evident among farm people such as family violence and child abuse.[60]

Ironically, while Extension people were called upon to extend support to farm families who might lose their land, some Extension workers were fearful of losing their own jobs. Given the difficult farm situation, Extension itself faced problems in that appropriations were cut resulting in a reduction of staff. During the early 1980s Extension, along with other state organizations, experienced at least four reversions of state funds. Robert Crom explained that because of state reversions and reduction of federal funds "we found a plateauing of resources at both the federal and state level at a time when inflation was still moving forward [with the result] that we had to reduce staff if we were to continue to keep the bank balance in the black." In response to this situation, Crom in November 1984, appointed a committee of twenty-six people (thirteen were staff and thirteen were constituent leaders) to do "what today we call strategic planning." With this report in hand, Extension over the next two years cut its staff by 60 professional positions. That reduced the total staff from about 430 to 370. Crom explained that Extension made cuts at all levels including county and area positions and from the ranks of the state specialists and administrative positions on campus. Some paraprofessional positions were also eliminated. At the same time officials reduced the number of area offices from twelve to seven. Reflecting on these reductions, Crom concluded, "We have gone through a very stressful time."[61]

For the general public, cuts at the county level were probably the most obvious. Before the 1960s many counties had three full-time employees—the agricultural director, the home economist, and a 4-H and youth worker. With funding reductions, however, split appointments became more common with a staff person serving two counties. Typically the home economist and the youth worker divided their time between two counties while each county had a full-time agriculturist. In southern Iowa, however, all three positions might be divided between two counties. Dan Merrick explained that the budget tightening of the 1980s meant that each staff member had to wear many hats. He cited one instance where an individual carried the title of County Extension Agriculturist/Community Resource Development Specialist/and 4-H and Youth Director. Merrick added, "You can imagine the frustration, the different training that person has to go to as opposed to myself as an agriculturist."[62]

While many farm families experienced severe stress because of financial difficulties, town residents sometimes found themselves in the same situation. In 1984 retail sales in small Iowa towns (less than five hundred residents) were down 14 percent leading to a loss of many businesses.[63] Even before the farm crisis of the 1980s, however, both Extension economists and community resource development specialists worked with small communities to help revitalize their economic life. Rural small town business districts had suffered as a result of the loss of nearby farm population and the development of large shopping malls in neighboring communities. A good system of roads, moreover, made it easy for small town residents to travel to larger communities. In small towns the farm crisis led to the loss of many businesses such as clothing, furniture, and drugstores; some communities even lost grocery stores and service stations. As ISU Extension economist Kenneth E. Stone pointed out, "When a store closes in a small community, a part of the town dies much as a dead limb on a diseased tree, usually never to come back." To help communities deal with these difficulties, Extension staff provided management training to local businesspeople.[64]

In Liscomb, for example, by the early 1980s the only major businesses remaining were the grain elevator and feed mill. Extension personnel helped local citizens evaluate possible alternatives and take a survey to determine local attitudes toward forming a community corporation to build a combination convenience grocery, restaurant, and service station. Community residents and nearby farm families then purchased $40,000 worth of shares and, along with a Small Business Administration (SBA) guaranteed loan they were able to build the facility. While the economic benefits are important to the community, as economist Stone has pointed out, perhaps the sociological benefits to the community are even more important. "For the first time in years, the people have a public and convenient meeting place for socializing while eating, shopping, or refueling."[65]

Later in the 1980s, Extension set up Community Economic Development workshops which also provided economic expertise for Iowa towns. By 1988, sixty communities had participated in the program. In Oskaloosa citizens managed to attract two new industries, build a shopping mall, and begin a Main Street renewal program after participating in the one-day workshop.[66]

The 1980s brought not only a new direction for Extension programs in rural communities, but also for programs in Extension agriculture. During the 1970s and early 1980s, Extension agriculturists had continued to emphasize production, believing that greater production of corn, soybeans, and livestock would solve economic problems. By the mid-1980s, however, changes were underway, both in the thinking of Extension personnel as well as that of other Iowans. Jerald DeWitt, Director of Agricultural Programs in Cooperative Extension since 1987, believes that the experiences of Extension agricultural personnel in the mid-1980s led to a recognition that a new direction was needed. DeWitt explained that when Extension staff presented programs around the state in 1984 and 1985, they were challenged directly by their constituents who asked, "Why can't you turn this thing around?" DeWitt acknowledged that Extension staff did not have the answers but they "were on the firing line." DeWitt believes that this was the first time that Extension had faced such confrontations. Previously "Everything we said had been accepted as truth, we were from [ISU], we had the answers. The 1980s proved us wrong and we lost our innocence during that period." The confrontations, according to DeWitt, left many Extension people devastated, but it caused Extension staff to "break out of some norms and do some things differently." One lesson that agriculturists learned was that "the hurts were deeper than just financial. As we got into the eighties, we found that not only was it [a loss of] profit, it was also emotional stress in our farm population."[67]

In addition to ASSIST and the Rural Concern Hotline, which DeWitt viewed as "a dramatic change and shift . . . and an intermingling of [Extension] resources," the Groundwater Protection Act of 1987 was a major departure point for Extension agriculture. In that year the Iowa General Assembly passed the groundwater act, which "literally shook us to our roots and provided us with immense opportunity to do business in a different manner." The act provided not for regulation of groundwater quality, but for the means to educate people to work for better groundwater quality. Two major elements in that program were demonstration and education, with Extension playing the key role in holding demonstrations, field days, and one-on-one activities with state farmers. DeWitt reflected that it came as quite a shock to him that, in effect, Extension in 1987 was really going back to Extension in 1914. In the 1980s Extension staff was high tech, with satellites, computers, and information networks, but here "we were going back to our roots." The result was that Extension had between one-half and three-quarters of a million dollars to "put on demonstrations in many counties on pesticide management, or no pesticide use, protection of groundwater, [and reduction of nitrogen] . . . a very intensive program." As DeWitt explained, in the past Extension had often been accused of trying to promote pesticide use and "suddenly we were in the camp of . . . trying to almost eliminate it."[68]

The major shift in the direction of some Extension agricultural programs did not come wholly as a result of the farm crisis of the 1980s, however. DeWitt believes that it really came about because of a variety of conditions that came together in the mid-1980s and produced "a teachable moment" that was recognized by many Extension staff. The first consideration was economics. Many people had been badly hurt by the 1980s farm crisis and were probably more receptive to new thinking. Secondly, Iowans were becoming more and more concerned about health and the environment. The State Geological Survey had been monitoring groundwater since the early 1980s and chemicals such as atrazine had been detected in the water supply. As DeWitt explained, "Suddenly there was an environmental concern which was wrapped around water quality; it wasn't an environmental concern wrapped around other things, but it was around water quality." About the same time the state legislature, which included environmentalists like Paul Johnson, passed the Groundwater Protection Act. DeWitt also noted that by the mid-1980s the state contained individuals like himself, extensionists Mike Duffy and Jerry Miller, and Johnson who had come of age in the 1960s and early 1970s when they had become concerned about environmental issues. By the mid-1980s, many of these people were in positions of authority where they could begin to act on their concerns. With all these factors operating, DeWitt believes that the outcome was a new day in Extension agriculture as staff began to support environmental issues and develop programs in sustainable agriculture.[69]

Extension agriculturalists also developed new programs that led to "partnering" between Extension and groups like the Practical Farmers of Iowa and Iowa Organic Growers and Buyers Association, which in 1980 were regarded as "fringe agricultural groups." DeWitt explained that in the late 1980s Extension hired an individual to work with the latter group full time in the Muscatine area. At the same time Extension agriculturalists helped the Practical Farmers of Iowa (PFI) secure money from the state legislature, which resulted in a person "who wears an Extension hat," resides on campus, and works full time as the PFI coordinator. In DeWitt's opinion, Iowa was the first Extension Service in the nation "to develop a formal relationship, where dollars were shared . . . with any type of farmers' environmental group." As DeWitt observed, had he been Director of Extension for Agricultural Programs in 1980, given his positive views on sustainable agriculture, he would not have survived.[70]

Throughout the 1980s ISU Extension, reflecting a national trend, also implemented a change in emphasis from programs to issues. This change has affected all four major program areas. Robert Crom believes this was a positive move and that Extension needed "to zero in on issues that are critical to the public agenda." He explained that "an issue is more focused than just good health. . . . We identify an issue such as restoring profitability to agriculture or water quality or family economic stability, or one that is diverging at the national level now called Youth at Risk." In effect, each program area such as home economics or resource community development resolves it. Crom believes that the issues approach is a more comprehensive way of dealing with a problem where education is involved.

> It lends itself also in the delivery sense in that it isn't a matter of going out with a set of meetings or doing a few radio broadcasts or using satellite up-link but it is a matter of planning all that in a more comprehensive sense. It is saying, all right, there are a number of sub-audiences out there that we need to reach, that we're going to make an impact on and what we need to do with this audience is different than what we need to do with that audience.[71]

Another change that affected Extension in the 1970s and 1980s was affirmative action. In reflecting on his seven years as head of Cooperative Extension, Crom believes that the organization made headway in this area, particularly in the 1980s. "I think we're a different Extension Service than we were ten years ago in terms of recognizing the gender concerns. We have a substantial increase in

FIELD DAYS at Iowa State University outlying research farms have been a traditional avenue for farmers
to keep current on new research and practices for
decades. Courtesy of the ISU Extension Communication Services.

the number of women who are county Extension directors. I think we have paid considerable attention to making sure that salaries are comparable regardless of gender. We have worked at affirmative action in recruitment of minorities." Crom added that he believed personnel in the four program areas "understand more about each other across those units and that we work in a [more] synergistic way."[72]

Elizabeth Elliott also reflected on gender changes among the Extension staff. She observed that Peggy Hafke of Woodbury County was the first woman hired as county director in the early 1980s and that by 1988 Cooperative Extension had over thirty female county directors.

> [Women] brought a really important element to the management of the county office. They've tackled some tough problems and they have brought . . . just a different viewpoint to looking at problems. And it is interesting now to go to a meeting of county directors. We had a series last fall and to see the interplay between the men and women and to see the men looking to the women for answers to some kinds of questions. It's really an evolutionary kind of thing.[73]

At the same time women have started moving into longtime traditionally male specialty areas such as agriculture, farm management, and community resource development.[74]

The increase in female directors is only one of a considerable number of changes taking place at the county level in the 1980s. Cass County director Dan Merrick stated that not only have changes taken place within Extension but also among the primary clientele that he and his co-workers serve. In his early days as an Extension director, Merrick would have farmers calling the Extension office, asking him to come out to their farm and identify some insect. Sometimes after he just returned from such a farm visit, another farmer from the same township would call, requesting the same type of assistance. Merrick explained that today a farmer is much more likely to call the Extension office and describe the insect himself, getting confirmation of the type of insect over the telephone. He used this example to underscore his belief that Iowa farmers today are very knowledgeable in all areas that affect their operations.[75]

In the 1980s county staff also continued to see a change in the type of clients seeking information. Merrick observed that at least half of his time was spent with nonfarm people who were interested in information on lawn care, gardens, shrubberies, and use of chemicals. He recalled a woman who called hysterically to report finding thirteen garter snakes in her garage. Merrick suggested that she get a hoe but she replied, "I can't get that close to it." He added that people have all types of requests such as how to get rid of bats, as well as painting and ventilation problems. He concluded, "We even get some people who just want to come in and talk about their personal relationships in the family. Those are areas that you would not expect in a job description."[76]

The clientele of Extension specialists in agriculture has also changed in the past decade or two. Regis Voss, an Extension soil fertility specialist in agronomy, explained that in the past several years a primary client of agronomy specialists has been the agribusiness community. When Voss started in his present position in 1964, the Extension Service was still the main source of information for Iowa farmers. That is no longer true, however, as trained agronomists and others with scientific training who work for fertilizer and chemical companies now have more contact with Iowa farmers than Extension. Because of that fact, several years ago Voss and other Extension agronomists decided that the agribusiness people should become a major client so Extension could help them remain current in their fields. Every fall Extension agronomists go out to each of the seven Extension areas and present a program called Update to the agribusiness clientele. They follow that with a series in late February in which they present two-day meetings providing in-depth material in areas such as soil fertility, entomology, and insect and weed management. Voss described these presentations as "a self-supporting endeavor" where participants pay a fee to cover costs of the meetings.[77]

A second change in Agronomy Extension, representative of changes throughout ISU Extension, is that specialists are now expected to be "good scientists *and* good educators." Voss, who coordinates Agronomy Extension, explained that in his field, some specialists have 50 percent of their time designated for research. They submit the same grants for funding projects as regular ISU faculty and other expectations are also much the same. Voss explained:

> From my point of view I expect all of our Extension staff . . . to be up-to-date, to conduct some research, to attend the professional meetings and essentially evolve as a recognized expert in their field.

In other words, in the North Central Region everyone of our staff ought to be recognized by their cohorts or contemporaries at other institutions as being outstanding or a knowledgeable individual.[78]

While the ISU Cooperative Extension Service has experienced both good and bad years throughout its seventy-five years of existence, perhaps more than any others the decades of the 1970s and 1980s represent the very best of times and the very worst of times. During the euphoric days of the early and mid-1970s, farm families enjoyed flush economic times. At the same time Extension was experiencing a great deal of success. After all, how could anyone complain about a system that worked? Iowa farmers were producing more corn, soybeans, and hogs than ever before and being amply rewarded for their efforts. While Iowans were beginning to pay some attention to environmental issues, the voices of concern were still muted. Like many Americans, Iowans seemed to believe that the good times would continue indefinitely.

By contrast, the late 1970s and 1980s witnessed almost a complete turnaround for roughly one-third of Iowa's farm population and many of the state's small town businesses. Although Extension seemed slow in responding to these changes, when they did act, they did so in a comprehensive manner, developing programs that covered every major aspect of the crisis. In effect, the 1980s called for a major response by Extension, probably taxing its staff and resources more than at any other time since the Great Depression. These demands came at a time when Extension's staff was being reduced.

Perhaps the experience of the ISU Cooperative Extension Service best reflects the basic nature of the organization. As Paul D. Warner and James A. Christensen point out in their assessment of Extension, the organization has not been restricted to one program or one activity, but rather "has been allowed to adjust to changing times." Probably there is no other period in Extension's history when this assessment has been more accurate than in the euphoric 1970s and the distressing 1980s.[79]

9

Seventy-five Years
of Change

By 1989, the Cooperative Extension Service had reached its seventy-fifth year; various celebrations were held around the country commemorating that event. A highlight was the publication of Wayne Rasmussen's national study, *Taking the University to the People: Seventy-Five Years of Cooperative Extension.* For three-quarters of a century, Extension had served (and continues to serve) as a primary source of education for rural Americans. The history of Iowa's Cooperative Extension Service from 1914 to 1989 includes both people and programs. It is a history of the Extension staff and the educational programs—dedicated to bringing about prosperity, innovation, and change—that have been disseminated to Iowa's rural and urban populations.

In reflecting on the history of Extension in Iowa, Marvin Anderson perceived three basic stages from Extension's beginning in 1903 to the time of his retirement as Dean of University Extension and Director of Cooperative Extension in 1972. Anderson described the first stage as a time when Extension personnel had to work hard simply to convince Iowa farmers of the relevancy of the organization.

In effect, county agents had to "sell" Extension to the people. The second stage, beginning around 1930, was a time "when hybrid seed corn and all the technology came out from our research that was a direct benefit to farm people." At this point Anderson viewed Extension as something of a transmission belt, carrying the new information to the farm population. Anderson recalled that by this time farmers were receptive to new information: "They were grabbing for it." The third stage, in the 1950s and 1960s, involved a more formalized educational system. Anderson described Extension officials then as the "architects of information education." Extension "dealt not just with transmission of facts but . . . with an educational process." Anderson acknowledged that it would be hard indeed to characterize the fourth stage of development as in the latter 1960s and 1970s when Extension was expanding rapidly into many new fields of activity.[1]

Anderson's observations underscore the continual process of change going on within Cooperative Extension through the years. In the 1910s and 1920s the first county agents were known as "crop doctors" because of their focus on crop production, particularly corn. During World War I there seemed to be agreement that every county needed a county agent. Home economists, on the other hand, were hired if funds were available. That view of the expendability of Extension home economists has persisted through the years. This perception also underscores Extension's longtime policy of putting far more resources into production agriculture than into work with farm women or youth. From the beginning of Extension, it seemed that many staff members saw increased production as the key to solving farm problems.

A major strength through the years has been Extension's ability to wear many hats, and to don them rather quickly. The organization has always possessed a flexibility that has allowed it to adjust to changing times. In World War I and II Extension's major responsibility was to help Iowans achieve record agricultural production. Given the use of the cooperator system in both world wars, information could be disseminated quickly to all farm families in the state. The needs of Iowa families were very different in time of peace, however, than in time of war. During the 1920s, with the drop in agricultural prices, Extension agents urged farmers to keep better records and join cooperative organizations, all in an effort to realize a greater profit from farming. At the same time home economists switched from emphasizing food conservation—as they had done during the war—to helping rural women increase their knowledge of nutrition, make their home and work schedules more efficient, and learn sewing and child care skills.

By the 1930s county agents' roles had changed again. With the passage of the Agricultural Adjustment Act in 1933, the federal government looked for an agency that could quickly help administer the AAA, particularly to inform farmers of the act's provisions and help them sign up for the program. County agents worked with the program in 1933, 1934, and 1935. In effect, Extension staff became promoters of a federal farm program.

During the 1920s and 1930s Extension agents worked to create interest in soil conservation, an effort that led to the organization of the Soil Conservation Service. As Wayne Rasmussen has pointed out, "Extension and the state agricultural experiment stations had established educational and research bases upon which a national soil conservation program could be built." The development of these practices points out an important aspect of Extension's work. At many times in Extension's history, the organization has taken the responsibility for developing a program that was later taken over by another agency or group. Cass County Extension Director Dan Merrick believes that Extension often gets people started and then appropriately "backs out the door" so staff can go on to another project. As Merrick acknowledged, helping a new group get started often involves identifying leaders or helping local people to develop leadership abilities.[2]

The decade of the 1950s again brought change to Extension. Beginning in 1953 as farmers experienced a drop in farm prices, Extension turned to staff and ISC faculty members, particularly economists, to analyze the reasons for the price decline and to provide guidelines for future action. Extension's role in the 1950s underscored a basic tendency: frequent reassessment of the organization and its mission. Sometimes evaluations were initiated by national studies such as the Kepner Report in 1948. Studies by national Extension committees were carried out at ten-year intervals in 1948, 1958 (the Scope Report), and 1968 ("A People and A Spirit"); this research typically provided an analysis of Extension's program areas and a statement of what Extension ought to be doing in the future. According to Marvin Anderson, the reports were one way that the federal Extension Service gave direction to state organizations.

A watchword during the 1950s was agricultural adjustment. Extension officials struggled to make changes in the Iowa farm sector that would result in higher profits for farm families. And agricultural adjustment in the 1950s seemed to rest upon this premise: expand or fail. Several Plans of Work by the state central administration in the latter half of the 1950s clearly spelled out the view that with fewer farmers, the more productive ones would be able to prosper, thus improving the farm economy. The 1950s remained a time of frustration as Extension officials sought ways to increase farm profits.

Some of Extension's most innovative work came in the 1950s. Extension economists Carl Malone and Wallace Ogg were pioneers in the field of public policy, which in turn put the Iowa Extension Service on the cutting edge in this field. As one former Extension official put it, "Public policy has been a landmark for ISU."[3] In his discussion of Extension's third stage of development, a more formalized educational system, Anderson perhaps had public policy work in mind. With these programs Extension had indeed moved beyond the conduit stage of information. Iowans received information on a public policy issue and then took part in discussions and decision-making processes. The basic purpose was still education but as Anderson described it, the Extension staff had become "architects of information education." These programs have not been carried out without criticism, however. Some in Extension believed that public policy offered only a pitfall as staff would be seen as advocates of particular policies. In later years Extension would be criticized for not becoming an advocacy group on issues such as the environment and sustainable agriculture.

The decade of the 1960s underscored a dominant characteristic of Extension: when times improve, concentrate on production agriculture. Perhaps Extension personnel shared the congenital optimism of farmers themselves, that increased production alone was sufficient to improve farm living. Yet when good times returned, programs designed to help families during times of stress were abandoned. One that received praise by almost every individual interviewed for this book was the Farm and Home Development Program; many former Extension staff members lamented its passing. Eldon Hans reflected that in looking back over his career, he wished he had worked harder promoting the FHDP because it was such an excellent program.[4] Although FHDP was initiated in difficult times, it was designed to bring about long-term planning that would help families manage resources through good times as well as bad.

In the 1960s Iowa Extension greatly expanded its range of services by responding to the needs of limited resource Iowans, particularly in urban areas. In 1968, the Expanded Food and Nutrition programs began for both urban adults and urban young people. Extension staff also began focusing on other needs of less fortunate Iowans such as housing, money management, and home maintenance. Even though the number of focus groups had been broadened, the basic purpose had not changed: Extension remained an educational organization that provided Iowans with scientific and technological information designed to bring about improvements in the quality of life.

It is interesting to view the programs developed by Extension in the 1960s in light of longtime perceptions that it was (and is) not sufficiently concerned with the problems of low income citizens.[5] In part at least, that view rested on the traditional association between Extension and Farm Bureau, an organization perceived as representing the interests of the nation's more prosperous farm families. Given the close association between the two groups, various positions by Farm Bureau (such as opposing programs of the Farm Security Administration, which provided aid to low-income farmers in the 1930s), seemed to represent Extension's views as well. And, undoubtedly, given the symbiotic relationship between Extension and Farm Bureau before 1955, the latter's views sometimes predominated.

At the same time this relationship led to confusion as to whether or not non–Farm Bureau members could take part in Extension programs. Apparently this confusion persisted into the 1960s. While it is understandable that ambiguity existed originally over the association between the two groups, it is difficult to see how a public institution could allow that notion to continue. As an organization with a primary mission of education, it seems that Extension should have made a greater effort to inform or educate the general public that anyone, regardless of Farm Bureau membership, could take part in Extension programs. And it seems that Extension had much to gain from correcting this misperception. Eradicating a false view would have helped Iowans see Extension as a grass roots organization created to help all rural residents, rather than one closely linked with a particular farm organization.

Like the previous decades, the 1980s also brought great change to the Iowa Cooperative Extension Service. While Extension had responded to agricultural depressions many times in the past, it seems that in the 1980s that response was more total. In previous hard times Extension's reaction typically came in the form of suggestions for concrete change or participation in a government program and ways to economize within the farm household. In the 1980s, however, Extension made a concerted effort, particularly through the Rural Concern Hotline and the Taking Charge program, to deal directly with Iowans' emotional needs. As Dan Merrick observed, this type of activity was not included in any county staff job description.

The recent farm crisis, as several Extension staff members observed, points out that the human dimension is always a part of any Extension situation and must be accommodated. In times of crisis, moreover, it often comes front and center and must be dealt with before financial or technical matters can be addressed. Don Broshar related a recent experience where Extension economists were discussing the difficulty of getting families to adopt some of the practices that would be helpful to them. Broshar added, "It is clear to me why that is. We are still trying to address a complex problem as if it is a technological problem." In Broshar's opinion, Extension needs not only to help staff become fine technologists but also "know how to work with and teach people." Broshar believes this change must come if Extension is to survive; otherwise the organization will not be relevant.[6]

In the 1970s and 1980s Americans began to express a growing concern about environmental issues, a concern that sometimes manifested itself in criticism of Extension policies. Some people charged that Extension was not moving quickly enough in promoting agricultural practices to lessen chemical use and promote reduced tillage. Sociologist Everett M. Rogers points out that "no-till farming" was adopted some fifteen years later in Iowa than in states like Kentucky and Virginia because researchers at the Iowa Agricultural Experiment Station and ISU Extension specialists opposed it in the 1970s. Rather, they believed that a modification of the practice called "minimum tillage" was better suited to Iowa. Farmers in Kentucky and Virginia began to adopt no-till practices in the 1960s. Although the Iowa Extension Service did not advocate this procedure, in 1970 a few farmers in Washington County heard about the practice from farmers in other states and through farm publications. By 1977 the Washington County farmers had started using the method. Two years later the county director there began to hold meetings on the subject. By 1980 some fifty farmers in the county had adopted the practice.[7]

In the 1980s, however, changes were forthcoming in regard to Extension and the environmental arena. Extension county directors and specialists in agriculture began to stress different approaches to reduce the amount of herbicides and insecticides applied to fields. One technique was to test a small area for insects, allowing that measurement to dictate the amount of insecticide applied to the entire field. No doubt in the 1960s and 1970s more chemicals were

AN EXAMPLE OF RIDGE-TILL FARMING, a soil conservation and fuel-saving practice which Cooperative Extension encourages. The practice became increasingly popular in the 1980s. Courtesy of the ISU Extension Communication Services.

applied than were needed since the overriding concern was maximizing production. But by the 1980s, however, the thinking of agricultural specialists was beginning to change. Regis Voss explained that Extension agronomists by the latter 1980s were encouraging farmers to use less fertilizer because given its application in the past ten years, nutrient levels had been increased to sufficient levels. He explained, "It's a case of a success story, [we encouraged] farmers to use fertilizer because it was very profitable for them and now we're trying to . . . unsell them. In other words, use soil testing differently." Voss added that agronomists are now saying to farmers, "you really don't need to apply any more fertilizer," and emphasizing that fact by pointing to profit savings and conservation of resources.[8] The financial bind many farmers experienced in the 1980s also encouraged them to take a more conservative approach in treating fields, thus reducing costs.

In the 1970s Jim Hightower's book, *Hard Tomatoes, Hard Times: The Failure of America's Land-Grant College Complex,* received national attention. Among his criticisms, Hightower charged that state colleges of agriculture ignored the consequences of the technological innovations they were making available to farmers.[9] While the merits of these criticisms will not be discussed here, it should be noted that organizations, such as Extension, dedicated to dispensing new scientific and technical information did not typically pause (at least before the 1980s) to question long-term implications of the information they were disseminating. Throughout its history the Iowa Extension Service has viewed itself as the organization that makes the technology transfer, bringing to farm families new information on thousands of subjects ranging from methods of treating corn borers to energy audits for farm homes. An important part of that dissemination of new information from the 1950s on was the urging by Extension of heavier use of chemicals such as DDT. Officials told farmers, in effect, yields would increase when they used certain chemicals. There were no ethics committees along the way, however, to assess whether new products or techniques would have some future detrimental effect on people or on the environment. Regis Voss, longtime Extension agronomist, commented on this fact: "Whether these things [use of farm chemicals] are good or bad . . . in terms of cropping patterns, size of farms, I guess I'll let somebody else judge that. Certainly the technology is permitting those things to happen."[10] In effect, the major emphasis has been that Extension serves as the conduit through which new information has been passed along to farm families and to farm business groups.

While Extension has gone through several major stages, one characteristic has remained throughout: Extension is an organization that retains great flexibility. While that flexibility is evident at different levels, the most apparent is the county level. A major strength of the organization has been the autonomy possessed by county Extension staff in responding to local people and local conditions. Extension officials express this autonomy in different ways. Dan Merrick stated that in Iowa, since there are one hundred different county offices, "We probably likewise have one hundred different approaches to the Extension program, though there may be some common threads." Eldon Hans observed that "changes come slow in Extension because there is quite a lot of freedom for individuals to function like they want." Interests of county staff also vary. According to county annual reports, there was (and still is) great divergence of interests. Some county directors stressed leadership while others emphasized community development. One state director recalled a young man just getting started as a county director who seemed to be only interested in beekeeping. Naturally, some staff have been more receptive to new programs than others. The late Arthur Johnson often recalled a director in southern Iowa who always responded to suggestions that he initiate new programs: "Just ignore them and eventually they'll go away."[11]

While the reluctance of some county staff to pursue new programs has, undoubtedly, been a source of frustration to area and campus specialists and state administrators, the autonomy possessed by county staff has given great resiliency and flexibility to the organization. County staff come to know their local area: Natural resources, as well as people themselves, vary from county to county; populations also vary within counties. Dan Merrick observed that it might take three years to develop a program in some townships and ten years in others.[12] The Extension system seems to have accommodated many different points of view among county staff members and between county staff and specialists.

There has also been room in the organization for individual initiative and incorporation of new ideas. State specialists could develop programs like Operation Ship Shape and energy audits for all Iowans while Bob Hall in Delaware County could reorganize meetings of Extension-sponsored groups to allow more time for planning. State Extension Services throughout the country, including Iowa, enjoy a relative freedom in regard to the federal Extension Service. Marvin Anderson commented on that fact, adding some control and direction comes through funding, but overall during his tenure as director "The federal [Extension Service] never really dictated what we should do."[13]

The flexibility inherent in Extension's structure has also helped account for its continued presence. Flexibility has allowed the organization to expand its programs to reach new audiences, evident first in the 1960s and even more so in the 1980s. Developing outreach programs or widening the circle of constituents has been vital for Extension, given the decline of the farm population. In 1991 census figures showed that the state contained just over one hundred thousand farms; at one point Iowa contained over twice that number of farm units. Fortunately for Extension, as Warner and Christensen observed, the organization has not been restricted to one program or one activity, but rather "has been allowed to adjust to changing needs." That Extension has done so helps explain the continued presence of an organization created to serve the farm population of the state, even when that population has declined significantly.[14]

While this book is not an institutional study per se, it is interesting to note that decision making is decentralized or fragmented rather than centralized within the state director's office. Some decisions are made within the county councils, the county directors' offices, the area offices and within the circle of state specialists. Still others are made by central administration. Elizabeth Elliott referred to the "friendly tension" that existed between field staff and state specialists. Several county directors, both past and present, noted that state specialists sometimes "seemed out of touch" with what is going on in the county. One former Extension staff member believed that all specialists should first work at the county level so they would better understand the needs and interests of local people. Given the type and range of decision-making processes, it is, in the view of a present county director, an organization that works from the bottom up, rather than the top down.[15]

While Extension has developed a myriad of successful programs through the years, some seemed to have attracted less notice than others. It is not surprising that agricultural programs have received the greatest attention, given the ever-increasing productivity of the Iowa farmer and the fact that production agriculture, at least until the mid-1980s, has been Extension's primary focus. However, countless programs in Home Economics Extension and 4-H have been particularly successful, even though resources have been far less in these fields; in effect, it seems that home economics and 4-H have done more with less. Both programs have relied heavily on volunteers, which was not the case in agriculture. In 4-H the challenge has been locating club leaders; in home economics, leaders established the mentality in the 1920s that the program needed volunteers to work properly. That mentality resulted in finding local leaders in the 1920s, 1930s, and 1940s, and more recently locating master volunteers to work with clothing construction, gardening projects, and food preservation. Home Economics Extension has made heavy use of local leaders and has used them creatively and effectively. Through the volunteer programs, personal empowerment has been an important part of both 4-H and home economics. It seems, in fact, that not only has Extension located volunteer leaders, but in many cases, has turned these people into missionaries for the organization. Countless numbers of Iowa farm women and men not only carried out their volunteer duties but did it with a fervor for Extension. At the same time, many older Iowans look back with great fondness on their 4-H days, convinced that 4-H had an extremely positive influence on their lives.

Extension has also succeeded through the years in attracting a staff with great missionary zeal for the organization. As Marvin Anderson related:

> I think one of the things about the people who were in Extension at my time at least, and preceding me, were mission spirit driven. They believed in what they were doing and they knew it was important. These [Extension Service retirees] although never wealthy, [with] modest salaries, are still driven to be community participants in the activities that are important.

Anderson noted that Paul Barger, a former county director, and a man now in his eighties, continues to write a column in his local newspaper because "people want to hear from him."[16]

One unheralded emphasis is Extension's successful development of leadership qualities; in effect, Extension has led the way in leadership programs throughout the state. In the 1920s and 1930s, farm women serving as local leaders for Home Economics Extension not only learned subject matter but also how to present the information to other farm women. Moreover, they learned how to organize groups and follow through with projects. The leadership qualities they learned through township and county Extension activities carried over into other activities within their communities. Leadership programs have been a part of 4-H. C. J. Gauger believes that leadership conferences for 4-Hers in the 1960s and 1970s ranked as

some of 4-H's most successful and worthwhile programs. Some
leadership programs have been independent such as Tomorrow's
Leaders Today, one that provides leadership training for people in
small Iowa communities. Beverly Everett, a prominent farm woman
from New Sharon, credits Extension for helping her develop
leadership skills and providing opportunities that led to her involvement in state, national, and international organizations.[17]

A major change in the past twenty years is that Extension is no
longer "the only game in town" in terms of education and services
to Iowans. Iowa now abounds with different groups that provide
services, ranging from community colleges to dozens of farm
businesses. While this has resulted in some Iowans feeling that
perhaps Extension has outlived its usefulness, former Iowa Extension
official Ronald Powers points out that it is an organization that does
far more than simply offer information. As Powers explained, some
organizations in providing only information are not providing
education. Powers made this prediction:

> There will come a time when people will say, "You know, we've got
> hundreds of sources of information but nobody who can explain
> this [material] or help me sort out or make choices and that's what
> we want . . . Extension to do, because that's what your job is."[18]

One additional observation is in order. Given Iowa's ideal
climate and soil base for agriculture, it was perhaps a given that
Cooperative Extension would flourish here. There were few other
places in the country where conditions were so well suited to the
successful development of an organization dedicated to providing
education to the farm population. Iowa's compact form of settlement
meant that, first of all, farms were close together, a condition that
made it easier for Extension personnel to visit farm people and draw
them to meetings. Compact settlement also made it easier to
disseminate information as evidenced by the cooperator system in
both world wars. Moreover, all parts of Iowa are engaged in
agriculture. Anywhere in the state, agriculture is a major concern;
and everywhere in the state there is major support for Iowa's leading
industry. Iowa also has been (and continues to be) homogeneous in
population. The state was settled primarily by immigrants from
western Europe and the British Isles as well as by individuals from
the northeastern United States where, it should be added, most
people had also originally come from western Europe and the British
Isles. Therefore, Extension did not have a disparate population to

LIVESTOCK PROJECTS have been a 4-H tradition since the early 1900s, and continue to be a vehicle for learning decision making as well as subject matter. Courtesy of the ISU Extension Communication Services.

work with; in effect, it did not face the sometimes difficult task of accommodating different cultures. Even wealth tended to be homogeneous as Iowa has not been a state of extremes in terms of income or land holdings. At the same time Iowa has always had a high literacy rate with a population that could easily benefit from printed material. Former Extension staff member Leon Thompson believed, in fact, that Iowa contained the proper intellectual environment for quick acceptance of Extension programs. Thompson observed that this right environment led to a "public permissiveness," particularly evident in accepting programs in public policy. This permissiveness had come about, Thompson believed, because of two Iowa publications, *Wallaces' Farmer* and the *Des Moines Register.* These publications have helped accustom Iowa's farm people to "seeing public issues discussed and analyzed."[19]

Throughout its many years, the ISU Cooperative Extension Service has provided a wide array of successful services to the people of Iowa. The Kepner Report issued in 1948 has perhaps captured the true essence of that service. "In short, whereas extension has done much for people, it is what extension has helped people to do for themselves that achieves the greatest results."[20] That statement perhaps stands as the best legacy to the Iowa Extension's seventy-five years of service.

Notes

ABBREVIATIONS: *ANR Annual Narrative Reports of County Extension Agents*
                IYA   Iowa Yearbook of Agriculture

Preface

1. "An Extension Service in Transition, 1956–1960" (Ames, Iowa: Cooperative Extension Service in Agriculture and Home Economics, Iowa State University and the United States Department of Agriculture cooperating. N.d.), pp. 14–15.
2. Ibid.

1. Open Country Iowa

1. David B. Danbom, *The Resisted Revolution: Urban America and the Industrialization of Agriculture, 1900–1930* (Ames: Iowa State University Press, 1979), p. 4.
2. Lewis Atherton, *Main Street on the Middle Border* (New York: New York Times Book Company, Quadrangle Books, 1975), pp. 245–49; also see Dorothy Schwieder, "Rural Iowa in the 1920s: Conflict and Continuity," *Annals of Iowa* 47(Fall 1983).
3. Earle D. Ross, *Iowa Agriculture: An Historical Survey* (Iowa City: State Historical Society of Iowa, 1951), pp. 118, 122.
4. Ibid., p. 129; and Schwieder, "Rural Iowa," pp. 109–10.
5. Thomas J. Morain, *Prairie Grass Roots: An Iowa Small Town in the Early Twentieth Century* (Ames: Iowa State University Press, 1988), p. 142.
6. Quoted in Morain, *Prairie Grass Roots,* p. 143.
7. Quoted in Schwieder, "Rural Iowa," pp. 114–15; and Morain, *Prairie Grass Roots,* p. 105.
8. Joseph Frazier Wall, *Iowa: A Bicentennial History* (New York: Norton, 1978), pp. 186–87; and Keach Johnson, "Elementary and Secondary Education in Iowa, 1890–1900: A Time of Awakening," Part 1, *Annals of Iowa* 45(Fall 1979):89–90 and Part 2, *Annals of Iowa* 45(Winter 1980):171–73.
9. Quoted in Morain, *Prairie Grass Roots,* p. 105.
10. Janice Nahra Friedel, "Jessie Field Shambaugh: The Mother of 4-H," *The Palimpsest,* 62(July/August 1981):99, 105.
11. Ross, *Iowa Agriculture,* p. 128.
12. Frederick Luebke, "Ethnic Group Settlement on the Great Plains," *Western Historical Quarterly* 8(October 1977):411.
13. An example of strong kinship ties can be found among the members of the

Ramsey Church in rural Buffalo Center, Iowa.

14. Clifford Drury writes of these types of activities in his personal account, "Growing Up on an Iowa Farm, 1897–1915," *Annals of Iowa* 42(Winter 1974):161–97.

15. Danbom, *The Resisted Revolution,* p. 4; and Gilbert C. Fite, *American Farmers: The New Minority* (Bloomington: Indiana University Press, 1981), p. 11.

16. Fite, *American Farmers,* p. 66.

17. Ross, *Iowa Agriculture,* p. 122; Allan Bogue, *From Prairie to Cornbelt: Farming on the Illinois and Iowa Prairies in the Nineteenth Century* (Chicago: Quadrangle Paperbacks, 1968), pp. 162–68; and Danbom, *The Resisted Revolution,* p. 5.

18. Herbert Quick, "The Women on the Farms," *Good Housekeeping* 57(October 1913):426–27; quoted in Danbom, *The Resisted Revolution,* p. 155.

19. For an excellent account of an Iowa farm woman's schedule in the latter nineteenth and early twentieth centuries, see Lizzie Fellows Heckart, "Four Seasons: Life on a Pioneer Van Buren County Farm," (Keosauqua, Iowa: *Van Buren County Register,* 1972):1–46.

20. Drury, "Growing Up on an Iowa Farm," p. 181; Deborah Fink, *Open Country Iowa: Rural Women, Tradition and Change,* SUNY Series in Anthropology of Work, ed., June Nash (Albany: State University of New York Press, 1986), p. 23–24.

21. Fite, *American Farmers,* p. 10.

22. Quick, "The Women on the Farms," pp. 426–27.

23. Morain, *Prairie Grass Roots,* p. 108.

24. See Fite, *American Farmers,* p. 12 for an example of this attitude. Also see Curtis Harnack, *We Have All Gone Away* (Garden City, New Jersey: Doubleday, 1973).

25. *Report of the Country Life Commission* (Chapel Hill, North Carolina, 1911), pp. 82–83, 103–6, 121–27.

26. By 1906 Extension models existed in states like Texas.

2. The Formative Years

1. Ralph K. Bliss, *Extension in Iowa: History of Cooperative Agriculture and Home Economics* (Ames: Iowa State University, 1960), p. 33; also see E. G. Ritland, "The Educational Activities of P. G. Holden in Iowa" (M.S. thesis, Iowa State College, 1941).

2. Ibid.

3. Ibid., p. 34.

4. Rosanne Sizer and William Silag, "P. G. Holden and the Corn Gospel Trains," *The Palimpsest* 62(May/June 1981):67; and Earle Ross, *Iowa Agriculture* (Iowa City: State Historical Society of Iowa, 1951), p. 125.

5. Ralph K. Bliss, ed., *The Spirit and Philosophy of Extension Work* (Washington, D.C.: Graduate School, United States Department of Agriculture and Epsilon Sigma Phi, National Honorary Extension Fraternity, 1952), p. 47.

6. Sizer and Silag, "P. G. Holden," p. 68; and Bliss, *Extension in Iowa,* p. 36.

7. Ibid.

8. Ibid.; and Ross, *Iowa Agriculture,* p. 125.

9. Bliss, *Extension in Iowa,* p. 43; and Sizer and Silag, "P. G. Holden," p. 70.

10. Sizer and Silag, "P. G. Holden," p. 70; and J. Brownlee Davidson, Herbert M. Hamlin, and Paul C. Taff, *A Study of the Extension Service in Agriculture and Home Economics in Iowa* (Ames, Iowa: Collegiate Press, Inc., 1933), p. 18.

11. Bliss, *Extension in Iowa,* pp. 48–49; and Sizer and Silag, "P. G. Holden," p. 70.

12. Kenneth Michael Lundeen, "Efficiency and Uplift: The Iowa Extension Service

and Business Agriculture, 1919–1935" (M.S. thesis, Iowa State University, 1976), p. 11.

13. Ross, *Iowa Agriculture*, p. 126; and *Annual Narrative Reports of County Agents and Home Demonstration Agents*, Clay County, Vol. 6, 1939, pp. 2–23. In 1939, Director Bliss asked each county agent to write a history of Extension in his or her county. These accounts provide valuable material on the early roles of county Extension personnel in the state.

14. Ross, *Iowa Agriculture*, pp. 126–27; and Bliss, *Extension in Iowa*, p. 66.

15. Ralph K. Bliss, "Personal Recollections of Ralph K. Bliss," typewritten manuscript, Special Collections, Iowa State University Library, n.d., pp. 8, 49, 71–99.

16. Bliss, *Extension in Iowa*, p. 100.

17. Bliss, ed., *The Spirit and Philosophy*, pp. 102–3.

18. Bliss, *Extension in Iowa*, pp. 100–101.

19. *ANR*, Clay County, Vol. 6, 1939, p. 4.

20. *ANR*, Bremer County, Vol. 4, 1939, p. 4; and Benton County, Vol. 2, 1939, p. 6; and Bliss, *Extension in Iowa*, p. 66; and Lundeen, "Efficiency and Uplift"; and *ANR*, Clay County, Vol. 6, p. 3, 4.

21. *ANR*, Black Hawk County, Vol. 3, 1939, p. 2.

22. Ibid.

23. *ANR*, Calhoun County, Vol. 4, 1939, p. 8.

24. Bliss, ed., *The Spirit and Philosophy*, p. 63.

25. *ANR*, Black Hawk County, Vol. 3, 1939, p. 5; and Clinton County, Vol. 3, 1939, p. 7.

26. *ANR*, Calhoun County, Vol. 4, 1939, p. 8; and Clinton County, Vol. 7, 1939, p. 9.

27. Davidson, Hamlin, and Taff, *A Study of the Extension Service*, p. 18; and *ANR*, Crawford County, Vol. 6, 1939, p. 7.

28. *ANR*, Butler County, Vol. 4, 1939, p. 3.

29. Bliss, *Extension in Iowa*, p. 72; *ANR*, Crawford County, Vol. 6, 1939, p. 16.

30. Bliss, ed., *The Spirit and Philosophy*, p. 2.

31. Ibid.

32. Bliss, *Extension in Iowa*, pp. 101–2; and *ANR*, Black Hawk County, Vol. 3, 1939, p. 3.

33. *ANR*, Black Hawk County, Vol. 3, 1939, p. 4.

34. Ross, *Iowa Agriculture*, p. 141.

35. Bliss, *Extension in Iowa*, pp. 113, 115; and Ross, *Iowa Agriculture*, p. 142; and Biennial Report of Agricultural Extension Work in Iowa, July 1, 1916 to June 30, 1918, p. 56. Since Iowa has ninety-nine counties it is assumed that there would be ninety-nine Extension offices in the state. However, there are one hundred because two Extension offices were created in Pottawattamie County, presumably because of the county's large size.

36. Ross, *Iowa Agriculture*, p. 142.

37. Bliss, *Extension in Iowa*, p. 124.

38. Ibid., p. 116.

39. *ANR*, Greene County, Vol. 12, 1939, p. 11; and Bliss, *Extension in Iowa*, p. 116.

40. *ANR*, Buena Vista County, Vol. 4, 1939, p. 5; and Crawford County, Vol. 6, 1939, p. 6.

41. Biennial Report of Agricultural Extension Work in Iowa, 1916 to 1918, pp. 25, 28.

42. *ANR*, Buena Vista County, Vol. 4, 1939, p. 6.

43. *ANR*, Black Hawk County, Vol. 3, 1939, p. 5; and Ross, *Iowa Agriculture*, p. 143.

44. Ross, *Iowa Agriculture*, p. 144; and Bliss, *Extension in Iowa*, p. 132; and Wayne Rasmussen, *Taking the University to the People: Seventy-Five Years of Cooperative Extension* (Ames: Iowa State University, 1989), p. 94.

45. Ross, *Iowa Agriculture,* p. 138.

3. A Decade of Expansion

1. Kenneth Michael Lundeen, "Efficiency and Uplift: The Iowa Extension Service and Business Agriculture, 1919–1935," (unpublished M.A. thesis, Iowa State University, 1976), p. 13; and Leland Sage, "Rural Iowa in the 1920s and 1930s: Roots of the Farm Depression," *Annals of Iowa* 47(Fall 1983):96.

2. Ralph K. Bliss, *History of Cooperative Agriculture and Home Economics Extension in Iowa: The First Fifty Years* (Ames: Iowa State University, 1960), p. 138, 140; Lundeen, "Efficiency and Uplift," p. 37; and Edmund deS. Brunner and E. Hsin Pao Yang, *Rural America and the Extension Service: A History and Critique of the Cooperative Agricultural and Home Economics Extension Service* (New York: Bureau of Publications, Teachers College, Columbia University, 1949), p. 77.

3. R. K. Bliss, *Extension Service Work in Iowa: Agriculture and Home Economics Annual Report,* July 1, 1920, to June 20, 1921, p. 5; and *IYA,* Part 12, "Excerpts of the Annual Report of the Extension Service in Agriculture and Home Economics," 1924, pp. 235–36. Even though Extension annual reports were produced every year, and were viewed as reports in a series, the name often varied slightly.

4. Earle Ross, *Iowa Agriculture: An Historical Survey* (Iowa City: State Historical Society of Iowa, 1951), p. 148; and Bliss, *History,* p. 142.

5. Bliss, *History,* p. 142.

6. Ibid., pp. 141–42; Ross, *Iowa Agriculture,* p. 153; and Bliss, *Annual Report,* July 1, 1920, to June 20, 1921, pp. 12–13.

7. Quoted in Lundeen, "Efficiency and Uplift," pp. 17–18; and R. K. Bliss, *Annual Report,* 1925, pp. 12–13.

8. Lundeen, "Efficiency and Uplift," p. 19; and Bliss, *History,* pp. 154–56.

9. Bliss, *Annual Report,* 1920 and 1921, p. 15. The Bureau of Agricultural Economics was created in the USDA in 1922, becoming the economic research bureau within the department. See Richard S. Lowitt, ed., *Journal of A Tamed Bureaucrat: Nils A. Olsen and the BAE, 1925–1935* (Ames: Iowa State University Press, 1980), p. 6.

10. Bliss, *Annual Report,* 1925, p. 7.

11. Joel Kunze, "The Bureau of Agricultural Economics' Outlook Program in the 1920s as Pedagogical Device," *Agricultural History* 64(Spring 1990):253–54.

12. Ibid., p. 260.

13. Lundeen, "Efficiency and Uplift," p. 46.

14. Dorothy Schwieder, "Rural Iowa in the 1920s: Conflict and Continuity," *Annals of Iowa* 47(Fall 1983):104–8.

15. C. H. Schopmeyer, "Extension Projects in Rural Community Organization," *Extension Service Circular* 43, (Office of Agricultural Instruction, Extension Service, Washington, D.C., May 1927), p. 3.

16. Brunner and Yang, *Rural America,* pp. 78–79; and Schopmeyer, "Extension Projects," p. 30.

17. Bliss, *History,* p. 161; and William Stacy, 1926 *Annual Report,* Rural Sociology Extension, Special Collections, Iowa State University Library, n.p.

18. Schopmeyer, "Extension Projects," pp. 6–7, 36; Bliss, *Annual Report,* 1920 and 1921, p. 15; and Stacy, 1925 *Annual Report,* Rural Sociology Extension, n.p.

19. Stacy, 1926 *Annual Report;* and *IYA,* Part 14, *Annual Report of Iowa Agricultural and Home Economics Extension Service,* 1929, p. 409. Following the writing of an annual

report, the Extension director summarized that lengthy report for a condensed report published in the *IYA*.

20. Stacy, 1925 and 1928 *Annual Reports*.

21. *ANR*, Benton County, Vol. 1, 1921, n.p.; and Bliss, *History*, p. 161.

22. *IYA*, Part 12, *Annual Report of Iowa Agriculture and Home Economics Extension Service*, 1924, p. 236.

23. Ross, *Iowa Agriculture*, p. 149.

24. Lundeen, "Efficiency and Uplift," p. 15.

25. J. Brownlee Davidson, Herbert M. Hamlin, and Paul C. Taff, *A Study of the Extension Service in Agriculture and Home Economics in Iowa* (Ames, Iowa: Collegiate Press, Inc., 1933), p. 78. It should be noted that Agricultural Economics, Industrial Divisions, Agricultural Divisions, and Agricultural Engineering was a part of both the Agricultural and Engineering Divisions.

26. *IYA*, Part 12, *Annual Report of Iowa Agriculture and Home Economics*, 1924, p. 232; and Bliss, *Annual Report*, 1920 and 1921, p. 18.

27. Bliss, *Annual Report*, 1920 and 1921, p. 20–21; and *IYA*, Part 12, *Annual Report of Iowa Agriculture and Home Economics*, p. 234.

28. *IYA*, Part 14, *Annual Report of Agriculture and Home Economics Extension*, 1927, p. 351.

29. *ANR*, Benton County, Vol. 1, 1929, p. 66.

30. Bliss, *History*, pp. 80–81; and Bliss, *Annual Report*, 1929, pp. 38–39.

31. Bliss, *Annual Report*, 1920 and 1921, pp. 22–25.

32. Davidson et al., *A Study*, pp. 105–6, 178.

33. Bliss, *History*, p. 162.

34. Ibid.; and *IYA*, Part 13, *Annual Report of Iowa Agriculture and Home Economics*, p. 297.

35. Neale S. Knowles, *Annual Report*, Home Economics, 1920, pp. 1–3, Special Collections, Iowa State University Library. All the *Annual Reports* for Home Economics for the 1920s are deposited in Special Collections, ISU Library. The report states that home economists also promoted Americanization but it is not clear what this entailed. Also, by the end of the decade, county home economics projects had become standardized, meaning that all townships in the county adopted the same project.

36. Ibid., 1920–1921.

37. Cora Leiby, *Annual Report* for clothing specialist. Included in the *Annual Report* for Home Economics, 1921–1922.

38. Quoted in Thomas Morain, *Prairie Grass Roots: An Iowa Small Town in the Early Twentieth Century* (Ames: Iowa State University Press, 1988), pp. 106–7. Emphasis added by author.

39. Leiby, *Annual Report*, 1921–1922.

40. *Annual Report* for food and nutrition specialist. Included in *Annual Report* for Home Economics, 1921–1922.

41. *Annual Report* for food and nutrition specialist. Included in *Annual Report* for Home Economics, 1920, 1921, and 1922.

42. Florence A. Imlay, *Annual Report* for Extension milk specialist. Included in *Annual Report* for Home Economics, 1920, 1921, and 1922.

43. Imlay, *Annual Report*, 1920.

44. Imlay, "Milk Projects," *Annual Report*, 1920.

45. Lundeen, "Efficiency and Uplift," pp. 33–34.

46. Gertrude Lynn, *Annual Report* for home management specialist. Included in *Annual Report* for Home Economics, 1921–1922, n.p.

47. Ibid.

48. Ibid. Not only did Extension bring programs to the farm, but sometimes provided women with opportunities to get away from the farm. During the 1920s home economists set up camps for rural women where they could spend a week away from their families and the daily routine of domestic and farm chores. Farm women participated in sessions where they heard lectures on farm living and domesticity, sang in choruses, took part in one act plays, and simply enjoyed entertainment put on by outsiders.

49. *ANR,* Allamakee County, Vol. 1, 1929, pp. 58–59.

50. Danbom, *Resisted Revolution,* p. 88.

51. *ANR,* Marshall County, Vol. 1, 1926, p. 3.

52. For a fictionalized account of farm women's visits to town, see Hamlin Garland, "A Day's Pleasure," *Main Travelled Roads.* Reprinted in 1962 by Signet Classic.

53. Jane Knowles, "The United States Cooperative Extension Service: The Origin of the Gender Gap," unpublished paper presented at the Conference of American Farm Women in Historical Perspective, New Mexico State University, Las Cruces, New Mexico, February 2–4, 1984, pp. 13–14, 30; Deborah Fink, *Open Country Iowa: Rural Women, Tradition and Change* (Albany: State University of New York Press, 1986), p. 96. Much the same view is expressed by Joan Jensen, *Promise to the Land: Essays on Rural Women* (Albuquerque: University of New Mexico Press, 1991), p. 18.

54. Bliss, *Annual Report,* 1920 and 1921, pp. 7–15.

55. Ibid.

56. Edith Zobrist and Esther Whetstone, interviews, Ames, Iowa, April 1989.

57. Zobrist and Whetstone, interviews; and Bernice Lund, interview, Ames, Iowa, April 1989.

58. Whetstone interview.

59. Herb Plambeck and E. Howard Hill, interviews, Ames, Iowa, April 1989.

60. *ANR,* Benton County, Vol. 1, 1921, p. 5.

61. Bliss, *Annual Report,* 1920 and 1921, pp. 10–13.

62. Whetstone interview.

63. Bliss, *Annual Report,* 1925, pp. 12–13, 43–44.

64. Ibid., pp. 10, 52.

65. Ibid., pp. 54–55.

66. Danbom, *Resisted Revolution,* p. 131; Lundeen, "Efficiency and Uplift," p. 48.

67. R. K. Bliss, *Biennial Report of Agricultural Extension Work in Iowa, 1916 to 1918,* p. 8; Bliss, *Annual Report,* 1925; and Bliss, *Annual Report,* 1929.

68. Dorothy Schwieder, "Education and Change in the Lives of Iowa Farm Women, 1900–1940," *Agricultural History* 60(Spring 1986):215.

69. Lundeen, "Efficiency and Uplift," p. 17; quoted p. 38.

70. Lundeen, "Efficiency and Uplift," p. 708; and D. B. Graves and Kenneth Thatcher, *The First Fifty: History of Farm Bureau in Iowa* (Lake Mills, Iowa: Graphic Publishing Company, Inc., 1968), p. 27.

71. While Extension and Farm Bureau officials certainly would have argued that Extension was created to help farmers achieve greater efficiency and greater productivity to increase their financial returns and to improve the quality of rural life, there are some scholars who argue differently. David Danbom believes that Extension was initiated mainly because urban citizens saw the inefficiency and disorganization of farming leading to higher food prices. Therefore, according to Danbom, agriculture needed to be reorganized and made more efficient so it could produce a cheap food supply for the nation. To that end, members of the Country Life Movement, composed of social thinkers, scientists, businesspeople, and government officials, pushed for the creation of an Extension Service. According to this view, concern for the welfare of farmers and their families was second, at best. See Danbom, *Resisted Revolution,* p. 3.

4. A Time of Trial

1. Leland L. Sage, "Rural Iowa in the 1920s and 1930s: Roots of the Farm Depression," *Annals of Iowa* 47(Fall 1983):96–97.

2. Theodore Saloutos and John D. Hicks, *Agricultural Discontent in the Middle West, 1900–1939* (Madison: University of Wisconsin Press, 1951), pp. 437–38.

3. Earle D. Ross, *Iowa Agriculture: An Historical Survey* (Iowa City: State Historical Society of Iowa, 1951), p. 164.

4. Saloutos and Hicks, *Agricultural Discontent,* p. 438.

5. Leland L. Sage, *A History of Iowa* (Ames: Iowa State University Press, 1974), p. 276; Saloutos and Hicks, *Agricultural Discontent,* p. 441. Saloutos and Hicks write that the "Cow War" was a part of the farm strike. It seems that the two were really separate incidents, with the Cow War helping to precipitate the farm strike.

6. Sage, *A History of Iowa,* p. 277.

7. Ibid.

8. Quoted in Saloutos and Hicks, *Agricultural Discontent,* pp. 436–37, 443.

9. Ibid., p. 443. This association is confusing because not all farmers taking part in farm strikes had joined the Farm Holiday Association. Therefore, it is incorrect to say that the association was always responsible for withholding actions.

10. Michael Lundeen, "Efficiency and Uplift: The Iowa Extension Service and Business Agriculture, 1919–1935," (unpublished M.A. thesis, Iowa State University, 1976), p. 52.

11. Lundeen, "Efficiency and Uplift," pp. 56–57.

12. J. Brownlee Davidson, Herbert M. Hamlin, and Paul C. Taff, *A Study of the Extension Service in Agriculture and Home Economics in Iowa* (Ames, Iowa: Collegiate Press, Inc., 1933), p. xi; and Lundeen, "Efficiency and Uplift," p. 57.

13. Ibid. The committee also recommended a close look at the association between Farm Bureau and Extension in light of the negative consequences of that relationship.

14. Lundeen, "Efficiency and Uplift," pp. 58–59, 60–61. The Extension study by Davidson, Hamlin, and Taff appears to have been a very thorough study and provides excellent material on the organization and activities of Extension up to 1930.

15. H. C. Wallace died unexpectedly in 1923.

16. Richard H. Roberts, "The Administration of the 1934 Corn-Hog Program in Iowa," *Iowa Journal of History and Politics* 33(October 1935):314; *IYA,* Part 10, *Agricultural and Home Economics Extension Service,* 1935, p. 290; and Ross, *Iowa Agriculture,* p. 173. Following the writing of an annual report, the Extension director summarized that lengthy report for a condensed report published in the *IYA.*

17. Quoted in Michael W. Schuyler, *Dread of Plenty: Agricultural Relief Activities of the Federal Government in the Middle West, 1933–1939* (Manhattan, Kansas: Sunflower Press, 1989), p. 51.

18. Lundeen, "Efficiency and Uplift," p. 63; and quoted in Schuyler, *Dread of Plenty,* p. 51.

19. Quoted in Saloutos and Hicks, *Agricultural Discontent,* p. 491.

20. Roberts, "The Administration," pp. 322–23.

21. Ralph K. Bliss, *History of Cooperative Agriculture and Home Economics Extension in Iowa* (Ames: Iowa State University, 1960), p. 165.

22. Ibid., p. 167; Roberts, "The Administration," p. 323; and Donald E. Fish, "The Emergency Years: Remembrances of a County Agricultural Agent in the Great Depression," *The Palimpsest* 72(Summer 1991):92.

23. Roberts, "The Administration," p. 325; and Bliss, *History,* p. 168.

24. Roberts, "The Administration," pp. 325, 327.
25. Ibid., p. 327; *IYA*, Part 10, 1935, p. 291.
26. Roberts, "The Administration," pp. 328, 330.
27. Bliss, *History*, p. 169.
28. Roberts, "The Administration," pp. 321, 331.
29. Bliss, *History*, p. 169.
30. Ibid., pp. 168, 171. In December 1935 Extension cooperated with the AAA in yet another way to create 100 county agricultural program planning committees. These committees then outlined cropping systems that would best maintain fertility and control erosion on the different soils in Iowa. County committees, made up of representatives of farm organizations and representatives of different farming areas, recommended on a county by county basis what amount of land should be put in some form of permanent vegetation. See *IYA*, Part 9, 1936, pp. 302–4; and *IYA*, Part 9, 1939, p. 349.
31. Lundeen, "Efficiency and Uplift," pp. 63, 65.
32. Quoted in Lundeen, "Efficiency and Uplift," pp. 66–67.
33. Ibid., p. 65.
34. Fish, "The Emergency Years," p. 99.
35. Bliss, *History*, p. 170; *IYA*, Part 10, 1935, p. 292.
36. *IYA*, Part 9, 1936, pp. 292–93.
37. Ibid., pp. 300, 302. Included in the insect infestations were grasshoppers, chinch bugs, army worms, and cutworms. County agents and Extension entomologists carried on insect control campaigns in thirty-six counties. See *IYA*, Part 9, 1936, p. 306.
38. Bliss, *History*, p. 172.
39. *IYA*, Part 9, 1936, p. 298.
40. Ibid., p. 299; Wayne Rasmussen has noted in *Taking the University to the People: Seventy-Five Years of Cooperative Extension* (Ames: Iowa State University Press, 1989), pp. 101–2, that when the SCS was first established, Extension officials and Farm Bureau wanted soil conservation agents put together with Extension agents, at the county level, to be administered jointly by state Extension directors and the SCS regional officers. In other words, Extension officials wanted full responsibility for soil conservation. Secretary of Agriculture Henry A. Wallace decided instead to have the soil conservation program administered locally through soil conservation districts, to be organized by Extension personnel. Extension was also to provide districts with educational help.
41. Bliss, *History*, pp. 213, 152, and 153; and *IYA*, Part 9, 1936, p. 300. In the fall of 1935 committees of representative farmers in each Iowa county were selected to develop a longtime program, which would provide for the use of cropping systems that would have a dual effect: prevent erosion and conserve fertility. This work was expanded in 1936 following the Supreme Court's decision to declare the AAA unconstitutional. In his 1938 annual report in the *IYA*, Bliss emphasized again the need for soil conservation measures, noting that soil losses in the past "had been enormous." See *IYA*, Part 10, 1936, pp. 293–94; *IYA*, Part 9, 1938, pp. 296–97. Bliss explained in 1938 that to help convince farmers of the need for remedial measures, the Extension Service would both teach and demonstrate the following: crop rotation in every county; strip cropping and contour farming where appropriate; development of better methods of handling pastureland in hill sections; grassing waterways to prevent erosion; use of lime; and use of phosphate.
42. Ross, *Iowa Agriculture*, p. 181.
43. Although she did not work with soil conservation, Louise Rosenfeld talked generally about this pattern of development in Extension. Interview, Ames, Iowa, May 3, 1988.
44. *IYA*, Part 9, 1937, p. 311; *IYA*, Part 9, 1936, pp. 304–5.
45. *IYA*, Part 10, 1935, p. 295; *IYA*, Part 9, 1939, p. 349.

46. Bliss, *History,* p. 174.

47. *IYA,* Part 10, 1935, p. 303; *IYA,* Part 9, 1936, p. 306; *IYA,* Part 9, 1937, p. 312.

48. Edmund deS. Brunner and E. Hsin Pao Yang, *Rural America and the Extension Service: A History and Critique of the Cooperative Agricultural and Home Economics Extension Service* (New York: Bureau of Publications, Teachers College, Columbia University, 1949), p. 77; and Gilbert Fite, *American Farmers: The New Minority* (Bloomington: Indiana University Press, 1981), pp. 62–63.

49. *IYA,* Part 9, 1936, p. 302; Louise Rosenfeld, interview, Ames, Iowa, May 3, 1988, tape 2, p. 9.

50. Rosenfeld interview.

51. Rasmussen, *Taking the University,* p. 103; *IYA,* Part 9, 1936, p. 316.

52. Bliss, *History,* pp. 179–80.

53. *IYA,* Part 13, 1932, p. 130.

54. *ANR,* Benton County, Vol. 1, 1935, p. 19; and Bliss, *History,* p. 171.

55. *ANR,* Adair County, Vol. 1, 1935, pp. 13–24; and *ANR of Benton County,* Vol. 1, 1935, p. 19.

56. *IYA,* Part 10, 1935, p. 315; and *IYA,* Part 9, 1937, pp. 324–35.

57. *ANR,* Benton County, Vol. 1, 1935, p. 1.

58. This criticism was included in Davidson, Hamlin, and Taff, *A Study of the Extension Service,* pp. 205–6; and *ANR,* Franklin County, Vol. 4, 1935, pp. 22–23.

59. *ANR,* Audubon County, 1935; Franklin County, 1935, Vol. 4, p. 23.

60. *IYA,* Part 9, 1934, p. 294; *IYA,* Part 9, 1936, p. 296; *IYA,* Part 9, 1939, p. 347; and *IYA,* Part 10, 1935, p. 312.

61. Rosenfeld interview, tape 1, p. 4. Because of its size, Pottawattamie County has always been divided into two parts, East Pottawattamie County and West Pottawattamie County, for Extension purposes.

62. Ibid., pp. 3, 5.

63. Ibid., p. 6.

64. Ibid., pp. 14, 16.

65. Ibid., p. 6.

66. *IYA,* Part 10, 1935, p. 315; and *IYA,* Part 9, 1939, p. 306.

67. *IYA,* Part 14, 1930, pp. 393–94; *IYA,* Part 9, 1939, pp. 358–59; *IYA,* Part 14, 1931, p. 260; *IYA,* Part 13, 1932, pp. 141; *IYA,* Part 9, 1936, p. 314; *IYA,* Part 9, 1940, pp. 392–93.

68. *IYA,* Part 14, 1930, p. 394; *IYA,* Part 9, 1938, p. 305; *IYA,* Part 9, 1937, p. 322; *IYA,* Part 9, 1939, p. 360.

69. *IYA,* Part 14, 1930, p. 395.

70. *IYA,* Part 14, 1930, pp. 393, 395.

71. Julia Faltenson Anderson, interview, Ames, Iowa, April 19, 1988, pp. 2–4.

72. Ibid.

73. *IYA,* Part 14, 1930, p. 295; *IYA,* Part 9, 1936, p. 313.

74. *IYA,* Part 10, 1935, p. 311; *IYA,* Part 9, 1937, p. 319.

75. Thomas Wessel and Marilyn Wessel, *4-H: An American Idea 1900–1980* (Chevy Chase, Md.: National 4-H Council, 1982), pp. 51, 56.

76. Ibid., pp. 56–57.

77. Bliss, *History,* p. 174; Deborah Fink and Dorothy Schwieder, "Iowa Farm Women in the 1930s: A Reassessment," *Annals of Iowa* 49(Winter 1989):580.

78. Ibid., p. 584.

79. Quoted in Fink and Schwieder, "Iowa Farm Women," p. 585.

80. Ibid.

81. "Musical Moments with American Composers," prepared by Fannie R. Buchanan, Extension assistant, Home and Community Development, Rural Sociology, Iowa State

College, No. C.D.-25.
  82. *IYA*, Part 9, 1937, p. 323.
  83. *IYA*, Part 9, 1936, p. 312; and *IYA*, Part 9, 1937, p. 318.
  84. Lundeen, "Efficiency and Uplift," pp. 67, 71.
  85. Rasmussen, *Taking the University*, p. 97.

5. "Food Will Win the War and Write the Peace"

  1. *IYA*, Part 9, *Annual Report of Iowa Agricultural and Home Economics Extension Service*, 1941, p. 444.
  2. *IYA*, Part 9, 1939, p. 347.
  3. Earle D. Ross, *Iowa Agriculture: An Historical Survey* (Iowa City: State Historical Society of Iowa, 1951), pp. 179–80.
  4. Gilbert C. Fite, *American Farmers: The New Minority* (Bloomington: Indiana University Press, 1981), pp. 77–78.
  5. *IYA*, Part 9, 1940, p. 378.
  6. *IYA*, Part 9, 1941, pp. 445–46.
  7. Ibid., pp. 443–44; and *IYA*, Part 9, 1942, p. 362.
  8. *ANR*, Greene County, Vol. 10, 1941, p. 174. It should be noted that by 1940, Director Bliss and other Extension officials had started using the term, county Extension director rather than county agent.
  9. *ANR*, Greene County, Vol. 8, 1941, p. 167.
  10. *ANR*, Fayette County, Vol. 7, 1942, p. 6.
  11. Each county Extension director, along with other county staff, annually put together a program or plan of work for the following year. *ANR*, Guthrie County, Vol. 10, 1941, p. 107.
  12. *IYA*, Part 9, 1942, pp. 363–65.
  13. Fite, *American Farmers*, pp. 83, 85.
  14. Ibid., p. 364.
  15. *ANR*, Fayette County, Vol. 7, 1942, p. 139.
  16. Anne Effland, "The Emergence of Federal Assistance Programs for Migrant and Seasonal Farmworkers in Post–World War II America" (unpublished Ph.D. dissertation, Iowa State University), pp. 11–12.
  17. The need for farm labor did vary from county to county. It is interesting that the Mahaska County director made no mention in his 1943 annual report of the need for farm labor while most of the other directors did. Wayne D. Rasmussen, *A History of the Emergency Farm Labor Supply Program, 1943–47* (Washington, D.C.: U.S. Department of Agriculture Bureau of Agricultural Economics, Agriculture Monograph No. 13, September 1951), p. 104.
  18. *ANR*, Marshall County, Vol. 7, 1943, p. 15; and *ANR*, Emmet County, Vol. 4, 1943, pp. 15, 16.
  19. *ANR*, Lee County, Vol. 7, 1943, p. 3. The Victory Farm Volunteers was an organization designed for young people. The program included providing summer work for high school and college students; it also involved some 4-H members. The Women's Land Army was carried on mostly by Extension home economists and involved all women working on farms. The program was designed to recruit women from towns and cities for farm work. See Wayne D. Rasmussen, *Taking the University to the People: Seventy-Five Years of Cooperative Extension* (Ames: Iowa State University Press, 1989), p. 110.
  20. *ANR*, Lee County, 1943, pp. 31–33.

21. Ibid., p. 4.

22. *ANR,* Marshall County, Vol. 7, 1943, p. 16.

23. *ANR,* Floyd County, Vol. 4, 1943, p. 7.

24. Ibid., p. 6.

25. *ANR,* Muscatine County, Vol. 7, 1944, p. 13; Rasmussen, *A History of the Emergency Farm Labor Supply Program,* pp. 226, 250, 261.

26. *ANR,* Page County, Vol. 7, 1944, p. 7; and Mary K. Frederickson, "Some Thoughts on Prisoners of War in Iowa, 1943 to 1946," *The Palimpsest* 65(March/April 1984):68–80; Rasmussen, *A History of the Emergency Farm Labor Supply Program,* pp. 96–98.

27. *ANR,* Page County, Vol. 7, 1944, p. 8.

28. *ANR,* Kossuth County, Vol. 4, 1944, p. 6.

29. *ANR,* Pocahontas County, Vol. 8, 1945, p. 4; *ANR,* Grundy County, no Vol., pp. 9–10, n.d.; and *ANR,* Fremont County, Vol. 4, 1945, p. 2.

30. *ANR,* Page County, Vol. 8, 1945, p. 8; and Edward Graff Papers, Special Collections, Iowa State University Library, 1942, p. 2.

31. *ANR,* Franklin County, Vol. 4, 1943, pp. 14–15; *ANR,* Johnson County, Vol. 5, 1944, p. 9; and *ANR,* Fayette County, Vol. 4, 1945, pp. 2, 8.

32. *ANR,* Ida County, Vol. 5, 1944, p. 12; and *ANR,* Johnson County, Vol. 5, 1944, p. 9.

33. *ANR,* Greene County, Vol. 10, 1941, p. 115; and *ANR,* Fayette County, Vol. 7, 1942, pp. 113, 121–22.

34. For example, see *ANR,* Floyd County, Vol. 7, 1942, p. 15; and *ANR,* Franklin County, Vol. 4, 1943, p. 13.

35. *IYA,* Part 9, 1942, p. 362; and *ANR,* Floyd County, Vol. 7, 1942, p. 21.

36. *ANR,* Greene County, Vol. 7, 1942, pp. 35–36.

37. Ibid.

38. *ANR,* Dubuque County, Vol. 4, 1943, pp. 10–11.

39. Ibid.

40. Ibid., p. 23.

41. *ANR,* Greene County, Vol. 7, 1942, p. 31; and *ANR,* Floyd County, Vol. 7, 1942, p. 21.

42. Marie Bishop, interview, Ames, Iowa, March 3, 1988, p. 7.

43. Ibid., p. 4.

44. Ibid.

45. Ibid., p. 8.

46. *ANR,* Floyd County, Vol. 4, 1943, p. 14; and Bishop interview, p. 5.

47. *ANR,* Floyd County, 1943, p. 14.

48. Louise Rosenfeld, interview, Ames, Iowa, May 3, 1988, tape 2, p. 3.

49. Ibid., p. 4.

50. *ANR,* Fayette County, Vol. 7, 1942, pp. 28–29.

51. Ibid., p. 31.

52. *ANR,* Kossuth County, Vol. 5, 1944, pp. 13–14.

53. Bishop interview, p. 8.

54. Ibid.

55. Ibid.

56. *ANR,* Kossuth County, Vol. 5, 1944, p. 16; *ANR,* Ida County, Vol. 5, 1944, p. 9.

57. *ANR,* Johnson County, Vol. 5, 1944, pp. 3, 15.

58. *ANR,* Jones County, Vol. 5, 1944, p. 17; and *ANR,* Palo Alto County, Vol. 7, 1944, pp. 19–26.

59. *ANR,* Johnson County, Vol. 5, 1944, p. 10; and *ANR,* Plymouth County, Vol. 7,

1944, p. 4.

60. *ANR,* Franklin County, Vol. 7, 1942, p. 12; and Vol. 4, 1943, p. 32.
61. Bishop interview.
62. *ANR,* Dickinson County, Vol. 4, 1943, p. 41.
63. *ANR,* Grundy County, Vol. 7, 1942, p. 5; and *ANR,* Dickinson County, Vol. 4, 1943, p. 21.
64. *ANR,* Hamilton County, Vol. 4, 1944, p. 7.
65. *ANR,* Dickinson County, Vol. 4, 1943, p. 15.
66. *ANR,* Kossuth County, Vol. 5, 1944, p. 5.
67. *ANR,* Franklin County, Vol. 7, 1942, p. 15.
68. Ibid.
69. *ANR,* Floyd County, Vol. 4, 1943, pp. 19–20.
70. *ANR,* Dubuque County, Vol. 4, 1943, n.p.
71. *IYA,* Part 9, 1942, pp. 364–65; *IYA,* Part 9, 1943, p. 3; *IYA,* Part 8, 1944, p. 335; and *IYA,* Part 8, 1945, p. 582.

6. Post–World War II

1. The full name for the Kepner Report (named for P. V. Kepner of the USDA who served as executive secretary of the committee) is *Joint Committee Report on Extension Programs, Policies and Goals* (Washington, D.C.: U.S. Printing Office, 1948). The publication was a joint effort by the U.S. Department of Agriculture and the Association of Land-Grant Colleges and Universities.
2. Leon Eugene Thompson, "Cooperative Extension And Public Affairs Education" (unpublished M.S. thesis, Iowa State University, 1964). Extension's reexamination was referred to as a "time of transition"; See also Philip Van Slyck and Warren Rovetch, "An Extension Service in Transition, 1956–1960" (Ames: Cooperative Extension Service, Iowa State University and the United States Department of Agriculture), nineteen pages. Although there is no date, it is clear from the material that it was published in 1960.
3. *ANR,* Palo Alto County, Vol. 7, 1944, p. 16; and Hamilton County, Vol. 4, 1944, p. 15. An additional concern was the poor condition of rural schools. During the war, they had been neglected, and discussion of rural schools was a part of many counties' agenda in the postwar period.
4. *ANR,* Jackson County, Vol. 6, 1945, p. 3.
5. Edward Graff Papers, ISU Special Collections, Parks Library, 1948, p. 5.
6. Ralph K. Bliss, *History of Cooperative Agriculture and Home Economics: Extension in Iowa—The First Fifty Years* (Ames: Iowa State College, 1960), p. 205.
7. Ibid., p. 206–7.
8. *ANR,* Dubuque County, Vol. 4, 1946, p. 13.
9. Ibid., p. 5.
10. Ibid., pp. 6–7.
11. Ibid., p. 14.
12. *ANR,* Dubuque County, Vol. 4, 1946, p. 6.
13. Bob Hall, interview, Oskaloosa, Iowa, February 25, 1988, p. 2.
14. Ibid., p. 3.
15. Dan Merrick, interview, Ames, Iowa, May 1, 1990, tape 1, pp. 4–5.
16. Hall interview, pp. 12–13, 15.
17. Bliss, *History,* pp. 202, 204.
18. *IYA,* 1951, Part 8, p. 419.

19. Ibid., p. 414.

20. *Basebook for Agricultural Adjustment in Iowa*, Part 1: "Agriculture in the Mid-Fifties," Special Report No. 20 (Ames: Iowa State College, 1957), p. 2.

21. Wayne D. Rasmussen, "The Impact of Technological Change on American Agriculture, 1862–1962," *Journal of Economic History* 22(December 1962):578; and Rasmussen, *Taking the University*, p. 120.

22. Graff Papers, 1952, p. 51.

23. D. B. Groves and Kenneth Thatcher, *The First Fifty: History of Farm Bureau in Iowa* (Lake Mills, Iowa: Graphic Publishing Company, Inc., 1968), pp. 199, 202–4; and *IYA*, 1954–1955, Part 8, pp. 341–43.

24. Groves and Thatcher, *The First Fifty*, p. 200.

25. Marvin Anderson, telephone interview, Ames, Iowa, February 28, 1992. Anderson served as ISU Dean of Agriculture and Home Economics and Director of Extension from 1966 to 1974.

26. Ibid. The county Agricultural Extension law called for the establishment of county Agricultural Extension districts; in effect, each county constituted a district. The law also called for the organization of an Extension council in each district or county "to cooperate with the ISC and USDA in conducting educational programs in agriculture, home economics and 4-H club work in the counties of the state." To replace the money previously obtained from Farm Bureau memberships, the law called for the levy of a tax in each county. See *IYA*, 1954–1955, Part 8, pp. 341–43.

27. Ibid., pp. 202–3.

28. Ibid., pp. 203–4.

29. *IYA*, 1954–1955, Part 8, p. 341.

30. Ibid., p. 343.

31. Ibid.

32. Ibid.; *ANR*, Crawford County, Vol. 4, 1955, p. 23; and Eldon Hans, interview, Ames, Iowa, February 18, 1988, p. 6.

33. Quoted in Edmund DeS. Brunner and E. Hsin Pao Yang, *Rural America and the Extension Service: A History and Critique of the Cooperative Agricultural and Home Economics Extension Service* (New York: Bureau of Publications, Teachers College, Columbia University, 1949), pp. 52–54. Brunner served as a member of the committee that issued the Kepner Report.

34. The charge to the joint committee was to review Extension's history, study basic problems of Extension, and make definite recommendations for future policies and activities of Extension. See Thompson, "Cooperative Extension," p. 32.

35. Thompson, "Cooperative Extension," p. 53. Extension officials at the University of Illinois held a workshop, Farm and Home Planning, in June 1948.

36. Lincoln David Kelsey in collaboration with Cannon Chiles Hearne, *Cooperative Extension Work*, 3d ed. (Ithaca, New York: Comstock Publishing Associates, 1963), p. 169.

37. *IYA*, 1952–1953, Part 8, p. 421; and *IYA*, 1954–1955, Part 8, p. 344.

38. *IYA*, 1954–1955, Part 8, pp. 344–45. In 1961 Minnesota, by comparison, had only 198 members who were new farmers out of a total participation of 1,799. See Wayne Rasmussen, *Taking the University to the People: Seventy-Five Years of Cooperative Extension* (Ames: Iowa State University, 1989), p. 124.

39. *IYA*, 1956–1957, Part 8, p. 303; and Charles Donhowe, "Certain Economic Principles in Farm and Home Development" (unpublished M.S. thesis, Iowa State University, 1959), p. 56a. According to Donhowe, 1,878 families participated in 1957–1958. By comparison, in 1956–1957, Minnesota had 1,209 families participating, Wisconsin 2,054, Illinois 2,377, Missouri 6,328, Nebraska 503, and South Dakota 444; Donhowe, p. 54.

40. *IYA*, 1956–1957, Part 8, p. 304.

41. *ANR,* Hardin County, 1955, Vol. 6, p. 2.

42. Ibid.; and Donhowe, "Certain Economic Principles," pp. 58–59. Extension officials set up the Farm and Home Development program to involve a specific number of farm couples each year. In 1954–1955, Congress appropriated special funds for the program which allowed for employment of additional staff including home economists, assistant Extension directors, and Extension youth assistants, in counties where the program had not yet been started. Couples took part in the program for a set number of years, after which the county staff recruited new couples. See Donhowe, "Certain Economic Principles," pp. 52–57.

43. *ANR,* Hardin County, 1955, Vol. 6, p. 11; and Donhowe, "Certain Economic Principles," p. 59.

44. *ANR,* Hardin County, 1959, Vol. 7, p. 23; and *IYA,* 1958–1959, Part 9, pp. 288–89.

45. Elsie Van Wert, interview, Garner, Iowa, February 11, 1988, p. 10.

46. Ibid.

47. For an in-depth study of Iowa farm women, see Deborah Fink, *Open Country, Iowa: Rural Women, Tradition and Change* (Albany: New York State University Press, 1986).

48. Thompson, "Cooperative Extension," pp. 121–22.

49. Ibid., pp. 41, 49–50.

50. Ibid.

51. Ibid., pp. 55–56.

52. Ibid., p. 74. The Farm Foundation had been established in 1933 from funds left by former president of International Harvester, Alexander Legg, and by former Illinois governor, Frank Lowden. See Thompson, "Cooperative Extension," p. 59. The Farm Foundation continued to be involved with public policy education for many years.

53. Ibid., p. 62; and *Discussing Public Policy,* a report of the North Central States Conference, University of Wisconsin, 1950, Forward and p. 1.

54. Thompson, "Cooperative Extension," p. 93. The Farm Foundation sponsored annual training conferences for Extension workers including agricultural directors, home economists, and other staff members in public policy education. These annual training conferences were continued at least into the early 1960s. See Thompson, "Cooperative Extension," pp. 68, 173.

55. Ibid., pp. 93–94.

56. Ibid., p. 95; and telephone conversation with Edna Ogg, wife of Wallace Ogg, long-time Extension agricultural economist who helped initiate public policy education in Iowa. Edna Ogg remembered that two sociologists, Philip Van Slyck and Warren Rovetch, were associated with the World Affairs Institute in New York. They provided the model for training local leaders to carry out the public affairs programs. The two sociologists first trained Carl Malone and Wallace Ogg who, in turn, developed the self-led groups. Van Slyck and Rovetch were also used as consultants for projects developed by the ISU Extension Service.

57. The state legislature appropriated $100,000 for this purpose. "An Extension Service in Transition," p. 6. Today this organization is known as CARD.

58. Ibid., p. 7.

59. Ibid., p. 8.

60. Ibid., p. 10.

61. Thompson, "Cooperative Extension," p. 10; and "An Extension Service in Transition," pp. 11–12. Officials had also worried that the heavy emphasis on social and economic issues related to overproduction in agriculture might "backfire" with those departments charged with making agriculture even more efficient. These fears also proved to be unfounded. See "An Extension Service in Transition," p. 12.

62. "An Extension Service in Transition," p. 11.

63. *Plan of Work—State of Iowa,* (Administration, Supervision and Staff Services, Extension Administration and Home Economics, 1957) p. A-2.

64. Ibid., p. 4. As Farm and Home Development was implemented during the 1950s and carried over into the early 1960s, leaving the farm was one option discussed with couples who did not have the capabilities for expanding their agricultural operation.

65. *Plan of Work,* 1957, p. 4; and *Basebook,* Part 2: "Prospects for the Years Ahead," p. 32.

66. Wallace E. Ogg, "My Career as a Public Affairs Specialist," 1989. (Unpublished excerpt from the memoirs of Wallace E. Ogg, "In Retrospect," which describes twenty-five years of Ogg's professional work.) Copy deposited at Special Collections, Parks Library, Iowa State University.

67. *IYA,* Part 10, 1960, p. 284.

68. *Basebook,* Part 2, p. 2; and *Plan of Work,* 1959, p. A-1.

69. Gilbert Fite, *American Agriculture and Farm Policy Since 1900* (New York: The Macmillan Co., Service Center for Teachers of History, 1964), pp. 25–26; and Bliss, *History,* Chapter 16.

70. "A Statement of Scope and Responsibility: The Cooperative Extension Service . . . Today." Prepared by the subcommittee of the 1957 Extension Committee on Organization and Policy, 1958, pp. 8–12.

71. Ibid., p. 10.

72. Quoted in Thompson, "Cooperative Extension," p. 54.

7. A Decade of Continuity and Change

1. *IYA,* Part 10, Fifth Biennial Report of Iowa Agriculture and Home Economics Extension Service, 1960–61, p. 286.

2. Ibid., pp. 285–86.

3. David May, interview, Guthrie Center, Iowa, May 19, 1988, p. 21.

4. Ibid.

5. David R. May, "A County Director Views Work with Low-Income Families," *Extension Service Review* 35(October 1964):176–77.

6. Ibid., p. 177.

7. *ANR,* Boone County, Vol. 1, 1961, p. 13; Adams County, Vol. 1, 1960, p. 15.

8. *ANR,* Floyd County, Vol. 4, 1964, p. 9.

9. Everett Stoneberg, interview, Ames, Iowa, February 22, 1988, pp. 3–4.

10. Ibid., pp. 2, 3, 10.

11. Ibid., p. 11.

12. *IYA,* Part 10, Seventh Biennial Report, pp. 263–64. TENCO included Appanoose, Davis, Keokuk, Lucas, Mahaska, Marion, Monroe, Van Buren, Wapello, and Wayne counties.

13. Ronald Powers, interview, Ames, Iowa, November 28, 1988, p. 3. Development of TENCO was followed a few years later by the creation of NIAD in the northern part of the state. *IYA,* Part 10, Seventh Biennial Report, pp. 263–64.

14. Powers interview, p. 2.

15. "TENCO is Combined Effort of People to Help Selves," *Ottumwa Courier,* June 26, 1967.

16. Ibid. In 1964, the Iowa Extension Service announced yet another change in the TENCO region, the establishment of a district Extension office with Roger Iverson as

acting district director. At the time, Director of Extension Anderson noted the change would permit "moving toward more specialized staff positions." See editorial, "TENCO Extension Unit," *Des Moines Register,* November 24, 1964. Anderson explained, "It is a new approach that will help us work more effectively with local people to plan and carry out educational efforts of a broader, area nature. We believe it will be a valuable supplement to the work of the individual county units." Also see "Iowa's TENCO Aids 10 Counties," *Des Moines Register,* September 8, 1962. TENCO had no treasurer and no money. The $2,000 needed to publish the recreation brochure was raised in a fund drive.

17. "Freeman Asks the Questions in Iowa," *Ottumwa Courier,* June 27, 1967.

18. May interview, p. 17.

19. Ibid., pp. 4–9.

20. *ANR,* Des Moines County, Vol. 4, 1961, p. 5; and Floyd County, Vol. 4, 1961, p. 4.

21. *ANR,* Franklin County, Vol. 4, 1961, p. 5.

22. *IYA,* Part 10, Seventh Biennial Report, p. 263.

23. *ANR,* Adair County, Vol. 1, 1961, p. 32; and Dubuque County, Vol. 4, 1961, p. 10.

24. *ANR,* Franklin County, Vol. 4, 1961, p. 13.

25. *ANR,* Allamakee County, Vol. 4, 1961, p. 44; and Des Moines County, Vol. 4, 1961, pp. 7–9; *IYA,* Part 10, Sixth Biennial Report, 1962–63; and *ANR,* Fayette County, Vol. 4, 1961, p. 12.

26. *IYA,* Part 10, Sixth Biennial Report, 1962–63, p. 290.

27. *ANR,* Guthrie County, Vol. 4, 1961, p. 19; and Dubuque County, Vol. 4, 1961, p. 12.

28. *IYA,* Part 10, Fifth Biennial Report, 1960–61, p. 288.

29. *ANR,* Dubuque County, Vol. 4, 1961, p. 17; Allamakee County, Vol. 1, 1960, p. 56; and Adair County, Vol. 1, 1960, p. 13.

30. *ANR,* Allamakee County, Vol. 1, 1960, p. 62; Appanoose County, Vol. 1, 1967, p. 17; and Franklin County, Vol. 4, 1965.

31. *IYA,* Part 9, Ninth Biennial Report, 1968–69, p. 301.

32. Paul C. Taff, *The Story of the Origin and Development of the 4-H Camping Center,* n.p., 1957, pp. 3, 4, 9, 14. The State Extension 4-H Club was composed of state Extension staff such as Taff and Barker and field agents.

33. Thomas Wessel and Marilyn Wessel, *An American Idea 1900–1980: A History of 4-H* (Chevy Chase, Maryland: National 4-H Council, 1982, p. 316; and see Paul D. Warner and James A. Christensen, *The Cooperative Extension Service: A National Assessment* (Boulder, Colorado: Westview Press, 1984), p. 49 for a discussion of the visibility of different Extension programs.

34. Ibid., p. 306; and Wayne D. Rasmussen, *Taking the University to the People: Seventy-Five Years of Cooperative Extension* (Ames: Iowa State University Press, 1989), p. 185.

35. "Iowa Poll," *Des Moines Sunday Register,* December 15, 1963.

36. "The New County Agent," *Des Moines Sunday Register,* December 15, 1963.

37. *Knoxville Journal,* February 4, 1964.

38. The call for combining the Extension Services at the three state-supported universities was debated and although there was no merging, the three institutions did work together to establish an educational center in southwest Iowa.

39. "Public Service Finance Workshops Begin Here," *Sioux City Journal,* February 20, 1964; and *IYA,* Part 10, Biennial Report, 1964–65, p. 265.

40. "Local Government Affairs is New Extension Program," *Iowa State Daily,* January 19, 1967; and *IYA,* Part 9, Tenth Biennial Report, 1970–71, p. 293.

41. Robert Crom, interview, Ames, Iowa, May 25, 1988.

42. A press release from the ISU Information Center, February 11, 1966, stated that Anderson had received three degrees from Iowa State College: B.S. in agronomy in 1939; M.S. in soil management in 1949; and Ph.D. in agricultural economics and soil management in 1955.

43. Russ Swenson, interview, Cedar Rapids, Iowa, February 3, 1988, pp. 16, 17, 19.

44. *IYA*, Part 9, Ninth Biennial Report, p. 296.

45. Ibid.

46. May interview, p. 21.

47. Swenson interview, pp. 22, 25.

48. Wallace E. Ogg, "My Career as a Public Affairs Specialist," 1989. (Unpublished excerpt from the memoirs of Wallace E. Ogg, "In Retrospect," which describes twenty years of Ogg's professional work.) Copy deposited at Special Collections, Parks Library, Iowa State University, p. 10.

49. Ibid., pp. 10–11. The research for the Iowa poverty study actually started in 1967. It had included a statewide household sample survey of six thousand residences, a statewide study of both private and public welfare programs in the state, an estimate "of the knowledge and attitudes toward welfare held by the key influential leaders who would be participating in workshops later"; and "An appraisal of the sociology and economics of welfare nationally" which would apply to Iowa. See Ogg, "Memoirs," p. 9.

50. Rasmussen, *Taking the University*, pp. 160–61. Money for the EFNEP came from Section 32 funds, allocated from customs receipts for the removal of surplus agricultural products.

51. *IYA*, Part 9, Ninth Biennial Report, p. 300.

52. "A Blue-Ribbon Recipe for Nutrition," *Des Moines Register*, May 12, 1989.

53. *ANR*, Boone County, Vol. 1, 1968, pp. 9–11.

54. *ANR*, Madison County, Vol. 1, 1968, p. 8.

55. *ANR*, Humboldt County, Vol. 4, 1969, pp. 11–12.

56. *IYA*, Part 10, Ninth Biennial Report, 1964–65, pp. 263–64.

57. *IYA*, Part 9, Tenth Biennial Report, 1970–71, p. 288. According to Wayne Rasmussen, that contrasted to 44 percent nationally in 1988, *Taking the University*, p. 121.

58. *IYA*, Part 9, Tenth Biennial Report, 1970–71, p. 288.

59. Stoneberg interview, p. 6.

60. Rasmussen, *Taking the University*, p. 120.

8. The Best of Times, the Worst of Times

1. Paul D. Warner and James A. Christensen, *The Cooperative Extension Service: A National Assessment* (Boulder, Colo.: Westview Press, 1984), p. 5. Even though Cooperative Extension became a part of University Extension in 1966, the remainder of this study deals solely with Cooperative Extension.

2. Ibid., p. 136.

3. Gilbert C. Fite, *American Farmers: The New Minority* (Bloomington: Indiana University Press, 1981), p. 202.

4. W. John Johnson, interview, March 1, 1990, tape 2, Ames, Iowa, p. 7.

5. Ibid.

6. *IYA*, Report of Cooperative Extension Service in Agriculture and Home Economics, Iowa State University, Part 9, Tenth Biennial Report, 1970–71, p. 288.

7. Ibid., pp. 288–89.

8. *IYA*, Eleventh Biennial Report, 1971–73, p. 184.

9. *IYA*, Part 9, Tenth Biennial Report, 1970–71, pp. 290–91; Wayne D. Rasmussen, *Taking the University to the People: Seventy-Five Years of Cooperative Extension* (Ames: Iowa State University Press, 1989), p. 134; William Carnahan, "Extension Trains Pesticide Applicators," *Extension Service Review* 46(July/August 1975):4; and *IYA*, 1975–77, p. 230. In 1976, more than 12,500 applicators completed written examinations to qualify for certification. According to Wayne Rasmussen, the new program was to "reduce the use and level of pesticides in the environment, reduce reliance on pesticides, and improve farm profits by increasing production through more efficient pesticide use." See Rasmussen, *Taking the University*, p. 135.

10. "Social Science Teachers Welcome Extension Materials," *Extension Service Review* 42–44(November 1971):10–11. The programs were held for three consecutive weeks with meetings lasting about five hours each. Two Extension staffers were involved with each presentation with over eight thousand adult Iowans taking part in the workshops. See "Social Science," pp. 10–11. Both programs were funded with a grant from Iowa Community Services under Title I of the Higher Education Act of 1965.

11. Rasmussen, *Taking the University*, pp. 191–93.

12. Ibid., p. 196.

13. Ronald Powers, interview, Ames, Iowa, November 28, 1988, pp. 7–8.

14. "When a Farm Shopping Innovation Approaches—Merchants Seek Extension's Help," *Extension Service Review* 39–41(June 1970):8–9.

15. "Fenton, Iowa—Small Town with Big Plans," *Extension Service Review* 39–41(July 1970):14–15.

16. Mary Yearns, interview, Ames, Iowa, March 29, 1990, p. 16.

17. "The Time Has Come," included in Program Development, Home Economics Extension, 1970–1979, in possession of Mary Yearns.

18. Elizabeth Elliott, interview, Ames, Iowa, May 10, 1990, pp. 3–4. At the same time, however, Elliott pointed out some difficulties with changing emphases in the program. She observed that ironically, the projects "were the very things that had brought many people into home economics. They loved their 4-H experiences in cooking, sewing, whatever. They came into home economics because they liked that." See interview, p. 4.

19. Elliott interview, pp. 14, 16.

20. Ibid.

21. Yearns interview, p. 5.

22. Elliott interview, p. 5.

23. Ibid.

24. A toll-free line in horticulture was also created. The change toward a program or issues approach is also apparent when one looks at the areas emphasized in home economics in the 1970s. In his biennial report for 1975–1977, Extension Director Charles Donhowe listed six program categories in home economics: human nutrition; consumer concerns; children and families; housing; health; and community development. See *IYA*, Biennial Report, 1975–1977, p. 232. Ten years earlier, the topics would have been more subject-matter oriented such as child care, food, canning, and home decorating.

25. Elliott interview, pp. 16–18. For an interesting technique used to carry out a needs assessment study (to determine future programs), see Kathleen Beery, "Which Comes First—Problems or Programs?" *Extension Review* (Winter 1984).

26. Yearns interview, pp. 10–11. The first program also resulted in Home Economics Extension getting approximately $125,000 worth of grants from the Energy Policy Council.

27. Ibid., p. 8; Linda Benedict, "Have Tools . . . Will Travel," *Extension Service Review* (March/April 1976):18–19.

28. Yearns interview, pp. 8–9.

29. Marjorie P. Groves, "Nutrition Fest—More Than Just Fun," *Extension Service*

Review 42(March 1972):12.

30. Marjorie P. Groves, "Kids Become Farm-City Ambassadors," *Extension Service Review* 42(January 1973):10–11.

31. Robert Crom, interview, Ames, Iowa, May 25, 1988, p. 8.

32. C. J. Gauger, interview, Ames, Iowa, March 15, 1990, tapes 1 and 2; tape 2, p. 4.

33. *IYA,* Thirteenth Biennial Report, 1975–1977, p. 233.

34. Ovid Bay, "At 50th National Congress . . . 4-H Looks Ahead," *Extension Service Review* 42–44(January 1972):3–4.

35. *IYA,* Thirteen Biennial Report, 1975–1977, p. 233.

36. Bay, "At 50th National Congress," p. 5; Rasmussen, *Taking the University,* p. 185.

37. Gauger interview, p. 21.

38. Ibid.

39. Marjorie P. Groves, "Regardless of Race, Creed or National Origin," *Extension Service Review* (May/June 1975):22–23.

40. Gauger interview, p. 16.

41. Fite, *American Farmers,* p. 208.

42. Mark Friedberger, *Farm Families and Change* (Lexington: University Press of Kentucky, 1988), p. 7; and Rasmussen, *Taking the University,* p. 125. In his study of the farm crisis, Friedberger believes that Iowa's farm families went through five stages: inflationary spiral, 1981; denial, beginnings of deflation, 1982–83; confrontation, build-up of advocacy, 1984–February 1985; beginnings of mobilization, 1985; beginnings of resolution, January 1986. Friedberger defines the confrontation stage as a time of "psychological violence against farm families, especially that violence brought on through paper" (foreclosure notices, farm sale advertisements, etc.), pp. 191, 200.

43. Friedberger, *Farm Families,* p. 196. This organization brought together farm groups including the National Farmers' Organization, the Iowa Farmers' Union, the American Agriculture Movement, and the United States Farmers' Association, along with some church and labor groups. See Friedberger, p. 196.

44. Quoted in Friedberger, *Farm Families,* p. 201.

45. Friedberger, *Farm Families,* p. 193.

46. Carolyn Bigwood, "Financial Fitness for Farmers," *Extension Service Review* 55(Fall 1984):14–15.

47. Johnson interview, p. 10; Rasmussen, *Taking the University,* p. 125.

48. Merlin L. Pfannkuch, "ASSIST Aids in Iowa," *Extension Review* 56(Summer 1985):4; Bigwood, "Financial Fitness," p. 14. Iowa officials estimated in 1984 that about one-third of Iowa farm families had "debts equal to 41 percent or more of their assets. About thirty thousand families located in all areas of the state [were] carrying 65 percent of the total Iowa farm debt." See Bigwood, "Financial Fitness for Farmers," p. 14.

49. Friedberger, *Farm Families,* p. 213; Johnson interview, p. 14. The hotline was still operating as late as April 1990. According to Wayne Rasmussen, Cooperative Extension around the country followed the same course (as Iowa), teaching farmers to "adjust their farming operations by cutting costs, shifting to different crops, finding new markets, or taking other steps that could improve income."

50. *Annual Report, Home Economics Extension,* 1985, p. 8, 9; Extension staff also developed a six-part home study course on stress management and put together publications on other problems facing farm families including family communication, dealing with creditors, and understanding depression. See *IYA,* Biennial Report, 1983–85, p. 886.

51. Elliott interview, p. 9.

52. *Annual Report, Home Economics Extension,* 1985, p. 7.

53. "Modest Home Makeovers: Helping Families Make Homes Livable," Extension

Publication EXT-13, May 1988.

54. Friedberger, *Farm Families,* pp. 218–22.

55. Johnson interview, pp. 12, 13, 15.

56. Dan Merrick, interview, Ames, Iowa, May 1, 1990, tapes 1 and 2; tape 2, pp. 9, 11, 12.

57. Don Broshar, interview, Ames, Iowa, May 10, 1990, p. 9.

58. Ibid., pp. 1, 2.

59. Ibid., p. 3.

60. Ibid., pp. 7, 8.

61. Johnson interview, p. 16; Friedberger, *Farm Families,* pp. 199–200; and Crom interview, pp. 21, 22.

62. Merrick interview, tape 1, p. 15.

63. Pfannkuch, "ASSIST Aids in Iowa," p. 4.

64. Kenneth E. Stone, "Reviving the Rural Retailer," *Extension Review* 54(Winter 1983):18–19; and "Better Business Management," *Extension Review* 54(Winter 1983):37.

65. Ibid.

66. Charles Gratto and Daniel Otto, "Community Economic Development Workshops," *Extension Review* 59(Winter 1988):25.

67. Jerald DeWitt, interview, Ames, Iowa, September 11, 1991, pp. 1, 2.

68. Ibid., p. 4.

69. Ibid., pp. 4–5.

70. Ibid., p. 5. Also see *Iowa Cooperative Extension Service Annual Narrative Report, FY 1987; Iowa Extension Service Annual Report, FY 1988;* and *Iowa Cooperative Extension Service Annual Report, FY, 1989,* all deposited in the Cooperative Extension Office, Curtiss Hall, ISU, for a more complete discussion of environmental and sustainable agricultural programs in the late 1980s.

71. Crom interview, p. 23.

72. Ibid., p. 24.

73. Elliott interview, p. 13.

74. Ibid.

75. Merrick interview, tape 2, p. 1.

76. Ibid., p. 3.

77. Regis Voss, interview, Ames, Iowa, May 24, 1990, pp. 7–9.

78. Ibid., p. 14; Many other areas of Extension including home economics have the same policy. Specialists are regarded as part of the ISU faculty and must receive tenure to retain their positions, the same as teaching and research faculty. For about a decade Extension persons in home economics have not been able to obtain tenure without a doctorate in their field.

79. Warner and Christensen, *The Cooperative Extension Service,* p. 5.

9. Seventy-five Years of Change

1. Marvin Anderson interview, Ames, Iowa, January 12, 1988, pp. 4, 14.

2. Wayne D. Rasmussen, *Taking the University to the People: Seventy-Five Years of Cooperative Extension* (Ames: Iowa State University Press, 1989), p. 100; and Merrick interview, tape 1, p. 4.

3. Powers interview, p. 12.

4. Hans interview, p. 16.

5. One assessment states that traditionally, the Extension Service has served middle

class, rural residents. See Paul D. Warner and James A. Christensen, *The Cooperative Extension Service: A National Assessment* (Boulder, Colo.: Westview Press, 1984), p. 21.

6. Broshar interview, pp. 9, 10.

7. Everett M. Rogers, *Diffusion of Innovations* (New York: The Free Press, 1983), 3d ed., pp. 147–48. Rogers describes no-till farming as "planting seed (usually corn or soybeans) into untilled soil by opening a narrow slot or trench of sufficient depth for seed coverage and soil contact, and using herbicides to control weeds and unwanted plants, thus eliminating such conventional methods of seed bed preparation and cultivation as plowing, disking, harrowing, cultivating, and so on."

8. Voss interview, p. 3.

9. James Hightower, *Hard Tomatoes, Hard Times: The Failure of America's Land-Grant College Complex* (Cambridge, Mass.: Schenkman Press, 1972).

10. Voss interview, p. 5.

11. Merrick interview, tape 1, p. 13; Hans interview, p. 13; Anderson interview; and private conversation with Arthur Johnson, August 1975, Ames, Iowa.

12. Merrick interview, tape 1, p. 3.

13. Anderson interview, pp. 7, 8. Anderson noted that each state Extension Service was required to submit an annual plan of work which had to be approved by the federal Extension Service. Federal auditors also came to the ISU campus to review and approve budgets. In his study of the history of public policy, Leon Thompson writes that in July 1916, Extension and land-grant officials held the "so-called Amherst Conference," to discuss relations between the USDA and Extension workers. The outcome "was to reinforce state control over extension work and to limit the power of the States Relations Service [a USDA committee]. Henceforth, all work within a state was to be done through the director of extension." See Leon Thompson, "Cooperative Extension and Public Affairs Education" (unpublished M.S. thesis, Iowa State University), 1964.

14. Warner and Christensen, *The Cooperative Extension Service*, p. 5.

15. Merrick interview, tape 1, p. 10.

16. Anderson interview, p. 13.

17. Gauger interview; Beverly Everett, interview, Ames, Iowa, April 2, 1991.

18. Powers interview, p. 23.

19. Thompson, *Cooperative Extension*, pp. 99, 100.

20. Quoted in Thompson, *Cooperative Extension*, p. 54.

Selected Bibliography

STATE DOCUMENTS

Annual Narrative Reports of County Extension Agents, 1916–1968. Special Collections, ISU Library.

Excerpts of the *Annual Report of the Extension Service in Agriculture and Home Economics,* 1924. Special Collections, ISU Library.

Annual Reports, Home economics, 1920–1930.

Annual Report of Iowa Agricultural and Home Economics Extension Service, 1914–1946. Cooperative Extension, Curtiss Hall, ISU, Special Collections, ISU Library, 1980–1989.

Annual Reports, Rural Sociology Extension, 1925, 1926, and 1927. William Stacy Papers, Special Collections, ISU Library.

Basebook for Agricultural Adjustment in Iowa, Part 1, 2, and 3. Special Report No. 20. Ames: Iowa State College, 1957.

An Extension Service in Transition, 1956–1960. Ames: Iowa Cooperative Extension Service in Agriculture and Home Economics, 1960.

Iowa Yearbook of Agriculture. Des Moines: State of Iowa, 1900–1983.

Modest Home Make-overs: Helping Families Make Homes Livable. Extension Publication EXT-13, May 1988.

Plan of Work—State of Iowa. Administration, Supervision and Staff Services, Extension Administration and Home Economics, ISU, 1950–1960.

Program Development. Home Economics Extension, ISU, 1970–1980.

FEDERAL DOCUMENTS

A People and a Spirit: A Report of the Joint USDA-NASULBC Study Committee on Cooperative Extension. Fort Collins: Colorado State University, 1968.

A Statement of Scope and Responsibility: The Cooperative Extension Service . . . Today. Prepared by the subcommittee of the 1957 Extension Committee on Organization and Policy, 1958.

Kepner, P. V. *Joint Committee on Extension Programs, Policies and Goals.*

Washington, D.C.: U.S. Printing Office, 1948.

Rasmussen, Wayne. *A History of the Emergency Farm Labor Supply Program, 1943–47.* Washington, D.C.: U.S. Department of Agriculture, Bureau of Agricultural Economics, Agriculture Monograph No. 13, 1951.

Schopmeyer, C. H. "Extension Projects in Rural Community Organization." *Extension Service Circular.* Washington, D.C.: Office of Agricultural Instruction, Extension Service, Vol. 43, May 1927.

MANUSCRIPTS

Bliss, Ralph K. "Personal Recollections of Ralph K. Bliss." Typewritten manuscript, n.d. Special Collections, ISU Library.

Graff, Edward. Private Papers. Special Collections, ISU Library.

Ogg, Wallace E. "My Career as a Public Affairs Specialist." Excerpt from Wallace E. Ogg memoirs, "In Retrospect." Special Collections, ISU Library.

Stacey, William. Private Papers. Special Collections, ISU Library.

NEWSPAPERS

Des Moines Register, 1963, 1964, 1989.
Knoxville Journal, 1964.
Ottumwa Courier, 1967.
Sioux City Journal, 1964.

BOOKS

Atherton, Lewis. *Main Street on the Middle Border.* New York: New York Times Book Company, Quadrangle Books, 1975.

Bliss, Ralph K. *History of Cooperative Agriculture and Home Economics Extension in Iowa: The First Fifty Years.* Ames: Iowa State University, 1960.

Bliss, Ralph K.; Symons, T. B.; Wilson, M. L.; Gallup, Gladys; Reese, Madge J.; and Schruben, Luke M., editors and compilers. *The Spirit and Philosophy of Extension Work.* Washington, D.C.: Graduate School, United States Department of Agriculture and the Epsilon Sigma Phi, National Honorary Extension Fraternity, 1952.

Bogue, Allan. *From Prairie to Cornbelt: Farming on the Illinois and Iowa Prairies in the Nineteenth Century.* Chicago: Quadrangle Paperbooks, 1968.

Brunner, Edmund DeS. and Yang, E. Hsin Pao. *Rural America and the Extension Service: A History and Critique of the Cooperative Agricultural and Home Economics Extension Service.* New York: Bureau of Publications, Teachers College, Columbia University, 1949.

Danbom, David B. *The Resisted Revolution: Urban America and the Industrialization of Agriculture, 1900–1930.* Ames: Iowa State University Press, 1979.

Davidson, J. Brownlee; Hamlin, Herbert M.; and Taff, Paul C. *A Study of the Extension Service in Agriculture and Home Economics in Iowa.* Ames:

Collegiate Press, Inc., 1933.

Fink, Deborah. *Open Country Iowa: Rural Women, Tradition and Change*. SUNY Series in Anthropology of Work, ed., June Nash. Albany: State University of New York Press, 1986.

Fite, Gilbert C. *American Farmers: The New Minority*. Bloomington: Indiana University Press, 1981.

Friedberger, Mark. *Farm Families and Change*. Lexington: University Press of Kentucky, 1988.

Garland, Hamlin. "A Day's Pleasure," in *Main Travelled Roads*. New York: Signet Classic, reprint, 1962.

Harnack, Curtis. *We Have All Gone Away*. Garden City, N.J.: Doubleday, 1973.

Hightower, James. *Hard Tomatoes, Hard Times: The Failure of America's Land-Grant College Complex*. Cambridge, Mass.: Schenkman Press, 1972.

Kelsey, David Lincoln in collaboration with Cannon Chiles Hearne, *Cooperative Extension Work*, 3d ed. Ithaca, N.Y.: Comstock Publishing Associates, 1963.

Lowitt, Richard S., ed. *Journal of a Tamed Bureaucrat: Nils A. Olsen and the BAE, 1925–1935*. Ames: Iowa State University Press, 1980.

Morain, Thomas J. *Prairie Grass Roots: An Iowa Small Town in the Early Twentieth Century*. Ames: Iowa State University Press, 1988.

Rasmussen, Wayne D. *Taking the University to the People: Seventy-Five Years of Cooperative Extension*. Ames: Iowa State University Press, 1989.

Rogers, Everett M. *Diffusion of Innovations*, 3d ed. New York: Free Press, 1983.

Ross, Earle D. *Iowa Agriculture: An Historical Survey*. Iowa City: State Historical Society of Iowa, 1951.

Saloutos, Theodore and Hicks, John D. *Agricultural Discontent in the Middle West, 1900–1939*. Madison: University of Wisconsin Press, 1951.

Schuyler, Michael W. *Dread of Plenty: Agricultural Relief Activities of the Federal Government in the Middle West, 1933–1939*. Manhattan, Kans.: Sunflower Press, 1989.

Thatcher, Kenneth. *The First Fifty: History of Farm Bureau in Iowa*. Lake Mills, Iowa: Graphic Publishing Company, Inc., 1968.

Wall, Joseph. *Iowa: A Bicentennial History*. New York: Norton, 1978.

Warner, Paul D. and Christensen, James A. *The Cooperative Extension Service: A National Assessment*. Boulder, Colo.: Westview Press, 1984.

Wessel, Thomas and Wessel, Marilyn. *4-H: An American Idea, 1900–1980*. Chevy Chase, Md.: National 4-H Council, 1982.

ARTICLES

Bay, Ovid. "At 50th National Congress . . . 4-H Looks Ahead." *Extension Service Review* 42–44(January 1972):3–4.

Benedict, Linda. "Have Tools . . . Will Travel." *Extension Service Review* 48(March/April 1976):18–19.

Berry, Kathleen. "Which Comes First—Problems or Programs?" *Extension Service Review* 55(Winter 1984):22–23.

Bigwood, Carolyn. "Financial Fitness for Farmers," *Extension Service Review*

55(Fall 1984):14–15.

Carnahan, William. "Extension Trains Pesticide Applicators." *Extension Service Review* 47(July/August 1975):4–5.

Drury, Clifford. "Growing Up on an Iowa Farm, 1897–1915." *Annals of Iowa* 42(Winter 1974):161–97.

Fish, Donald E. "The Emergency Years: Remembrances of a County Agricultural Agent in the Great Depression." *The Palimpsest* 72(Summer 1991).

Friedel, Janice Nahra. "Jessie Field Shambaugh: The Mother of 4-H." *The Palimpsest* 62(July/August 1981):98–115.

Grotto, Charles and Otto, Daniel. "Community Economic Development Workshops." *Extension Service Review* 59(Winter 1988):25–26.

Groves, Marjorie P. "Nutrition Fest—More Than Just Fun." *Extension Service Review* 42–44(March 1972):12–13.

_____. "Kids Become Farm-City Ambassadors." *Extension Service Review* 42(January 1973):10–11.

_____. "Regardless of Race, Creed or National Origin." *Extension Service Review* 47(May/June 1975): 22–23.

Hanson, Louie. "Fenton, Iowa—Small Town with Big Plans." *Extension Service Review* 41(July 1970):14–15.

Heckart, Lizzie Fellows. "Four Seasons: Life on a Pioneer Van Buren County Farm." Keosauqua: *Van Buren County Register,* 1972.

Johnson, Keach. "Elementary and Secondary Education in Iowa, 1890–1900: A Time of Awakening." Parts 1–2. *Annals of Iowa* 45(Fall 1979):87–109; (Winter 1980):170–75.

Kunze, Joel. "The Bureau of Agricultural Economics' Outlook Program in the 1920s as Pedagogical Device." *Agricultural History* 64(Spring 1990):252–61.

Luebke, Frederick. "Ethnic Group Settlement on the Great Plains." *Western Historical Quarterly* 8(October 1977):405–30.

May, David. "A County Director Views Work with Low-Income Families." *Extension Service Review* 35(October 1964):176–77.

Nelson, Don. "When a Farm Shopping Innovation Approaches—Merchants Seek Extension's Help." *Extension Service Review* 39–41(June 1970):8–9.

Quick, Herbert. "The Women on the Farm." *Good Housekeeping* 57(October 1913):426–36.

Roberts, Richard H. "The Administration of the 1934 Corn-Hog Program in Iowa." *Iowa Journal of History and Politics* 33(October 1935):307–75.

Sage, Leland. "Rural Iowa in the 1920s and 1930s: Roots of the Farm Depression." *Annals of Iowa* 47(Fall 1983):91–103.

Schwieder, Dorothy. "Education and Change in the Lives of Iowa Farm Women, 1900–1940." *Agricultural History* 60(Spring 1986):200–215.

_____. "Rural Women in the 1920s: Conflict and Continuity." *Annals of Iowa* 47(Fall 1983):104–15.

Sizer, Rosanne and Silag, William. "P. G. Holden and the Corn Gospel Trains." *The Palimpsest* 62(May/June 1981):66–71.

Stone, Kenneth E. "Better Business Management." *Extension Service Review* 54(Winter 1983):83–84.

_____. "Reviving the Rural Retailer." *Extension Service Review* 54(Winter 1983):18–19.

Wallize, John A. "Social Science Teachers Welcome Extension Materials." *Extension Service Review* 42–44(November 1971):10–11.

THESES AND DISSERTATIONS

Donhowe, Charles. "Certain Economic Principles in Farm and Home Development." M.S. thesis, Iowa State University, 1959.

Effland, Ann. "The Emergence of Federal Assistance Programs for Migrant and Seasonal Farmworkers in Post World War II America." Ph.D. dissertation, Iowa State University, 1991.

Lundeen, Kenneth Michael. "Efficiency and Uplift: The Iowa Extension Service and Business Agriculture, 1919–1935." M.S. thesis, Iowa State University, 1976.

Ritland, E. G. "The Educational Activities of P. G. Holden in Iowa." M.S. thesis, Iowa State College, 1941.

Thompson, Leon Eugene. "Cooperative Extension and Public Affairs Education." M.S. thesis, Iowa State University, 1964.

INTERVIEWS

Anderson, Julia Faltenson. Ames, Iowa, April 19, 1988.
Anderson, Marvin. Ames, Iowa, May 7, 1991.
Arnold, Floyd. Ames, Iowa, February 25, 1988.
Barger, Paul. Waterloo, Iowa, February 18, 1988.
Bishop, Marie. Ames, Iowa, March 3, 1988.
Broshar, Don. Ames, Iowa, May 10, 1990.
Crom, Robert. Ames, Iowa, May 25, 1988.
DeWitt, Jerald. Ames, Iowa, September 11, 1991.
Elliott, Elizabeth. Ames, Iowa, May 10, 1990.
Everett, Beverly. Ames, Iowa, April 2, 1991.
Gauger, C. J. Ames, Iowa, January 30 and March 15, 1990.
Hall, Bob. Oskaloosa, Iowa, February 25, 1988.
Hans, Eldon. Ames, Iowa, February 18, 1988.
Herriott, Cleon. Cedar Rapids, Iowa, February 3, 1988.
Hill, E. Howard. Ames, Iowa, April 24, 1989.
Johnson, W. John. Ames, Iowa, February 20 and March 1, 1990.
Lawrence, Roger. Ames, Iowa, January 18, 1988.
Littlefield, Kenneth. Sac City, Iowa, January 15, 1988.
Lund, Bernice. Ames, Iowa, April 24, 1989.
May, David. Guthrie Center, Iowa, May 19, 1988.
Merrick, Dan. Ames, Iowa, May 1, 1990.
Nicholson, Betty. Primghar, Iowa, January 16, 1988.
Plambeck, Herb. Ames, Iowa, April 24, 1989.
Powers, Ronald. Ames, Iowa, November 28, 1988.

Rosenfeld, Louise. Ames, Iowa, April 22 and May 3, 1988.

Schmoll, Lois and Merlyn. Lake Mills, Iowa, February 11, 1988.

Soults, Maurice. Ames, Iowa, September 17, 1987.

Stoneberg, Everett. Ames, Iowa, February 22, 1988.

Swenson, Russ. Cedar Rapids, Iowa, February 22, 1988.

Van Wert, Elsie. Garner, Iowa, February 11, 1988.

Voss, Regis. Ames, Iowa, May 24, 1990.

Whetstone, Esther. Ames, Iowa, May 16, 1988, and April 24, 1989.

Yearns, Mary. Ames, Iowa, March 29, 1990.

Zobrist, Edith. Ames, Iowa, April 24, 1989.

Index